Praise for *On Butterflies' Wings*

"A delightfully uplifting memoir that shows the power each one of us has to change the world."

DR. HELENE GAYLE, FORMER CEO OF CARE

"On Butterflies' Wings" is a book that will inspire you to follow your own dreams with commitment and passion. Not knowing what is around the next corner or who you may meet when you arrive, only adds wonder to the adventure."

REP. DENNIS KUCINICH

"Tania is a modern-day Marco Polo."

GEN. ISMAEL ALSODANI

"Tania is the Scheherazade of aviation."

SHIRINE GILL

"Tania is a Universal soul. She can be anywhere in the world and feel right at home. Maybe knowing Tania is like going to Heaven without the inconvenience of having to die first."

FRANK BARWAH, EXECUTIVE FILM PRODUCER

"With her eagle eyes, Tania enables us to experience the world from the skies with depth and focus. She captures different slices of our planet as she interacts with national leaders and people from all walks of life. *On Butterflies' Wings* offers insightful commentaries about our world today. A unique, powerful and easy to read book."

PROFESSOR KANTATHI SUPHAMONGKHON, 39TH MINISTER OF FOREIGN AFFAIRS OF THE KINGDOM OF THAILAND

On Butterflies' Wings

An Anthology of International Escapades

TANIA ANDERSON

Foreword by Al Topping

Published by Travels with Tania

ISBN (paperback): 978-1-964083-00-1
ISBN (ebook): 978-1-964083-01-8

Book design and production by www.AuthorSuccess.com

Printed in the United States of America

This is a work of creative nonfiction. All the events in this memoir are true to the best of the author's memory. Some names and identifying features have been changed to protect the privacy and identity of certain parties. The author in no way represents any company, corporation, or brand mentioned herein. The views expressed in this memoir are solely those of the author.

To my beloved parents Nike and Glenn,
who taught me everything they knew.

"Everyone and everything around you is your teacher."
–Ken Keyes

Free Offer

As a free gift to readers of my book, I am offering a bonus chapter. Download a compelling story entitled *Superstowaway! Don't ask me about the mile-high club, ask me about stowaways—it's a much better story.* Growing up disadvantaged in northern Nigeria, my affable, intrepid housekeeper Suley was determined to embrace a brighter future for himself at all costs. That he did, with grit, grace, and a burning desire to be part of the American dream.

https://taniaanderson.vip

Contents

Foreword

by Allan Topping

As part of Pan American World Airways' management team during the Vietnam War, I was director of South Vietnam and Cambodia for Pan Am. On April 24, 1975, I organized the last civilian flight out of Saigon.

In the '80s, I was asked to recruit new flight attendants for our iconic international airline. At that time, we flew to every continent except Antarctica. Touring numerous US cities, we were about to interview more than 30,000 applicants, not an easy task.

The new hires had to be cosmopolitan, natural-born diplomats, *au courant* regarding present worldwide events, impeccably dressed in proper decorum, and preferably college-educated. It was a plus if they had lived abroad, but they also were required to select a foreign language and then pass the written questions and oral exam by our language professor, Dr. Joseph Bator. Sign language would qualify. All the boxes had to be checked.

Our distinctive airline had close ties to the CIA, and often experienced international incidents or attempted coups. It was essential that our crews had to be trustworthy and reliable, as you will discover in this memoir.

When I hired applicants in the '80s, Pan Am still flew to more than 82 countries, but times were difficult, as the company was losing money and had begun selling off valuable assets.

My focus was on first impressions. The second the candidate walked into the room, I imagined them in our Adolfo uniform walking down the aisle of a 747. It was not only their appearance that mattered, but also their demeanor and eloquence. Miniskirts were taboo.

Tania described her exceptional education at one of England's best schools and her previous travels to the European continent, the Caribbean, and South America as a traveler.

I hired her on the spot. Her eyes glistened, then she let out a slight gasp when I asked, "What would you say if I told you we are going to send you to Miami for training this Sunday?"

She went on to experience as much as she could in her short six years with Pan Am, requesting trips to countries that were going through a metamorphosis: Berlin as the wall was being chipped away and it looked as if East and West Germany would be reunited, flying into Moscow in the middle of the coup d'états attempt to overthrow President Gorbachev, flying White House press charters alongside Air Force One, and spiriting American military into a Middle Eastern war zone only weeks after Saddam Hussein of Iraq had invaded Kuwait. The peril of possible poisonous gas-filled SCUD missile attacks from Iraq was evident.

Tania's thirst for adventure in foreign lands while befriending people from multiple cultures was only heightened by her Pan Am experience. On the sorrowful day, we went bankrupt, she was flying a White House press charter, carrying President Bush, Sr. down to Florida.

After recovering from Pan Am's devastating demise, she picked up the mantle and ran into her future with it.

Tania coordinated crews made up of former Pan Am flight attendants to fly into Nigeria. After befriending a tribal chieftain and his brother, she set about carving out a new life in Africa. This culminated in being feted at three palaces, two elaborate ones built from Italian marble, and the third made from brick and plaster of mud, at the Emir's compound.

Then, after months of soaking in the culture, an abrupt misunderstanding arose. Tania had to suddenly make an alarming escape, and late one night fled Nigeria alone.

She also spent time working in India, meeting Mother Teresa at her home in Calcutta.

Back in America, Tania ingratiated herself on Capitol Hill by lobbying as a volunteer for causes dear to her heart. She supported legislation for international human rights and, domestically, rights for airline crews.

On the 30th anniversary of her hire date with Pan Am, Tania emailed me.

"Al, I heartily thank you for hiring me at Pan Am 30 years ago, which I'll never forget. You changed the trajectory of my life forever."

And I replied, "You had that 'something special' we were looking for."

The following is Tania's captivating story.

Allan Topping, Pan Am Director
South Vietnam and Cambodia 1972-1975
July 19, 2023

Introduction

"You call it the world, we call it our home!" we used to chant as Pan Am crews zipped along the airport concourses of the world's most famous cities.

Born an only child into an aristocratic family among spies and diplomats (often those two professions were interchangeable), writers, legislators, adventurers, and royals, I suffered from several major setbacks in my childhood. At six, my parents' marriage exploded into an acrimonious divorce. Three years later I took the witness stand in their custody battle over me, which was entirely abnormal at the time. My stepfather's alcoholism reached a crescendo, sending my mother into near poverty as he lost one job after another.

Slowly dying of emphysema, my beloved father set the stage for my future by consulting with a Dutch Countess about a distinguished English boarding school.

While my American friends were attending football games and proms, I was shipped off to a co-ed school in England at fourteen. After three months, I rushed back to my father's bedside in Virginia as his life ebbed away. He died two days after Christmas. Devastated, I was determined to carve out a good life for myself, which was his dearest wish.

Returning to England, it was sink or swim, and I felt completely out of place. However, I developed a strategy. I befriended the Americans first, the foreigners second, and the Brits last.

My progressive school, Millfield, was a smorgasbord of prominent scions and offspring of Hollywood "A" listers and politicos, including royals from about eight countries. Rumor had it that Queen Elizabeth once considered sending Prince Charles to Millfield. The present King

Rama X of Thailand was in all my classes the first year. I befriended some aspiring luminaries, most of whom are dear friends to this day.

When my four high school years ended, I returned to the States feeling rudderless. I had become more European than American. What would I study in college, how would I shape my future? Had my father lived, I am certain he would have pushed me to attend law school.

At American University, I majored in political science and international studies, with minors in psychology and sociology. Fresh out of school, I sought employment with the State Department. With stars in my eyes, I dreamed of being a diplomat, to represent America and affect change on the global stage. It was not meant to be. After failing the foreign service exam twice, I plunged into a long depression, working odd jobs but keeping my eyes open. After a series of interviews with the CIA, I got cold feet. I am far too much of a free spirit for sneaking around the world spying on others, although I am quite sure that is what two of my godfathers did, and perhaps my own father during World War II.

Then at 32, the iconic Pan American World Airways hired me, catapulting my lifestyle into the stratosphere. Overnight, the airline became my north star. They flew to 82 countries on every continent except Antarctica. Pan Am was also the unofficial flag carrier of the US decades before Air Force One was built. Suddenly, I could fly around the world on my own terms and reconnect with my cosmopolitan friends while making new ones.

Pan Am also had a close relationship with the CIA, often getting "advanced recon" info about impending coup d'états or dangerous uprisings. This was evident when I flew into Moscow during the 1991 attempted coup against President Gorbachev. At times the current news reflected my trips abroad—flying soldiers into Saudi Arabia for Desert Shield, helping strangers chip away pieces of the Berlin Wall to speed up its demise, and a White House press charter the day Chief of Staff John Sununu handed his resignation to President George H. Bush. That was the same day my cherished Pan Am went bankrupt.

After Pan Am's demise, I was forced to strategize an entirely new life path, and that I did.

My thirst for adventure and exploration had only intensified, so I signed up for the Hajj operation when a Nigerian businessman, Chief Kabo, chartered two American Boeing 747s to transport Muslim pilgrims from Nigeria to Saudi Arabia. In subsequent years, I flew the Hajj out of Saudi Arabia and India, bringing me into contact with old friends and a serendipitous greeting with His Holiness the Dalai Lama, in New Delhi. When in the States, I worked as a volunteer lobbyist on Capitol Hill concerning international human rights "for those who do not have a voice."

I always look for the soulful common denominators that bind humankind, and this has taken me to the ends of the Earth. I have met golden souls along the way whom I have admired since my youth. Some dazzling surprises arose which I never saw coming.

So, what is this book all about and why should you read it?

I want to share with you the golden opportunities that arise when you have a positive attitude along with an open heart. The day I met Saint Teresa, my colleagues told me she was in Rome, but my intuition yelled "Go!" Hours later, I found myself being blessed by her in her home.

When I heard that President Nelson Mandela was going to be honored at the US Capitol by President Bill Clinton, I called the only legislator I knew personally, Congressman Jerry Kleczka, and he gave me an invite.

But I have also stepped up to the plate in my job as an international flight attendant when the outcome was entirely uncertain: transporting soldiers into war zones, flying into Sheremetyevo Airport in Moscow when it was surrounded by tanks during the 1991 attempted coup against President Gorbachev, and slipping into East Berlin through the wall as it was being dismembered but still closely watched by armed guards and the notorious Stasi.

I hope this book will inspire you to follow your own spirit and intuition, allowing them to lead you on your journeys. I have for many years; they have served me well and will forevermore.

If you are a millennial or Gen Z, my wish is that this memoir will inspire you to realize your own dreams of how a grateful heart and mindset is the key to a world full of adventure.

And, if you are a boomer like me, I hope my stories bring fond nostalgia to you on your own stroll down memory lane.

October 9, 2023

Mother Teresa at home

1

Meeting an Angel on Earth, Mother Teresa

The lady's voice on the other end of the line was good-natured. "Missions of Charity, Washington, D.C., may I help you?"

"Yes, I would like to inquire about Mother Teresa's shelter for the lepers in Calcutta."

Anticipating a trip to India, I wanted to gather some information about how Mother Teresa's numerous shelters there were operated.

"This is Sister Ann Therese speaking. Will you be traveling to India soon? In Calcutta, we have a home for unwed mothers, a shelter for handicapped children, and a Home of Hope for the elderly and infirm. Missions of Charity has several soup kitchens around the city. A sanctuary for leprosy patients is an hour's drive outside Calcutta. We have two orphanages in addition to the Home for the Destitute and Dying, which is located in Kalighat."

Sister then asked what my plans were, if I was married or single, Catholic, and why I was interested in the lepers. I was disconcerted to see that, after decades, many tropical countries still put leprosy on the back burner. Funds are frequently given for the research of other diseases while leprosy is ignored. Leprosy, a disease frequently mentioned in the Bible, was not being addressed properly, and should have been "cured" by now. Minimal research has been conducted over decades, possibly because of an apathetic attitude from the public as well as the medical field. An American doctor once told me that they only spend about 20 minutes in medical school on Hansen's disease, the medical term for leprosy. I was shocked to discover that America had built two "leper colonies," one in Carville, Louisiana, and the other founded by Father Damien located in Molokai, Hawaii. At both sites, patients were forcibly removed from their families and relocated to a life of complete isolation from society. In some developing nations, it is common to see people with the disease, fingers and toes missing, out in public among groups of pedestrians. Flying in Africa, I have even had some as passengers who reached up for their lunch tray with badly deformed fingers and skin lesions.

"Tania, when you visit Calcutta, we'll have someone show you around the facilities and answer all your questions. Thank you for your interest. Goodbye," added Sister Ann Therese.

☙

"You know that Mother Teresa left for Rome yesterday to see the Pope, don't you?" Sammy, the "Wacky Paki" said, smiling, closing the door after me as I slipped into the taxi.

Wiping the sweat from Calcutta's steamy heat from his brow, he leaned onto the windowsill. "You'd have a much better time if you just stayed with us at the pool. They will be cooking *tandoori* chicken with basmati rice and we are going to have a 'mai tai' party this afternoon."

I was tempted. The heat was so oppressive that within an hour of taking a cool shower, you were stinky again. Venturing out took real determination, and our hotel provided a welcome oasis. "Even a blind rooster can find a kernel of corn every now and then," one of our pilots joked, relieved that we had been booked into such a nice hotel.

Out of 44 colleagues—two Boeing 747 crews—I could not persuade even one person to join me to visit Mother Teresa's home, a mere ten-minute ride away.

For the two previous weeks, we had been flying the Hajj, which is the Muslim Pilgrimage, out of New Delhi to Jeddah, Saudi Arabia. Now our crews were positioned and ready to fly nearly 15,000 passengers from the area of Bengal, in eastern India, to Jeddah. Over three months, we were scheduled to transport a total of 40,000 Indians.

Sammy, a Boeing 747 captain, was the main liaison between our US-based charter company and Air India. They had leased our two B-747s for the Hajj operation to fly from New Delhi, Mumbai, and Calcutta to Jeddah. Sammy had grown up in Pakistan, spoke Urdu and Hindi fluently, and knew all the traditions, including the "dos and don'ts" from that part of the world. Having lived in New England for many years, he also knew American customs and habits intimately. He did not mind his nickname, rather he relished it, as it testified to his valuable contribution to our operation, which continually featured many facets and unexpected occurrences, inevitable when East meets West.

Once, about halfway through our five-hour flight from New Delhi to Jeddah, I walked into the cockpit to see if the pilots wanted anything to drink. Sammy was speaking with Air Traffic Control (ATC) and his accent sounded much stronger than usual. I thought he was having a little fun and making a joke. Nothing could have been further from the truth. He was actually speaking with the Control Tower in Shiraz, Iran, as we flew overhead, directly over southern Iran. They had no idea that there was a bunch of Americans operating this particular flight. Our designator was from Air India, and Sammy's central Asian accent fit the bill perfectly.

"You sure you won't change your mind?" Sammy asked, in a teasing way.

I declined. "I know that the newspaper said she left for Rome yesterday, but I would still like to see where she lives and learn more about Missions of Charity."

The taxi began to weave in and out of the heavy traffic. A rail-thin man approached my window, selling fragrant jasmine garlands. Always a big spender, I purchased two for a total of ten rupees, about 16 US cents total, to complement my red dress. I gazed out of the window and watched families of three or four, all perched on one single motor scooter, riding along, saris waving in the breeze. Nobody was wearing any head protection. I was always concerned that the long saris would get caught in the scooter, with everyone crashing down. Rickety carts carried heavy loads of wood and supplies, hauled by obedient water buffalo who weigh as much as a small SUV. Giant bundles of laundry were balanced on women's heads. Snake charmers sat cross-legged with their sidekicks, the ever-present mongoose. The weasel-type performer was always ready to engage in warfare with the serpent nearby, usually the highly poisonous cobra. Visions of Rikki Tikki Tavi, the intrepid mongoose depicted in Kipling's *The Jungle Book*, flipped through my mind.

A large billboard showed a familiar Indian figure addressing throngs of white-robed citizens. The quotation said, "I have nothing new to teach the world. Truth and non-violence are as old as the hills." -Mahatma Gandhi.

Tall trees provided shade above Mother Teresa's multi-storied home, while shorter mango trees supplied fruit from the garden. The entryway's stone floor had been worn in the middle by the endless groups of visitors who had called from every corner of the Earth. Thanks to the stone floor and walls, the foyer was cool. I sensed some electricity in the air. Wiping my sandals on the welcome mat, I spied a small group of Americans right inside the entrance, speaking in excited whispers. I have heard this sound too many times in my life not to recognize the fact that something special was going to happen, and soon. You hear it whenever someone well-known is in the vicinity, and in anticipation of their presence, people whisper loud enough to let the others in on the news, but not too loud to be an embarrassment. This "chu, chu, chu" can be heard any time when prominent politicians, presidents, spiritual leaders, royalty, "A list" actors, or performers are about to make an appearance. But Mother Teresa was most certainly in a category by herself.

Approaching them and sounding typically American, I asked, "Hey you guys, what is going on?"

All five flashed bright smiles. One of the ladies said something I shall never forget. Sometimes, even simple statements seem to freeze time for a second or two. Then you take that special moment and add it to the rest of the unforgettable and significant occurrences that are already filed away in that distinct part of your imagination and memory. I like to think of it as an uplifting collection of impressions that I have strung together, and can readily access, when I find it necessary to cheer myself up for some reason later.

"Mother Teresa cancelled her trip to Rome yesterday," she said happily, relishing the welcome news. "She will come out of her quarters in about 20 minutes and will meet with everyone upstairs."

I am not quite sure exactly what went through my mind, but it was something like, *Jackpot!* I thrust my hand into my purse to make certain that I had brought along a spare roll of film to capture this golden opportunity. I had.

"Thanks for the great news, how breathtaking to meet her in person!" I exclaimed. "I couldn't get any of my colleagues to join me because they had heard she had left India. Now, here I am, by myself, and I am going to meet one of the greatest human beings on the planet along with all of you."

We headed up to the second-floor veranda and I had a little time to look around.

The veranda was square, so it was easy to spot all the activity in the courtyard, adjacent rooms, and the hall where Mass was offered. Mother Teresa's private quarters ran along the entire length of the building. Below, the courtyard was bustling. Volunteers from all over the world were helping with the endless chores that come with running an oversized residence.

Throughout the year, the spacious home continuously welcomed endless streams of visitors and pilgrims, *also* hailing from all points East and West. I could only guess how many nationalities were represented at any given time. Giant pots used for soup clanged as they were washed *en masse* with scores of kitchen utensils. This superlative operation was as organized as an anthill. Each person knew exactly what their duties were. Guests often came from Europe to visit, then, impressed with this sacred place, completely changed their plans to stay and volunteer for a few months.

I lingered there watching the activity below. No doubt I was in a spiritual vortex as I stood in the center of a place where God was actively working through all of the devoted sisters and volunteers. In a room close by, a simple graduation ceremony was being held, congratulating 34 sisters who had just completed their studies. Missions of Charity would be sending them abroad to carry on Mother's work. At that time, in 1996, there were already 517 missions in more than 100 countries, including the United States. Originally from Albania, Mother Teresa had run the Mission for nearly 50 years.

A color painting depicted Mother Teresa with her arms around dozens of children representing the world's major ethnic groups. With their arms in the air, they emerged from the top half of our planet. Doves flew out into all directions above the Earth. The caption read "Mother of Mankind." It appeared to come to life as I studied it. Now I was just moments away from meeting one of history's greatest figures, a *living saint*, one of the most admired humanitarians of all time.

I peeked in on the sisters who were holding evening Mass. All were lined up in orderly rows on their knees, each wore the well-known blue and white saris which the sisters from Missions of Charity wear. The words next to a crucifix above said, "I thirst." The chalice, or ciborium, which contains the host, or body of Christ, had been placed in the middle of the altar. Fresh tropical flowers on both sides of it complemented a statue of Mother Mary, who had a garland of fragrant gardenias around her neck. A dozen white candles lit up the white silk cloth that covered the holy table. As a backdrop, the setting sun shone golden light through the windows on either side.

Next to the entrance, words under a small painting of Mother Mary noted, "May 1996—The Holy Father's Intentions." Below those words read: "That all parish activities through Mary's intercession contribute harmoniously to spiritual renewal" and "That Mary's example help Christian women achieve their unique role of the evangelical mission of the Church."

Beneath a medium-sized crucifix, a picture of Mother Teresa holding hands with the Pope had been placed. The caption read, "Let us make the Church present in the world of today."

Next to the photograph, a handwritten sign had instructions for volunteers:

Welcome to Nirmal-Hridayi. Today we are invited to serve our brothers and sisters who are here with us. May the presence of Jesus shine through us as we bring them his eternal love and joy. You may arrive at 7:45 a.m. and we will start our day with prayer. Specific duties will be assigned by Sister Dolores, beginning with serving breakfast. We will finish work and leave at noon. Do not take any photographs without permission.

Nothing is so little that God does not care, nothing so small that he is not concerned. God cares for each of us as though we were the only object of His love. However small I am, God's love seeks me out. God Bless you. All for Jesus.

A schedule for inter-faith prayers was posted, led by a Jesuit priest. Buddhists, Hindus, Muslims, Parsees, and Sikhs would all come together to pray and engage in enlightening dialogue to forge better understanding between the groups.

As we waited, one of the sisters explained how Mother Teresa was always concerned about social justice and fairness for all citizens. The Indians particularly believed in Mother's divine goodness and the way in which she devoted herself completely to Jesus. "We do not have to wait for Rome to canonize her, we already know that she is a saint," the sister added.

While taking in the sights, I also kept an eye out for any movement from Mother Teresa's room, ready to slip into position at whatever point she emerged. I strained my eyes and could see her speaking with a few sisters.

At last, there was an uptick in activity, and a flurry of sisters blew out of Mother Teresa's quarters. As this heavenly icon emerged from her door, I tried to fully absorb each moment in an attempt to etch it into my memory for the rest of my years. She walked along the balcony, stopping to speak to each single person. In turn, she listened intently to what every individual expressed to her. Pleased to see that she was taking her time with one and all, I knew that I would also be able to spend a few precious and unforgettable moments with her. As she proceeded on to the next pilgrim, I was delighted to observe the reaction of the previous one. Some just exclaimed their excitement in the myriad of languages spoken that day, while others instantly glowed as if they had been touched by an earthbound angel. A few were so overwhelmed that they fell silent, at a loss for words, while they tried to assimilate the magnitude of their brief encounter with Mother Teresa.

The diminutive icon occasionally adjusted her sari as she walked. I had seen photos of her with Princess Diana and knew that she was petite. Standing right next to Diana, at 5'11 tall, I guessed that she was about

4'9, because at five feet, she would have at least reached Diana's shoulder.

Closely observing Mother Teresa move among the group, I was unaware that Sister Ann Therese was watching me out of curiosity. Now 1996, it had been five years since the telephone conversation in Washington, but neither of us knew what the other one looked like.

I studied Mother and my first thoughts were: *Look at how the Almighty works. Many of the greatest benefactors and peacemakers for mankind on this Earth are neither tall nor imposing. Imagine Gandhi, also small and thin in stature, and what he did for this world. God, if I did not know who she was, I would just think she was someone's grandmother. It just illustrates once again how the "Lord works in mysterious ways." Saints are among us everywhere, and often you do not truly know who is doing His work.*

Mother Teresa's medium-brown eyes, full of multi-dimensional light and depth, were crowned by dark, arched eyebrows. Her visage exuded the feeling of warmth and love for her fellow human beings, regardless of their station in life. Anyone could approach her. She appeared to have arthritis and carried a small leather-bound book in her left hand. Her blue and white sari was fastened at her shoulder with a gold-colored safety pin. She always wore this simple, one-dollar white sari to identify with the poor, reminiscent of the humble clothes Gandhi had worn. All the sisters' saris were made by the patients at the Mission of Charity's leper colony. A rosary with the crucifix dangled from her left shoulder. She had deep lines in her face as if she carried the weight of the world on her shoulders. Walking slowly, she looked vulnerable. Having recently suffered from bouts of malaria and heart trouble, she would only live for another sixteen months.

She must have felt debilitated because she had also been hospitalized with a broken collarbone the previous month. Frail-looking but a real stalwart, the discomfort had no bearing on her spirit. An American philanthropist who had brought medical supplies from the States for her shelters told me that despite her pain, she had insisted against doctor's orders on having him, along with his group, admitted to her hospital room so that she could thank them personally.

Finally, Mother Teresa, often referred to as "the saint of the gutters," walked directly toward me, nearing the end of the impromptu line. Greeting me in a gentle voice, she welcomed me to her home. "I am so thrilled to meet you that I can hardly put it into words," I told her. "I was so happy to hear that you cancelled your trip to Rome yesterday. I feel so incredibly blessed to be in your presence."

I motioned with my hands towards my collarbone, patting it, to be sure that she would understand me, as I was not certain how fluent she was in English. "How are you feeling, Mother? I certainly hope that you are not in any pain, and that your collarbone is completely healed. I pray for your full recovery."

She smiled and nodded. Glancing skyward momentarily, she said that she felt much better, thanking God that she was not in too much discomfort.

Reaching into my purse, I felt glad that we had been paid our per diem the day before. She graciously accepted the donation. I was immediately impressed with the fact that if I had handed her a five-dollar bill and someone else had handed her two "Uncle Bens," ($200) she would have been equally respectful to both of us, just as if we had given her the same amount.

"Whatever you do for the well-being of the needy is beautiful to God," she said to me, like what she had expressed to the others who had given her an offering.

Indicating that she wanted to bless me, she was ready to place both of her hands on my head. At nearly six feet tall, I had to bow over quite a bit. Bending my knees, I felt her gentle hands touch my head. Leaning in, she whispered a blessing for me as the other pilgrims watched. As her energy flowed into mine, it began to gently surge throughout my body. I sensed that a kind of ethereal cleansing was taking place, as if I was standing under a soft waterfall. I experienced a refreshing, tingling sensation with goosebumps all over. I was instantly aware that I would receive the benefit of her touch for many more years to come. For a few precious moments, time absolutely stood still for me.

She stood back a bit and fiddled for something in a pocket located in her sari. There had to be a few valuable sections in there—at least one for spur-of-the-moment donations and another one for small gifts. She brought out a fistfull of silver medals. Mother Mary was on the front of each one, along with the inscription, "Oh Mary conceived without sin pray for us who have recourse to thee."

So grateful that she had given me about a dozen blessed medals, I planned to take them back to America for friends who were ill with serious diseases to cheer them up. Later, after giving all of them away, I kept exactly one.

Thanking her profusely in a quiet, reverent voice, she acknowledged my gratitude by nodding. She glided by to speak with the Irish couple standing behind me. It was difficult for me to comprehend the experience, to take it all in. I grappled with the impact of what had just happened. I felt overwhelmed, but in an uplifting, enlightening way. Simply said, Mother Teresa had taken my breath away. I cannot imagine anyone on the planet not being profoundly moved by having met her, even if they had no idea who she was. An extraordinary human being in every sense of the word, Mother Teresa had shone a radiant light on the world for decades.

One of the sisters asked what part of the States I was from. As soon as I said the Washington, D.C., area, she chuckled and said, "I lived there for five years."

Within seconds, we figured out that we had previously met over the phone.

It was Sister Ann Therese. Absolutely beautiful, she had one of those timeless faces which you could not tell if she was 38 or 58 years old. Her golden-brown skin had an eternal glow that came from within. Her brown eyes were bright and shone when she spoke. She looked like a resplendent bride every time I saw her in subsequent visits. Over the years, I have noticed this "timeless look" on the faces of devotees of God's work no matter what religion they practice. Having come into contact with thousands of Muslims during the Hajj operations, it was also a joy for me to observe this look of kindness and devotion to others in many of the Islamic pilgrims I have met along the way.

"Tania, I noticed that you had a camera but did not have a photo taken with Mother Teresa," she said.

"I was so overcome by meeting her that I completely forgot," I replied, laughing at myself, "but I would also not want to bother her." Sister replied, "Oh, she will not mind. Get your camera ready and I will ask her for you."

I will be forever grateful that she did ask Mother Teresa to take a photo with me. It was a very thoughtful gesture on her part, to invite me to spend a few more precious moments in the presence of this celestial individual who meant the world to millions, and will, *ad infinitum.*

⤴

Back at the hotel, I ran straight into Sohan, one of our fellow Air India flight attendants, in the lobby. The word had got out all over Calcutta that Mother Teresa was still in town. My co-workers had surmised that I had experienced the great fortune of having visited the right place at the right time.

"Tania, we have been waiting for you with eagle eyes," he began. "Everyone wants to hear all about your meeting with Mother Teresa."

Smiling at the idiom about a predator's vision, I replied, "I know you have been, Sohan, but I will tell you tomorrow. Right now, I just want to return to my room and remember what an extraordinary day this has been for me."

Up in my room overlooking the hotel's tropical courtyard, I hungered for some peaceful time to absorb what a unique day it had been for me. I longed to contemplate and reflect upon the meaning. I lit some sandalwood incense and put on some Hindi music at a low volume. The indelible impression of this momentous day continuously danced in my thoughts. Running an imaginary videotape of the experience through my mind, I wanted to examine my feelings more closely. The benefit of this remarkable encounter had entered into my soul to be with me forever.

Removing the garland of jasmine from around my neck, I took a big sniff of the aromatic little white flowers. Wrapping them in a colorful Indian scarf, I carefully packed it away. It had now become a cherished souvenir. Selecting one of the medals Mother had given me, I placed it in a silk pouch nestled in my purse. From time to time during my travels, I show it to others, inviting them to hold it. Every single day since that blessed meeting, I have carried it, and shall, always.

⤴

Mother Teresa was canonized by Pope Francis 1 on September 2, 2016.

My father with native Indians

2

Earning My Wings in Spyville, USA

Rumor mongers hissed about what a shame it was that Glenn and Nike were never going to have any children. Married for over nine years, there was no kid in sight. In the fifties, practically the first thing on a marriage agenda was to procreate. So far, they had been out of luck.

A business trip to Caracas, Venezuela, changed all that overnight. My parents savored every minute of exploring this tropical destination with its exotic flora and fauna. My father spoke Castilian Spanish so that paved the way, making the trip even more enjoyable and enriching. Even though my mom suffered from a painful broken ankle, Mother Nature had finally won out.

When they returned to their home in McLean, Virginia, just outside Washington, D.C., my mother instinctively knew that she was expecting a child. She was right. Me. I just wanted to enter the Earth's vibration in a roundabout way. I had been conceived in Caracas, a rather cool place to begin the process of coming into this lifetime.

Eight godparents, four men and four women, all close friends, took active roles in my life, so "my village" was set at an early age. Elva Licklider, my mother's best friend and the most generous, kind lady you could ever meet, was my favorite. You could depend on her for anything. She never had any children, so I was just like her daughter, and could discuss anything with her in confidence.

My parents entertained often in Troxell Hall, the custom Tudor mansion that my father built in his late twenties. As you entered through the front door, the first thing you noticed was that the dark

Senator Estes Kefauver of Tennessee attended a large party which included Mrs. Glenn Anderson of Fairfax County, Virginia

My mother with Senator Estes Kefauver

wood-paneled living room shot straight up to the second-story ceiling. Parallel wooden balconies ran alongside the bedrooms upstairs. Three large stone fireplaces on the first floor kept us warm in the dead of winter. Situated on twelve acres of dense forest along Georgetown Pike, it was close to the well-known girls' school, Madeira.

Born in 1900, my father Glenn grew up behind Troxell Hall, not far from the rushing falls of the Potomac River. Dark-complexioned, he was photographed in 1905 grinning widely with local Native Americans surrounding him. He not only fit right in but could have easily been taken for one of them. My father was naked, and one striking young Indian lady who resembled a dark version of Bo Derek had her arm around him, strategically positioning some flowers right in front of his privates. Hence, my father was introduced to another culture at the tender age of five.

My father (left) at the US Supreme Court

As an attorney, he served before the US Supreme Court, and as an architect, he built more than 100 Tudor townhouses called "Foxhall Village" in Washington, D.C., before he reached the age of thirty-five. In those days, our nation's capital was rather intimate, and key people were acquainted. Politically active, my parents knew First Lady Eleanor Roosevelt, General Douglas MacArthur, and Senator Harry Byrd from

Elva (left) Mom (right) at Troxell Hall

Virginia personally. An old friend, Senator Estes Kefauver of Tennessee, consulted with my father for advice during his presidential bid in 1956. From a bright room in the White House overlooking the south lawn and Washington Monument, my parents would join the venerable First Lady for tea, French pastries, and animated discussions about the politics and events of the day.

Daddy always had a keen interest in aviation and space. On clear nights, he would hoist me up onto his shoulders, taking me for a ride

Mom with Princess Tatiana Abkhazi

out onto the front lawn. He loved pointing out the various constellations and even one of the early satellites as it raced across the sky.

My mother Nike had a light complexion, blazing crystal-blue eyes with natural dark lashes, and blonde hair which she fixed in the same style as actress Hedy Lamar. She always wore the 18-karat gold orchid necklace with a matching bracelet my father had purchased for her in Caracas.

While my father was befriending Native Americans as a young boy, my mother also spent her formative years with ethnic people miles away

Princess Tatiana and me

in the Caribbean, living in Port-au-Prince, Haiti, with her family of diplomats. The innocent little towhead was quite the contrast to the islanders but learned Patois. Easily adapted to the colorful island life, she loved the sound of drums.

She adored and respected all living things. To make me laugh, she would lean out of the bedroom window and imitate a wolf's cry just to get the neighbors' dogs to howl back. When they came to visit Teddy, our Great Pyrenees, she lavished them with treats. She saved snacks

By Joe Heiberger, Staff Photographer

Teddy, the stay-at-home who used to be quite the gadabout, braces himself for a pat on the head from his little mistress, Tania Anderson, 28 months, of McLean, Va.

Yours truly with Teddy

for tiny chipmunks and put saltlicks out for grazing deer. A florist, she often whipped up creative arrangements and centerpieces for our parties using all types of bright, fragrant flowers.

Her daily column, "Town and Country," was featured in the society section of the newspaper. She was a freelance writer for *National Geographic* magazine, the *New York Times,* and women's magazines. Absorbing volumes of information about different cultures and customs, she spoke with authority about unusual destinations as if she had traveled there. Always eager to meet others from foreign lands, she loved to hear endless stories of their lives abroad, drinking in all the details.

My parents frequently threw joint soirees with the then-Secretary of State Dean Acheson and his wife, entertaining an eclectic group of friends at Troxell Hall. Princess Tatiana Abkhazi of Russia, one of my godmothers, and her husband John Shields, whom we saw often, were frequent guests. Baron and Baroness van Lynden of the Netherlands, our cherished neighbors, were with the Dutch Embassy. Joey was originally from Scotland, and her husband Willem was a submarine commander. Their beautiful, multi-lingual daughter Antoinette was my good friend, and we played together often. A Polish countess and a French countess were also regular guests, along with an Irish American taxicab driver and his family, who were old confidantes.

Prince and Princess Pignatelli, friends of my parents, usually brought their blonde son Paul along to play with me. The guests kidded at how I looked more Italian than Paul with my dark, Mediterranean appearance, and how cute we looked playing together, as his light coloring was like my mother's. A good sprinkling of politicians, restaurateurs, and intelligence agents rounded out the guest list of this international milieu.

The topic of conversation often centered on current world events. Diverse political opinions were expressed throughout the evening. Large buffets were served while guests spread themselves out among the three large first-floor parlors. The aroma of popular French perfumes wafted through the air as they mingled.

Even my pets were foreign and exotic. Zaner was a lush seal point Siamese cat with "Elizabeth Taylor" violet eyes. As Zaner navigated the crowd, my father, observing his large, dark brown, velvet-looking balls, joked that you could not deny that Mother Nature had a sense of humor. Teddy was a gentle Great Pyrenean from the mountains of southern France bordering Spain. To everyone's delight, Teddy allowed Zaner to sleep on top of him, cozily nestled in his thick white fur while he snored away.

My best friends were Diane Parks and her brother Marty, who also lived in McLean. Three generations of their family had been friends with my family since the 1930s. Diane, Marty, and I scurried all over their grandmother Evelyn's famed Tower House located high on a bluff overlooking the Potomac River. Looking for trouble, we combed through the snake-infested forest like wild banshees with Herman, their cocker spaniel. Covered in red blistering skin from poison ivy, we always came home with imaginative stories of exploration. Inside the house, we built "forts" made from sheets, naturally decorated with grandma's fine China and crystal. Diane still likes to say, "Tania and I were babies together!"

In those days, invitations arrived from the White House, plainly addressed to "Mr. and Mrs. Glenn Anderson, Troxell Hall, McLean, Virginia," definitely an address from a simpler era.

Daddy's forefathers were from Catalonia, in eastern Spain, and my mother's side was mostly from Ireland. Both hot-headed, they argued frequently. You might say that it was the "Latin temper" versus the "Irish temper." They shouted at each other often, much to the lament of their mutual friends. Just like a car with no brakes, once they got going, nobody could stop them. One summer night when I was four years old, I remember one such blowout. Returning from a party, I was wearing my favorite maroon velvet dress with a white lace collar. Cruising along Swinks Mill Road in our 1951 Pontiac convertible with the top down, I was standing up in the back seat (that is right, no seatbelts!) trying to balance myself while gazing at the star-lit sky.

Suddenly, the fireworks started, and the screaming began. Earlier that day, my father had found several—but severely bent—heirloom sterling silver spoons in the flower beds. My mother had been using them to dig up the soil for her beloved roses. By the time my father stopped the car behind our house, the argument had escalated to the stage where my mother jumped out, slamming the door so violently that it shattered all the glass in her window.

However, they agreed on many positive things. Both viewed humankind through an almost identical perspective. Strong feelings concerning equal rights and the universality of mankind were paramount. Respecting cultures very unlike our own, their powerful belief in human rights, and kind regard towards our fellow human beings was always evident. Empathy, understanding, and justice were frequent topics of conversation when I was growing up. The words "fair and equitable" often ring in my mind to this day. Both were gifted with a marvelous sense of humor; they loved to entertain friends with infinite amusing anecdotes. Storytelling was the lifeblood of their parties.

"Ain't no fools, ain't no fun," my father used to laugh, as he loved to tease.

Years before I was born, my parents threw a large masquerade party. All the guests were gathered downstairs with libations and hors d'oeuvres. Everyone was asking where in the hell my father was. Always notoriously late, and hearing the complaints from below, he sashayed out onto the balcony off his bedroom, carefully surveying the animated group. Overlooking the entire downstairs from above, my father was stark naked. Not a stitch, quite *risqué* for the 1940s. To the shock and raucous laughter of the guests, he declared, "Quit complaining, everyone. Have another cocktail and I'll be down in a minute!"

My parents both acutely understood the frustration that comes with being bullied. Years before Legal Aid, my father was offering advice *pro bono* to others in trouble. One day, a Black colleague named Barbara called him, almost frantic. She was so upset that her voice hit a sharp pitch as she continually mispronounced his name after I answered the phone.

"Mister Annerson, Mister Annerson, I bought a wig from Garfin-kel's, and it was real expensive. I spent far too much money on it, so I was shocked when I washed it only once and it nearly fell apart. It looked horrible! I promptly took it back to the store and they refused to refund my money." She went on to explain how the employees had been extremely rude and mean. "Can you do something for me?"

My father got the name of the nasty department store clerk and dashed off a quick letter on his attorney's stationery to the general manager. When Barbara returned the foul wig a week later, she was greeted with all smiles, no questions. They could not hand her refund back fast enough.

We always patronized the local vegetable stand on Old Georgetown Pike that was owned by a small Black family who also lived in McLean. I remember well the head of the family, Lewin. A kindly man, he was tall and slender, always attired in a well-worn straw hat to complement his denim overalls.

On quiet Sunday afternoons, my father would invite Lewin over for some Old Virginia Gentlemen whiskey, and they would discuss the latest. My father wanted a pulse on everything that was going on around us, including the African American community and their concerns. As good friends, they enjoyed each other's company immensely. While playing with my dolls, I could hear the tone of their conversation being punctuated with frequent laughter.

When I was five, my parents took me to the funeral of Lewin's cousin at a modest, wood-paneled church located next to a large field not far from our home. As we approached the entrance to the church, we could hear the harmonious voices of the choir, declaring their love for the deceased. The church was jammed with mourners. The only White people there, we joined the others on the steps trying to see if we could squeeze ourselves inside. Everyone was beautifully dressed in their "Sunday best," as they used to say. Men wore pin-striped dark suits. Women wore black, neatly pressed dresses with matching hats and shoes accompanied by gloves. This showed respect for the deceased, the church, and each other.

The funeral was a metaphor for my parents' marriage, which ended within months of that event. Still in love with my mother, my father was deeply distressed, but the marriage was *over*. By the time I was seven, my mother had remarried and moved to Charleston, South Carolina. Her new husband, Bevo Middleton, included me on their honeymoon to Nassau, Bahamas; my first trip off America's mainland. After getting over the initial shock that the Bahamians were racing down the "wrong" side of the road, I was excited to explore this resplendent and sunny

British colony, as it was then. We befriended a family from New York City. Their daughter and I spent long hours playing with the colorful lizards and swimming in the calm turquoise-blue waters surrounded by brilliant tropical flowers. Spectacular sunsets held their bright hues like a canopy over the island for a long time after the sun had faded from the horizon.

◡◦

At a young age, my new stepfather Bevo had been happily adopted by Mrs. Robert E. Lee, III. When she passed on, he inherited rare artifacts from the estates of both George Washington and Robert E. Lee, allowing him to buy an 1874 Victorian mansion in Charleston, South Carolina. On the first floor, hand-painted murals on the ceiling illustrated each room's function. The parlor's artwork depicted fairies playing musical instruments, while delicate flora provided nectar for butterflies. In the dining room, cherubs feasted on fruit along the ceiling above the dining room table. Two outside balconies ran alongside the entire length of the house. An elevator operated from the dining room up to the main bedroom, and meals could be loaded onto a dumbwaiter in the kitchen to be whisked upstairs. Fearful that I would get stuck in the elevator playing, my mother was quick to brief me that it was not a toy. A circular balcony known as a widow's peak atop the house provided a spectacular view of the surrounding area. That same balcony can still be seen from Google Earth. A carriage house containing stalls for the transportation of the day—horses—was behind the residence.

Bevo and my mother opened a museum utilizing the first-floor rooms to display memorabilia from his inheritance. In those early, heady days of my mother's second marriage, life was good, and she radiated her newfound happiness. Now surrounded by prominent members of Southern aristocracy, they entertained often on Rutledge Avenue. Even though she had been born a Yankee, my mother felt a strong affinity with the South, and devoured books about the Civil War. Now she was living in a city well-steeped in America's history, residing in a museum loaded with historic artifacts.

As our guests sipped mint juleps in frosted silver goblets, my mother relished exploring her new environment. As the goblets clinked, the sound of her voice and their laughter echoed throughout the cavernous rooms of our house.

The celebratory mood would be short-lived, however. Despite a grand opening ceremony and some favorable write-ups in newspapers and magazines, there were not enough visitors. Even though my mother's marriage to Bevo had a promising beginning, life began to unravel quickly. Drinking excessively, he tried in vain to hide his habit from my mother by constantly eating mints to obscure his putrid vodka breath. When he pressed the car's brakes, several small bottles of cheap screw-top wine rolled forward, hitting his feet. "Bevo! When are you going to lay off the dragon sweat?" my mother would bark.

My mother hired a beautiful, vivacious, 26-year-old lady, Helen Meyers, a native of Charleston, to keep me in line and look after me when they went out on the town. Helen, with her patient demeanor, fondly remembers how I used to dress our three boxers, Butch, Boo-Boo, and Queenie, in some of my clothes and scarves. For me, it was pure heaven to get into bed with three pliant canines and my Barbie dolls to play house.

Recently, I called Helen to ask if she could remember any rambunctious behavior on my part. To my surprise, she said I was pretty good, despite my hyper-energetic reaction to all the upheaval after the divorce.

Every few months, I was shuttled on flights back and forth between my father's home in McLean and my mother's in Charleston. Years later I would laugh and say, "I was the original UM (unaccompanied minor)."

In those days, I would have accumulated substantial frequent flier miles, had they existed.

My mother's young marriage disintegrated as my stepfather slammed down the booze, losing one job after another. Selling off the precious historical artifacts from his inheritance at bargain-basement prices just to keep them afloat infuriated my mother. In that era, when many couples stayed in miserable marriages "for the sake of the children," it seemed as if my mother was headed for divorce number two.

By age nine, our lives continued on a collision course. Attending my father's alma mater, Maret, an exclusive French school in Washington, D.C., my grades were dreadful: four Ds and two Cs. A big believer in education, my father was dismayed. Academically, I was putting in a dismal performance, but on the positive side, and true to my nature, I was making friends with kids from faraway and unusual lands—Egypt, India, France, and Saudi Arabia.

Most weekends, my father took me to Clarence Westbrook's jazz restaurant in northeast D.C. Lifelong friends, my father and Clarence discussed business matters while I got my muzzle into a large, juicy T-bone steak with crispy fries, accompanied by a Shirley Temple with multiple cherries. Popular with African Americans, Clarence's restaurant was always packed, and rightfully so. The food was delicious and the live jazz always relaxing. This is where my love of jazz was born, and thoughts of his lounge bring back fond memories. On the brink of puberty, I was engrossed as couples embraced while slow dancing, wondering if I would enjoy swaying to the beat when I got older. The men usually wore sports coats, while the ladies were decked out in form-fitting dresses or blouses with tight, knee-length pencil skirts. The atmosphere and music were uplifting, providing a welcome escape for its patrons. During the early sixties, the living was *not* easy for Americans of color, so Clarence's place was a welcome and pleasant oasis in a segregated environment.

Soft red, pink, and yellow light illuminated the walls. Whenever the live music stopped, someone always fed coins into the jukebox. The dancing never ended.

Clarence was a White man with blue eyes and solid white hair, a few years older than my father. His great restaurant had deservingly earned the respect of the Black community. The melodic energy in his restaurant flowed with relaxed ease, and even though I always fell fast asleep in the car on the long ride home, I never turned my father down when he suggested that we visit Clarence. To this day, whenever I hear jazz, I am transported right back to Clarence's smoky restaurant, the décor, the styles from the '60s, the dancing, the flirting, and the oversized grilled steaks.

To expose me to a wide variety of beneficial learning experiences, my father occasionally took me to political events. One day, he drove me up to Capitol Hill to meet some senators, but not without some really careful prepping first. I was a bit hyperactive, to say the least, so my father made certain that I knew exactly what was expected of me, primarily to be polite. He bought me a beautiful blue chiffon knee-length party dress to wear for making the rounds. I was clearly instructed to curtsy when introduced to anyone on "the Hill," as we call it in D.C. To my father's great relief, when introduced to Senator Estes Kefauver, whose presidential campaign my father strongly supported and advised, I curtsied right on cue.

As the court date approached, I became increasingly restless and unruly. Not to blame them, but this was made worse by the fact that my parents were now embroiled in a hostile custody battle over me, to be played out in the Fairfax, Virginia, courthouse. Given nine days off from school, I sat in the attorney's office nearby for endless hours while the testimonies dragged on. Terribly bored, I was completely unaware of the highly charged emotional drama taking place across the street. Inside the courtroom, witnesses' emotions were just about ready to boil over.

While several of my godparents watched intently from the stiff, uncomfortable benches, Bevo took the stand to testify that I would have a better life with him and my mother. He declared under oath that I had bonded with him so well that I wanted to change my surname to Middleton. That was the *ka-boom* statement that sent my father right over the edge. Red-faced, with his eyes bugging out, my father flew into a rage, jumping out of his seat. Still in love with my mother, his emotions were compounded by the fact that he was horrified at the thought the judge might ship me off 700 miles away to be under the care of my unemployed, alcoholic stepfather. In those times, unless the mother was an unfit kook, the great majority of custody cases were ruled in her favor.

Rising from the witness stand after his testimony, Bevo casually strolled out of the courtroom. My father immediately stormed out after him into the hallway, roaring, "You lying, perjuring bastard! You're under oath, you know! You son of a bitch!"

His rage superseded the thought that he could be held in contempt of court. The entire courthouse resonated and shook from my father's wrath.

The next day, I took the stand. In the early sixties, it was almost unheard of for a child to testify in a custody case. The attorneys were gentle in the way they posed their questions, but it was difficult for me to observe all the raw emotions up close now that I was actually inside the courtroom. Dear Elva, my favorite godmother and mother's best friend, looked as if she would burst into tears any minute if one more angry word was said. She loved both of my parents deeply. It was heart-wrenching for her and became even more acute when each one pressed her for support. While certain friends of my parents looked teary-eyed, some faces became contorted when lies were told. Still others just studied the scene quietly, sad and pensive, perhaps contemplating the result of all the accusations.

The entire process had a visceral effect on everyone involved and it showed on their strained features. I felt strongly conflicted about the outcome of the trial, as I adored both of my parents. Like a true Piscean, I constantly daydreamed as I sat on the hard wooden seat. I contemplated how our lives had been. It seemed like it had been decades since we had thrown the lively parties at Troxell Hall, where I used to run from guest to guest trying to get attention, as if I did not have enough already. In the wintertime, each lady's fur coat was carefully placed on the beds upstairs as they arrived. Frolicking in them, I would back up a few feet just to take a running leap into the entire pile. Then I would try them on, one by one, starting with my favorites. Edith, a close friend, said the first time she saw me, I was four years old. I had selected someone's luxuriant fox coat, which dwarfed me, and was descending the sweeping staircase slowly, trying desperately not to trip, looking to see who noticed first.

Imagining the future, I visualized myself sweeping down that staircase like a princess bride in my ravishing wedding gown to greet the guests in the home my beloved father had built. These not-too-distant memories played through my mind like a video as the testimonies dragged on and I tried to get lost in my own pleasant thoughts.

Suddenly, the noise of the gavel crashing down jerked me back to the stark reality of the dank courtroom. Now, in that barren, unsightly room, I realized that only *three* years had passed since my parents and I had lived together. It seemed like a lifetime. All of our lives had changed dramatically. The first time I saw *Kramer vs. Kramer*, those same emotions raced to the surface again. I almost said out loud in the theater, "I could have written the screenplay to this, as I have lived through this experience and know exactly how it feels, frame to frame."

A smoker, my father stepped into the hallway in between testimonies and puffed away furiously, pondering the ugly situation we were all embroiled in. Constantly coughing and suffering from emphysema, he had only five precious years left to live.

One afternoon after the two-week trial, Daddy strolled slowly into the attorney's office while I was reading a kid's detective book. His face was ashen, with the downcast look of defeat. He alternated between studying my curious face and the floor.

"Well, that's it," he sighed in a quiet voice, "I lost the case. The judge gave full custody to your mother."

With no idea what to say, I stayed quiet to let him think it through for a few minutes. "You will be flying to Charleston next week," he added, hugging me while managing a slight smile. "I have done everything that I could."

By the time I was thirteen, my father's physique had dramatically changed. In his youth, he had been so striking that Metro Goldwyn Mayer had offered him a contract to star in films. He was 6'3" with a medium build, his thick black hair parted on the side. With a mustache and deep brown eyes, he would have been perfectly cast as a gangster. Double-breasted suits with wingtip shoes and a fedora hat made up his signature look. He had even dated Jean Harlow for a while and was scandalized that she never wore a brassiere when they went out on the town together. That was sexy stuff in the 1930s. Platinum blonde Jean, with her carefully coiffed angel-type hair and perfectly made-up porcelain skin, was one of the most sought-after actresses in Hollywood. She always wore feminine, silky, alluring gowns, and my father would go cuckoo with desire, usually getting a hard-on, according to my mother. They must have been quite a pair, making the grand entrance at parties together, Jean with her sultry decolletage and my father with a rocket in his pocket.

Now hunched over, his face was drawn. His eyes were losing their luster as the life began to ebb out of his body, bit by bit. Constantly hacking away, it was necessary for him to always carry a handkerchief. Now, instead of being perfectly proportioned, he was scrawny and gaunt. Watching him rapidly go downhill tore my emotions to shreds. Even in grammar school, I used to snatch cigarettes out of his lips right after he lit up. It was as if I knew that this would be the villain to drain and ravage his life.

⌒◎

Realizing that he was on his way out of this world, he made careful plans for my future. He approached our old friends from Holland, the van Lyndens, to inquire about European schools. Antoinette's mother Joey suggested Millfield, a progressive boarding school in Somerset, England. This would be the seventh school I would attend in my short life.

My life was about to be irrevocably changed forever.

At fourteen, I was embarking alone on an entirely new phase of my existence, at a school in Europe, across the Atlantic Ocean, far from American shores. I was also going to lose my beloved father during my very first semester there and could sense it. My heart was breaking, but I tried hard to stay positive.

⌒◎

After bidding a tearful goodbye to my friends and family, I flew up to Idlewild (now JFK) Airport in New York, a 35-minute flight. My father had arranged through friends at Air India for me to fly on their B-707 to London by myself.

The Air India representative ushered me into the Maharaja Lounge to wait for my trans-Atlantic flight. The hostesses in the lounge were all wearing saris in a variety of my favorite colors. I felt right at home. As I sipped a Coke with cherries, I distinctly remember looking across the tarmac at the aircraft that was going to whisk me across the ocean to begin an entirely new chapter of my being. "My life will never be the same after today," I thought, simultaneously feeling spellbound and apprehensive.

After a delicious spicy curry dinner, the navigator snaked his way back, plunking himself down next to me in the darkened cabin. What's easier than trying to shark an unescorted 14-year-old girl on the plane you are in charge of? Becoming scarlet-faced as he tried to make some small talk, I had not yet acquired the expertise to tell a homely guy to drop dead. As he moved closer to "make out" (as we used to call it), I declared in a loud voice, "Buddy, who's flying the plane? You need to get lost! I have got to get some sleep for London!" He skulked away as other passengers stared.

Life at Millfield School took me far, far away from the happenings in America. While in London, I stayed with my guardians, who lived on the trendy Abbey Road made famous by The Beatles. Guardians were required to look after all foreign students while in London. Traveling on the train down to Somerset's countryside, I arrived at my new boarding house with 19 other maidens, or so I thought.

My new English school had 800 boys and 230 girls from more than 65 nations. Classes held only six pupils, so students and teachers all knew each other well. Initially, I did not mesh well with the English. They were constantly making fun of my American accent and slang expressions. "She says she wants to raid the icebox!" an English gal sniffed before bursting out laughing.

I huffed, "We invented it and I will call it whatever I like!"

Another lass looked down her nose and demanded, "Tell me why you always say, 'what a riot' and 'what a blast!'"

These were popular American expressions at the time, and they had traveled across the Atlantic with me. A new environment, indeed. Scandalized to learn that dozens of them had already been "deflowered" by age 15 (this *was* 1966 after all), one pale-faced English girl turned the tables on me. Howling on the bus, she announced, "Oh, my! Tania is still a virgin!"

As some of the girls cackled, I sank down into the plush seat. I was also agitated they were always asking me what the hell the Yanks were doing in Vietnam, as if, at age 14, I had any articulate answers. All it did was hurt my feelings and make me feel more like an outsider. But before long, I was making friends with students from cultures far different from those in the West.

His Royal Highness, Prince Mahidol Vajiralongkorn, the crown prince of Thailand, was in my class of six students that very first term. Four months younger than me, he had thick dark hair, a smooth complexion, and medium-colored brown eyes. Initially, all I could recall about Thailand was the popular film *The King and I,* and our affectionate feline Zaner. What I did not know, but my mother would have informed me, was that Prince Mahidol was considered a demi-God in his native land. His mother, Queen Sirikit, a strikingly beautiful woman, and her husband, King Bhumibol, ruled for more than 50 years. The king had been the world's longest-serving monarch until his passing in 2016. When commoners are in the presence of the king and queen, they can never be above the monarchs in stature, so they must crouch down, even when they are seated on an aircraft in flight. A Thai flight attendant at Pan Am once proudly showed me a photo of her in the upper deck of the B-747, squatting down to be lower than Queen Sirikit.

As a prince and a commoner, Mahidol and I truly came from two diverse ways of life, but that did not stop a friendship from budding. High-energy and impetuous, I pulled the same hijinks I had learned from my school in the States just a few months earlier. When the teacher was not looking—which was not too often—I would show Mahidol cartoons from the newspaper and then send him a cute message scrawled on crumpled paper. After a few moments, he would flash me a mischievous look, and we would continue our kidding of each other.

Mahidol loved tennis, and I would go down to the courts to just watch him. One day, he came out and smiled for me while I took photos. As we laughed and joked, I snapped away with my brownie camera. Months later, when my mother saw them, she kidded, "Darling, if we ever have any financial difficulty, we can always sell these photos to *LIFE* magazine."

However, she was obviously pleased that I was befriending such distinguished classmates.

Despite its reputation as a progressive boarding school with extraordinary opportunities, Millfield could also be a dumping ground for gifted offspring of wealthy parents while they sorted out their private lives back home. The dorms did not have central heating, sometimes just a warm pipe that ran alongside the wall. Tasteless rice and ordinary potatoes with tough meat were served at most meals. The toilet paper was just like tracing paper, and I wrote my parents letters on sheets about six feet long just to prove the point. The archaic corrugated iron huts where we had some classes featured wrought iron stoves in the center. We took turns shoveling fuel into them for warmth; a scene from days gone by. I remember watching my classmate Amir from Persia all bundled up, lifting filthy coal and wood into the fire to keep us all warm. I am sure that this duty was not exactly what his parents had in mind when they sent him to the most expensive prep school in Europe, but we all prevailed somehow.

On weekends, all students were required to take part in some sporting activity. We cheered for our Millfield teams at polo matches, swimming competitions, and rugby games. Slender horses raced across the challenging and wet green hills of Somerset in steeplechases. At the stables we visited the horses, chatted, and brewed hot tea.

My father signed me up for riding lessons, which cost extra. Grooming the horses, cleaning out their hooves, and polishing their saddles was mandatory. Boys took turns scooping out the stables and "mucking the heap"—no exceptions. They pitch-forked the formidable mountains of horse dung, regardless of their title or who they were—whether prince, sheikh, count, sultan, lord, or commoner.

Once Queen Sirikit made an unannounced surprise visit to see His Royal Highness Prince Mahidol at my school. She was not allowed to meet with him right away. It just happened to be his turn that weekend for clean-up after lunch. After having traveled over 6,000 miles, the queen was politely informed that she would have to kindly wait, and her son would be out in less than an hour. You cannot beat British discipline.

In 2016, after King Bhumibol's passing, HRH Prince Mahidol ascended to the throne as King Rama X.

Also swimming around in my randy teenaged mind was the probability of choosing a compatible boyfriend with over 800 lads in my school. After all, I only had to compete with 229 other young lasses—not bad odds.

"Salaam alay kum" (Peace be unto you) was the greeting. I whirled around to see a boy my age, my height, with lively brown eyes and a welcoming smile. I had no idea what it meant. "Excuse me?" I asked, a little perplexed.

"Oh, you don't speak Arabic," the young man replied, looking both surprised and disappointed at once. Hearing my accent, he asked, "Are you American?"

"Why, of course." We introduced ourselves, and instantaneously a great, life-long friendship was born.

Maamoun Zahid from Saudi Arabia also took riding lessons with his brothers. He had a natural gift for riding, and I was envious. As much as I adored horses, I was never a good rider. Maamoun could gallop away while showing us some tricks. It must be in his blood, I thought. While he was out ripping along the fields at a break-neck pace, I was assigned to an elderly gentle white horse named Fantasy; just my speed.

Spending loads of time together in between classes, I was fascinated by the way he addressed me, always referring to me as a young woman. I still thought of myself as just a tall girl, but he had an entirely different perspective. He spoke to me in a way that I cannot imagine any American teenaged guy speaking to a teenaged girl. It was unusual, enticing, and made me oh-so-curious to explore our friendship more.

Trying to get a frame of cultural reference, I recalled my little girl-friend Khalida, also from Saudi Arabia, whose father was Ambassador to the US. We had been at Maret school together at age nine, and I distinctly remember visiting her vast home in Northwest Washington. She was a darling girl, and we got along well. Once when she ran off to get some toys, I was left alone in the living room for a few minutes. Something on the wall caught my eye. Over the stone fireplace, five formal portraits hung together. Her father was positioned in the middle, with two women placed on each side. Glaring at them, I instinctively knew that theirs was an ethos vastly different from our own. Thankfully I kept my mouth shut for the plethora of questions I had until Daddy picked me up. Then I burst out with different types of inquiries all at once. Laughing, my father haltingly explained a little about polygamy. Scandalized, I asked how a man could possibly wrangle his life with four women under one roof, not to mention all the screaming kids? Now that I knew Maamoun, perhaps at some point he'd fill in all the details.

On Saturdays, we attended polo matches or steeplechases, usually accompanied by our friends from various African nations. Cold for months on end, the weather's dampness easily penetrated our bones. Soon I realized why the English drank so damn much hot tea. I began sucking down about eight cups a day myself, just trying to stay warm. I sympathized with my friends from hot countries. If I was freezing, how were they dealing with it? To top it off, we did not have a scrap of central heating in this elite school. Every night the hot water for baths ran out after 30 minutes. Rather than take a cold bath, I would skip it all together and stay stinky, later shivering while trying to fall asleep.

I almost got into trouble with Maamoun during the early days of our friendship, but my offense was completely unintentional. At a sporting event, I decided to capture the fun on camera. Maamoun was walking in front of me, and I called out his name. He swung around and I instantly snapped his photo. He was furious, but I had no idea why. "You are not allowed to do that!" he bellowed. His face was screwed up, and he was obviously upset. I felt guilty, but for what? "You cannot capture my image in a photo!" he exclaimed.

I apologized, and when he calmed down, he explained to me that in their culture, photos of people's faces are forbidden. I promised never to take his photo again. When it was developed, I could instantly see how infuriated he was, but he also instinctively knew that I would never make him angry on purpose. I just did not know the traditions of his country but was certainly beginning to learn them.

During that first term, I wrote to both of my parents frequently. I like to think that my father derived some real satisfaction in knowing that even during those early days in England I was adjusting well to new customs with exotic friends. In my own naïve way, I related tales of my days spent with an international collection of students and teachers. Through my letters, I am certain that he got a good idea of how I was settling in as he read the descriptions of my transformed life 3,700 miles away.

As a parent, he made an enormous sacrifice to set me free during his final days on this Earth, while he spent silent and bleak sub-zero nights sitting entirely alone in front of the fireplace at Troxell. As the life in his body began to dissipate, he deteriorated rapidly in the large, now empty house. Too weak to climb the stairs to the bedroom, he slept upright in an over-stuffed chair in the dining room. Giving a child complete freedom under these circumstances must be one of the biggest sacrifices a parent can make. In essence, what he had envisioned and planned for so carefully was taking root, as I became more confident while settling down in England. Now it appeared as if my future would be set on another, much less perilous, course.

One of the strongest psychic impressions I have ever had was during a short stay in London that November at my guardian's flat on Abbey Road. My father had been consistently writing to me that he was fine, not to worry about him, that friends were looking after him. Then one day, as I was ironing, I began to weep quietly. I knew in my heart that he did not want me to fret about his health, thinking that my grades would be affected by my concern. Through Millfield, he had scheduled a Christmas skiing trip to Grindelwald, Switzerland, but the distinct impression washed over me that it was imperative for me to return home or I might never see him again. Traveling back to school from London, I went directly to ask the Bursar to cancel the Swiss trip and to arrange for me to return to the States. Accommodating, they made the plans as requested.

My first return from abroad marked the beginning of many times that my arms would be laden with gifts and souvenirs from another country. As I emerged from Customs, my jaw dropped with shock. My emaciated, disheveled father was sunken into a wheelchair. With a single glance at my father in that broken condition, my heart plummeted to the airport's linoleum floor and shattered into thousands of tiny pieces. Clarence was on his right. My mother and Bevo were standing on the other side of the metal apparatus.

As I rushed towards my father, all the Christmas gifts fell and scattered on the floor. Valiantly struggling, it took every ounce of energy he had to get up out of his wheelchair to hug me. As we embraced tightly, I immediately realized that I was completely holding him up. His bones were protruding from an old shirt that looked like it had not been changed in days. I was crushed to see my father in a nearly paralyzed state.

My mother and Bevo went to great lengths to be cordial to my father, as if everything was entirely normal. Thankfully, for everyone's sake, the welcome home went smoothly and there was no sniping of any kind. It was the first time that all of us had been under the same roof together since the custody battle at the courthouse five years previously.

On Christmas Day, I went to see my father at the hospital. Trying hard to keep the tears at bay and stay upbeat, I had so many stories to tell that I did not know where to begin. He listened intently as I animatedly described everything about life at Millfield. Even though he was desperately ill, he must have gained some pleasure in those final hours, hearing that his dreams for me had been realized. The seeds he had planted so carefully were well on their way to bearing fruit.

After spending that frigid and icy Christmas afternoon with him, describing my new teenaged life in England, the time came to leave. After a prolonged goodbye, a big hug and a kiss, I left the room. Shuffling down the hallway, I abruptly stopped. Creeping back, I quietly stood in the doorway. My father had his back to me, facing the foggy window. He was coughing violently and shaking, but he could sense something. He slowly turned around to face me.

"Merry Christmas, Tania," he said, managing a weak smile.

"Merry Christmas, Daddy," I replied, running in for another warm hug. Using my childhood nickname, he asked, "You know that I love you more than anything else in the world, don't you, Noonie Mice?" He had said those empowering words to me many times in my short life.

Three days after Christmas, my mother ascended the spiral staircase to my bedroom, wailing. Dead asleep, I was immediately awakened by her sobs. She sat next to me on the bed, taking my hands in hers. It took her a moment to speak, as she gathered her thoughts.

"Darling, last night your father got sick, very sick," she said slowly, "and he died. I am so sorry."

With her blood-shot blue eyes, she looked right into mine as I gasped and burst out crying. My head started to spin, as I thought, *died, died, died!* Even the sound of the word in my mind was alien. My father, larger than life, has left us, so completely *final.*

I was only fourteen. Both my parents were supposed to still be alive, to nurture me and guide me until I could confidently set sail by myself. What path could my life possibly take from here now that the captain of my ship had vanished? Feeling a wave of fear about the unknown came over me, and I began to tremble. I had always felt that I could not go on living if something happened to my father. My eyes scanned the ceiling, as if looking for answers to this horrendous news.

Looking at her bright blue eyes filled with tears, I realized in that instant that deep down, she had really loved my father despite all the bitterness after their divorce. We embraced, holding each other tightly for some time.

Now a significant chapter in her life was also ending with my father's death.

3

Walking on Air—
I Became a Pan Amigo

From a tender young age, I was always searching the sky for the first evening star to make my "wish du jour," as my father described it. He taught me that way of visualizing. It felt mystical to me, and I carefully pronounced the words as if it was a mantra. Perhaps it was my first mantra. "Star light, star bright, first star I see tonight. I wish I may, I wish I might, have the wish I wish tonight." If I appeased the heavens carefully enough, possibly my fantasies would be granted. My father took great delight in observing the look of wonder on my face, as he, too, was intrigued by the heavens.

As a young child, I developed a fascination of foreign lands. I pored over books with tales of life in unusual locales, richly illustrated with colorful renditions of natives from other lands wearing their national costumes. For hours I studied pictures of how their villages looked, what kinds of animals they had, and how they appeared to live life in surroundings sharply contrasted with ours. Even at preschool age, I felt in my bones that one day Fate would lead me to numerous exotic destinations, many where I have lived in previous lifetimes. I just wasn't certain what the catalyst would be.

Before graduating from American University with a B.A. in political science and international studies, I took the foreign service exam. I failed. I took it again. I failed once more. It appeared that I was not destined to be a diplomat. I interviewed with the CIA, but that didn't feel right. Disappointed and discouraged, I moved to San Diego for a few years, living with old friends near the Pacific Ocean while becoming a party animal.

After I returned to Washington, D.C., a full-page ad for Pan American World Airways jumped out at me one day. Interviews were being held at the Mayflower Hotel, where my parents had attended endless special occasions of yesteryear. Living in a tiny 150-square-foot room only two blocks from the hotel, I just happened to have a sky-blue suit, Pan Am's color, and got my tail down there tout de suite the next morning.

It was obvious that the interviewer did not like me at all. Perhaps my "type" reminded her of someone who had betrayed her. When she said with a half-smile, "We'll call you," we both knew that she was lying. *Pan American World Airways!* I thought, as I walked slowly up the street, feeling dejected. I was determined to be hired. Having lost out with the State Department, I was not going to let *this* opportunity slip by me. Then I had an idea. I had noticed much confusion in the hotel suite, so I decided to go back the next day, wearing a different suit. Thinking of the sky, I chose a white summer suit with a cobalt-blue silk blouse.

This time, the interviewer was a friendly lady named Mary. We hit it off right away. She looked over my application and resume, asking me all kinds of questions. Later I learned that if you had anything on the application about having lived or studied in a foreign country, it was a big plus. That was precisely what Pan Am was looking for in their new hires—as opposite of the "cookie cutter" flight attendant spectrum as they could find—diverse and sophisticated applicants who could seamlessly step into the role of diplomat as if it was second nature. This group craved adventure.

The only glitch was when she said, "I see that your language is Spanish—wait just a minute," as she fumbled with some papers.

I remember thinking *oh, no, I haven't studied Spanish in a blue moon, don't tell me I will be busted for this detail!* She instructed me to translate nine or ten lines. The gods must have been with me, for I passed with no trouble.

"I'd like you to meet another interviewer," Mary said, and there stood Al Topping, a tall, handsome Black man with a ready smile.

"Come in, Tania, have a seat."

Asking more detailed questions about my experience, he was curious about my studies in England. I had no way of knowing, but Al was one of the "famous" employees at Pan Am.

In 1975, he was the station manager in Saigon when the communists were pressing into the city. Complete chaos reigned, as South Vietnam was collapsing all around them. While the American Navy was dumping helicopters off their carriers into the sea to make room for refugees, Al was planning a decampment of his own. Desperate citizens pressed against the fence surrounding the airport, pleading to be let in, while Al was inside his frenzied office, trying to hammer out a viable plan of escape. He was in continual, direct contact with his bosses in Hong Kong, Honolulu, and Pan American's operations in New York. Pan Am's Chairman, Bill Seawell, was also in constant touch with President Ford. Approval for the inbound flight to land at Tan Son Nhut Airport—now closed to all commercial aircraft—came directly from President Ford.

In the harrowing last days before Saigon's final fall to the North Vietnamese, Al had the arduous responsibility of deciding on which day the very last civilian flight would evacuate the exhausted, distressed people. Al chose April 24, 1975. The Boeing 747 would fly out as many Pan Am employees, family members, and citizens as it could hold. If scheduled too early, precious relatives would be left behind, but if it took off too late, it could be shot down, causing a catastrophic incident. An abundance of artillery surrounded the airport as encroaching shots were continually heard. On board, tensions mounted as the aircraft awaited permission from the tower for departure. Hundreds in the cabin fell completely silent. Al later said, "It seemed like an *eternity* before we received clearance for take-off."

Screaming down the runway, Al, sitting behind the captain, was ever so grateful that the airstrip was clear of debris. The B-747 was precariously heavy, dangerously overloaded with 113 passengers more than its normal capacity of 350. Safely airborne, *Clipper Unity* flew them all to freedom in America. Today, many Vietnamese credit Topping for saving their lives.

His heroics did not go unnoticed by Hollywood, which cast James

Earl Jones as Al and Richard Crenna as Captain Dan Hood in the film *Last Flight Out*.

Had I known any of this at the interview, I would surely have been intimidated, but all I wanted that day was to be hired. "So, Mr. Topping, when do you think I might hear from Pan Am?" I meekly asked.

The stoic Al then turned to me and said the words I shall never forget, "What would you say if I told you we are going to fly you down to Miami for training?"

I think in that instant I saw my whole future pass before my eyes. I inherently knew that my life would never be the same again. I was on the launch pad to my destiny just by hearing those simple words. After the interview, I floated right out of the room and through the chic hotel's lobby like a fairy.

Until I reported for training, everything I looked at, thought about, smelled, saw, or felt seemed heavenly different. Leaving the hotel, charging up Connecticut Avenue to join my friend Chris Beakey for lunch, I discovered for the first time in my life what it truly means to feel as if you are "walking on air." I was so damned excited I just wanted to chat anybody up to tell them the great news, to share my new-found happiness with them. That clear, crisp, February day became Utopia in an instant. The gates of opportunity had flung wide open for me. I began to see in my mind's eye what it would be like to travel the world while looking up all my old pals from Millfield School. My thoughts raced at 100 miles per hour with all the possibilities that lay ahead. By the time I caught up with Chris, I had reached a peak of elation, and like a whirling dervish, could hardly complete a sentence without interrupting myself with a new idea.

Being hired by Pan Am was like suddenly eloping. Like a jealous spouse, Pan Am controlled your hours, days off, and destinations. To my buddies, it was just as if I had suddenly and unexpectedly run off and gotten hitched. Weeks later, a gay friend confided, "I can't help it, Tania, I'm jealous of Pan Am. They took you away from me."

Friends gave me survival guides full of advice for what to do in God-forsaken countries during uprisings, kidnappings, medical emergencies, and disasters. Another handed me a list of all the nations on the State Department's current bulletin warning Americans not to visit, which I nicknamed their "caca list." My new airline flew to nearly every destination mentioned.

In the "old days," Pan Am took out full-page congratulatory ads in the hometown newspapers of all the flight attendants they hired, running photos of them proudly wearing their new uniforms. In many cases, they became instant mini-celebrities, especially if they came from a small town where everyone recognized them.

I traveled in first class down to Miami for training, eagerly studying the worldwide route system. Pan Am flew to at least 80 countries. Checking in at the hotel, as I put my little monkey fingers out for the key, the desk clerk pointed, saying, "Oh, no, the bellman will take your luggage upstairs. Please go that way."

As I entered, a gaggle of my new supervisors greeted me. Quickly ushered to the ladies' room, I was asked to pee in a jar for a drug test. Later I learned that two male recruits had decided to celebrate their new jobs in an unorthodox way on the flight to Miami. Squeezing into the lavatory, they puffed on a celebratory marijuana joint, immediately setting off the shrill smoke alarm. Upon arrival, they were promptly flown back home on the next departing flight—this time in economy class.

The entire hotel was buzzing with kinetic excitement and anticipation. There was so much to learn about our new airline culture and tons of people to meet. We enthusiastically jumped on the buses to go to class like a bunch of exuberant kids roaring off to summer camp. The beauty of it for me was that nearly everyone had strong international backgrounds and cosmopolitan interests like mine. "The more exotic, the better," I joked.

My second stepfather Archie laughed out loud after I was hired and exclaimed, "Tan! You have found your niche; you are a square peg in a square hole!"

Mother was also thrilled for me, knowing well that I was exactly in the perfect setting, advising me, "If you don't get a husband and career out of this, you're not my daughter!"

Now, joyfully ensconced in a new international menagerie of colleagues, I happily told her, "Pan Am has just recruited all my new closest confidants," a statement which rings true to this day, as several of my classmates became life-long friends.

Kevin McDonald from Saint Louis was one such person. From the minute we were introduced and shook hands, we became inseparable. Elegant, with distinguished features and model-good looks, Kevin and I felt as if we had known each other forever. We dove right in, eagerly exploring and embracing Pan Am's vast universe together.

Three days after we arrived, the drug tests were back. Up on my floor, Pan Am supervisors were knocking on numerous doors, saying, "You have been dropped from the program."

Dozens of new employees were unceremoniously fired. One morning I even heard the maids exclaiming, "1015, se fue! 1021, gone!" going right down the list.

I survived.

In training, certain Federal Aviation Administration (FAA) regulations had to be memorized. Eight new airplane configurations were studied, along with detailed emergency procedures for each jet, which comprised only a fraction of the training. It was almost overwhelming. Engrossed for long hours with frequent exams, we were studying, eating fast food double-time, in class, or dead asleep, resting up for the next round of fresh information. You could flirt with your new co-workers, but you had to be quick about that, too. We extinguished different types of fires. Evacuations were conducted, jumping two stories down steep rubber slides where Velcro caught our butts at the bottom. We set up emergency rafts in pools to practice ditching, delegating authority to "survivors," and utilizing every item in the survival kit. We administered oxygen, simulated in-flight childbirth, assisted the disabled, and learned to identify nitroglycerin and crudely made bombs. Pretty soon life without a seatbelt felt like wearing a micro-mini skirt with no panties. Yikes!

In conversation, Pan Am people only said the name of the city, i.e., Rangoon. It was automatically understood that you knew the country and location.

Our manual contained one chapter with evacuation procedures in ten languages. Another section on protocol had a detailed list of how to properly address every dignitary imaginable, whether royal, religious, or political. Manners and demeanor were taught, such as how to light a cigarette like a lady. Also imperative was the proper pronunciation of the wines from Pan Am's vast cellar. Passing language tests, both written and oral, including 400 words in key airline vernacular from the *International Airline Phrase Book in Six Languages* was also required for graduation. Dr. Joseph Bator, the well-known multi-lingual professor and author of the book, tested each one of us personally. If you failed, you had one month to pass, or you were knocked off the payroll until you did. Talk about pressure. Who wants to return home with their tail between their legs?

Out of 30,000 interviewed, 1,500 were hired. Five months later, the number had been whittled down to just 525. And I was one of the lucky ones.

On St. Patrick's Day, at the culmination of training, I took my "Q-Flight" (qualification flight) with my friend Sabine Ackman Bradshaw. While she was confident, I was super nervous, obsessed that one wrong answer would send me back to D.C. to eat some crow. Dividing us up into groups, the instructors took us around to each door on the B-747, asking us meticulous questions. In the cockpit, we were queried about the equipment and how we would utilize it. I distinctly remember the instructor asking me a specific question about the upper deck exit. Not 100 percent certain, I answered haltingly, but Sabine gave me a knowing wink that I was on the mark.

At long last, the final day of training arrived. In an exuberant graduation ceremony, it was symbolic for me to have my wings pinned onto my lapel. Finally sanctioned, I felt accepted into the world of aviation. Eyes glistened for the freshly-minted flight attendants. We relished clapping for each other as wings were affixed to each person's uniform. For me, it was a graduation ritual of another kind. Our new class had now joined into the indomitable spirit that was the true Pan American World Airways.

After cake and punch, but before flying us up to our New York base, there was one last procedure, and it was *not* fun. The instructors had warned us about it in advance. Because Pan Am flew to all parts of the world, we had to be injected with every inoculation for traveling abroad: yellow fever, cholera, tetanus, hepatitis, diphtheria, and typhoid. The typhoid shot alone would kick your ass, and they knew it. If it made you ill, you could cancel your first trip and it would not go against your record. They lined us up like the military, ready to be jabbed. At every station, they had ammonia tubes to break, to stick up under your nose if you passed out. The typhoid shot was painful for nearly everyone. It felt as if a giant Maine lobster had gotten hold of my upper left arm and would not let go. For three nights, I could not sleep on that side, but I was determined not to call in sick.

Right out of training, Pan Am's all-encompassing culture was about to devour me entirely, and it *did*.

Flying up to New York on a chartered Boeing 727, we were delighted to enjoy one last treat: the rare St. Elmo's fire. Luminous, electric fingers from lightning crawled across the cockpit windscreen. Veins of purple-colored static electricity from the storm continually wiggled up the glass for more than an hour while we took turns going to the cockpit to view the free light show.

My baptism-by-fire inaugural flight was scheduled to Germany on a jumbo jet. After a tiring seven-hour journey across the Atlantic, the gusty wind chopped at our aircraft as we approached Munich, pitching us all around. In the enormous 747, if you are seated in the aft section, the motion has a fishtail effect, making it feel more turbulent than the front section. Held down by their seatbelts, everyone's heads bobbed up and down every time we hit more rough air. With their noggins swinging to and fro, they reminded me of prairie dogs on the lookout from their dugouts, or whack-a-moles. Many also had their palms over their mouths to muffle the sounds of fearful yelps. Buckled into my own jump seat at the back of the airplane, I looked out the window. The visibility was dreadful. Our pilots came within 200 feet of the runway but could not see more than half a mile. In the thick fog, they executed a missed approach, aborting the landing. The four engines groaned loudly as they pulled the nose sharply up in the driving wind. Diverting with a plane full of 425 passengers, we headed to Frankfurt.

Ringing in my ears were the last words that the lead instructor in Miami had said to the room full of neophyte flight attendants, "Fasten your seat belts, team, because you are in for the ride of your *life!*"

In 2005, at the 30-year Saigon Airlift reunion in Washington, D.C., I approached Al Topping as he was finishing dessert. As the reunited Pan Amers from Vietnam and America swirled all around us, I had the honor of thanking Al personally for hiring me, tearfully telling him, "That day, you changed the course of my life forever, something I shall never forget." He stood up and gave me a long hug.

Disbelief at the Brandenburg Gate in Berlin

4

Beneath the Crumbling Berlin Wall

Eyeing my passport suspiciously, the East German guard at Checkpoint Charlie scowled. "Why do you have the name Tania, a Russian name, when your middle name is von Traeschler, a German name?" he demanded in a thick Teutonic accent, seemingly annoyed.

Crossing back into West Berlin, we had visited Ceclienhof Palace, the site of the Potsdam conference, in East Germany. After World War II ended, British Prime Ministers Churchill and Attlee met with President Truman and Soviet Premier Stalin, all of whom represented the victorious powers of the war, to discuss post-war arrangements in Europe. Germany was to be divided into four parts: one portion run by the British, one by the French, one by the Soviets, and one by the US.

Seven teenagers and our group leader from the States, Barb, were on a 1969 summer tour of eight countries in Europe. Abruptly ordered off the van, we watched as two guards, one on each side, walked alongside the vehicle. Holding poles with mirrors, they were making certain that some poor bastard had not tried to escape by desperately strapping himself underneath. Understanding his possible contempt for the Russians and royalty, I downplayed the connection with my Russian godmother, Princess Tatiana Abkhazi, telling him that I had been named for a family friend. I explained that my middle name had come from the Bavarian part of my father's family. Rifling through my purse, the guard found a teenager's girly stuff—tampons, love notes, lipstick, breath mints. My face flashed red as he nosily went through its contents with his dirty fingers. Nobody had ever trespassed through my purse before, at least not that I knew of. He looked sinister and distrustful. After his colleagues had finished searching the van, he waved us on with a disapproving look as if he was doing us a big favor but was not quite sure if he should let us go. At the time, Checkpoint Charlie was the main crossing point between East and West Germany. I felt some fondness for Charlie, the iconic spot for thousands of Berliners. Charlie certainly had been front and center as a witness to the desperation of a divided Berlin during those tumultuous years. Yet the name still sounds odd to me since the Wall finally came down that jubilant night of November 9, 1989.

But on that hot July day in 1969, I could have never imagined in my wildest dreams that one day the 96-mile-long Wall would ever meet its demise. Wooden platforms in West Berlin had been built so that people could peer over the fortified, nine-foot-high divisive barrier, which carved a swath right through the heart of the city. The other side was bleak, dark, polluted, and heavily represented by monstrous examples of Stalinist-era architecture. Dominated by enormous gray buildings, devoid of any pleasing design, the walls of the Soviet offices were rife with asbestos and other toxic materials, both inside and out. The depressing 90-foot-wide death strip in between the two walls was exposed, raw, and loaded with land mines. In addition to the 302 watchtowers, carefully positioned Klieg lights blazed brightly at night, making a successful escape almost impossible. Menacing German shepherds slunk alongside the guards, itching to tear an escapee apart. "Shoot to kill" orders had been issued.

Over the years, thousands of distressed people risked their lives by attempting to escape to the West, only yards away. In the no-man's desolate land in between the two Walls, valiant fugitives were cut down in a hail of gunfire, only to bleed to death, unassisted and unable to reach the far wall. More than 136 brave souls were annihilated as they attempted to reach freedom.

However, there were some successful escapes of the 5,000 who tried to flee. A narrow tunnel was dug beneath a graveyard in East Berlin. Pretending to honor the dead, "mourners" would arrive with bunches of flowers, only to disappear underground. Once the police caught on, it was hastily sealed up. Two intrepid families secretly bought yards of nylon cloth, fashioning it all into a hot air balloon which could hold four adults and four children. One black evening they drove to a barren field and lifted off. The wind whisked them over the trees, but after a mere 23 minutes of flight, they panicked when the gas burner died. Upon landing, they rejoiced when they realized they were on West German soil.

Hastily constructed in August 1961, the Wall immediately separated countless families, some of whom did not see their relatives until decades later.

⌒

Safely back in West Berlin, I did not even want to climb the platform for a peek, as I had this cartoonish image in my mind that some disgruntled East German guard or Stasi agent, tired of being gawked at by tourists on the western side of the Wall, might let go with a few rounds and blow my head off.

The Stasi, or secret police of East Germany, were free to be objectionable whenever they felt like it. A tightened rein and extensive dossiers were kept on all East German citizens. People disappeared all the time without explanation or redress. Thousands rotted in desolate prisons, held without charge. Adding thousands of informers to its enormous force, the Stasi had about one spy for every six civilians. The tentacles of this poisonous regime wiggled in every direction. When it became apparent that the Wall would cease to exist, most Stasi officers, not surprisingly, hastily fled like cowards.

⌒

Decades later, when East and West were reunited and the inquiries heated up, it seemed as if there had only been a handful of them. "Stasi? I don't know any Stasi!" shouted the headline in one local paper. Remaining personnel denied their horrific roles in carrying out the orders of an iron rule. Unfortunately, after World War II ended, the dreaded knocks at the door were continued by the Stasi and their well-trained canines, terrorizing the public right up until the Wall's destruction.

In the East, while the Stasi continually gathered "evidence" to charge people with crimes against the State, West Germany had developed a powerhouse economy with one of the West's strongest currencies, the Deutschmark. As the East Germans puttered around town in the Trabant (nick-named the "Trabi"), dispersing plumes of noxious black smoke, making queer sounds, and running as if it was powered by a lawn mower, the West Germans cruised in world-class luxury cars along their unscarred *autobahnen* at 125 miles per hour. But the pain of separation was devastating and always evident. When the Wall was hastily built in August 1961, homeowners who had been on vacation lost their houses in an instant, seized by the authorities for their own enjoyment. If they had relatives on the other side of the Wall, contact was extremely difficult and discouraged. Their beloved families may have lived less than a mile away, but it might as well have been ten thousand.

A ruthless puppet of "Red" Russia, communist leader and atheist Eric Honecker made life hell for most East Germans. Now living under the oppressive Soviet-controlled regime, life for East Berliners as they had known it disappeared. The ruling authority combined the political creed of communism with the German respect for regulation, thus creating the climate for a wickedly efficient administration.

I bet our tour guide from behind the Iron Curtain that summer day was an agent, as well. In between quick notations on the historical sites we visited, she blasted us with non-stop communist diatribes about how wonderful life was in the East. No explanation was necessary; we could easily see for ourselves. She bitterly complained about Western countries—all our violence, decadence, and exorbitant prices for goods. I hope that she felt better after pouring it out on a bunch of kids just trying to learn a little something about European history. Perhaps she was trying to cover her ass if one of *us* reported that she had not represented the East appropriately. Otherwise, she would have had to face the consequences. Pure paranoia was part of everyday life in that totalitarian regime.

Pan Am shared a rich history with Germany. It flew to Frankfurt, Hamburg, Berlin, Stuttgart, and Munich from five US gateway cities. Flights to other cities within Germany were called the Internal-German Service (IGS), which also carried Luftpost (German mail) on our Boeing 727s. Frankfurt was a major hub for us; the springboard for Moscow, the eastern bloc capitals, the Middle East, Africa, Pakistan, and India.

Pan Am also played an historic role in the 1949 Berlin Airlift operation, when Captain George Price, piloting a DC-3, made five unofficial flights into Tempelhof Airport in Berlin, taking in much-needed vital supplies. He was reprimanded upon his return to Frankfurt, as the flights were unauthorized, but his invaluable contribution to the Airlift made a lasting impression on the grateful Berliners.

In 1948, during a secret mission flying DC-3s for Pan Am, Price described to me how he transported unique cargo loads out of Frankfurt to London. The Berlin banks were becoming panicky about the billions of dollars worth of gold bullion in their possession, afraid that Stalin might consider the prospect of seizing it from them. Under the watchful eye of machine gun-toting guards, the gold was boarded onto a late-night train in Berlin to be transported overland to Frankfurt, where it would be airlifted to safety in London. Price emphasized that the undertaking, which he nicknamed *Operation Plymrock,* was well-oiled; the ground personnel were superb in their efficiency. Only the military and Pan Am knew about the flights, as it was the only airline that operated them. Barely three years after the bloodiest war known to mankind, two former archenemies, the Americans and Germans, collaborated effectively to transport the cargo. Each flight had about $3.7 million worth of gold; a tidy sum back then. In 1948, an ounce of gold was $35.

"It wasn't packed neatly," Price told me, "The ingots were placed in duffel bags with piles of sawdust to protect them. The plane was absolutely stuffed with gold; every inch was occupied with a bag. I have photos of some of the ingots—unbelievable! The gold was so bright. Formidable weather was also a big concern, as the visibility during winter was treacherous, sometimes as bad as 150 feet. We nicknamed those thick foggy conditions 'Niagara Falls.' Before takeoff, the airplane doors were sealed shut and all the bolts were tightened, so if we had to evacuate for an emergency, we would have had to squeeze out of the cockpit windows, if possible. We were instructed to keep flying, no matter what, even if there was a fire on board. Thankfully, we did not endure any potshots from the Russians. Even *they* realized that such an action could easily re-ignite another war. The pilots were thoroughly trained and knew the airport layouts well. The ground crews and aviators were most certainly up to this unusual task. After just a few trips, we had transported millions of dollars worth of pure gold," Price added.

"We never lost an airplane, but we did lose one, single, ingot," he concluded, laughing. "That single piece was stealthily swiped by a military man during the day when the fog had moved in and the ground visibility was almost zero."

⌒⊙

Berlin-related tales became hot topics among my colleagues as the austere conditions at the wall began to relax a bit. One weekend, my roomie Kevin McDonald and I flew over "the pond" to attend the Paris Air Show with two VIP tickets. Strolling past the best fighter jets the world has to offer on our way to the VIP tent, we compared stories.

"Tania, did you hear about what happened to the crew who went out to dinner in Berlin last week?"

I wondered which way the story was going to go. "Did something lousy or wonderful happen?" I yelled, as a loud MIG-29 zoomed overhead, showing off.

Fourteen hungry crewmembers had gone to dinner and ordered everything from sauerbraten with sauerkraut to pastries, along with beer and wine. At the end of the meal, the waiter put down the check. As they were beginning to figure out the exchange rate, an older man came to the table. He promptly grabbed it. They just assumed there was a mistake in the addition. Proceeding to tear the bill up into little pieces, he said, "I own this restaurant, and I have always felt deeply grateful to Pan Am for dropping supplies to us during the Berlin Airlift in 1949. After the War, conditions were horrendous for civilians. We had no medicine and extremely limited provisions. People were starving. In the streets, they were killing domestic animals to eat. Ordinary civilians were chopping down trees for fuel during the harsh winter. Then Pan Am flew in with food and vital supplies. You do not have a bill; dinner is on me tonight. Thank you, Pan Am."

⌒⊙

During this time, my cousin Ras Smith and his wife Cathie were working as diplomats with the US Mission in Berlin. As the country was still divided, it was not called an embassy but served the same function. Once they invited me to dinner at their spacious home in the Zahlendorf section of the city. Ras was the chief of the political section. Cathie, who worked in management, oversaw the logistics when the "spy exchange" took place on the Glienicke Bridge that connected Potsdam with West Berlin. Several East German and Russian spies were exchanged for Natan Sharansky, a Soviet dissident and anti-communist who later became a member of the Knesset in Israel.

Giving me a tour of their house, they showed me the fortified bomb shelter in the basement, containing an enormous vault with a combination lock for former stolen or acquired Nazi valuables. Shortly afterward, we sat down to sample some tasty German cuisine. During our conversation, we discussed Pan Am's fragile financial health. Ras advised me that once the Wall was history, Lufthansa would take over the profitable Pan Am internal German routes. My heart sank as I listened to him. Already in such dire monetary straits, I could not bear the thought that we would lose another valuable source of income. Regrettably, Ras was right.

In the late 1980s, Hungary began to quietly look the other way, allowing East German refugees to cross into their country, traveling unimpeded onto West Germany. It was a roundabout way to get there, but certainly beat the alternative. Word of the exodus began to leak out, and stories on the nightly news trumpeted joyous family reunions after more than 25 years of separation. A steady stream of refugees continued to flee East Germany, as many realized that the Soviets were evidently not halting the emigration.

My colleagues were bidding madly for Berlin trips so they could see with their own eyes what appeared to be history in the making. Many either hailed from Germany or had relatives there, so now they could see first-hand what was happening and judge for themselves. Our crew lounge in New York was constantly abuzz with spirited accounts of how life was rapidly being transformed in Berlin. Nearly every returning crew member had fistfuls of concrete "rocks" chipped from the now-disintegrating Berlin Wall. Animated stories were told about the determined hundreds stationed along the Wall with hammers and other instruments, continually hacking away. Large pieces, particularly those marked with graffiti, were coveted. By sharing their tools, everyone accelerated their mutual desire to expedite this historic demolition.

Lusting for a trip to see for myself, I bid like crazy for Berlin and got one. Jim Pepe from Denver, a fellow flight attendant and a good friend, joined me as we headed straight for the Brandenburg Gate. Jim, tall with thick brown hair and light eyes, had a wonderful sense of humor and a love of animals. I often stayed in New York with him and another friend of ours, purser Jim Shaughnessy. They had adopted a gentle stray pit bull, Bo-Bo, and Merle, a chunky black-and-white cat who resembled a miniature Jersey cow. She continually hissed, taking swats at Bo, acting as if he was out to get her, even though that was the last thing on his mind. He was completely perplexed as to why she was so upset. After a jet-lagged trip abroad, it was hilarious to watch them.

Jim Pepe and I loved flying European trips together. Fun and articulate, he was also wonderful to our passengers. He was someone I could really count on when those trans-Atlantic flights were demanding, hyperactive, and oh-so-full. "An ass in every seat, a face in every window," we used to joke after an exhausting flight.

Gypsies wearing bright head scarves were selling souvenirs from yesteryear—Soviet coins, military pins, and trinkets from World War II. Stamps, flags, military uniforms, hats, and relics from the dreaded Stasi could also be purchased. Something caught Jim's eye and he began to laugh. A T-shirt teasingly said, "Will the last person out of East Berlin please remember to turn off the lights?"

Continuing onto Checkpoint Charlie, rumors circulated that even Charlie would go at some point. As dull-colored Trabant cars lined up to enter West Berlin, the small but well-renowned station did not look as significant to me as it had in 1969. Now it looked like a trailer. A simple sign above it read, "Allied Checkpoint Charlie," with the flags of Britain, France, and the US. The stark difference this time was the ambiance. Inside, the French guards were smiling, even allowing us to try on their military hats. We then posed with two East German guards. One looked amused, the other did not. The dour one was probably contemplating when he was going to bail out from being a spy and make a run for it before the inquiries and inevitable trials would begin. French troops nearby happily posed for photos in the sunshine under a sign which said, "*Vous Sortez du Secteur Americain,*" (You are leaving the American Sector), also translated into German and Russian. Endless European languages were spoken in excited and zealous tones from the throngs of people. Something positive was certainly in the balmy air; perhaps the anticipation of better times to come, and it was ever-so-welcome.

Now the Wall had some deep inroads from the excavation which yielded large ready-made souvenir rocks. People savored the ritualistic sensation that they were contributing something to the Wall's demise, after all the sorrow it had caused over the decades. In a sense, the atmosphere was permeated with that grief, but also punctuated with optimism. Some portions had colorful graffiti art for long stretches, almost like murals. Other parts were dull and ugly, a real eye-sore. Numerous languages had been scribbled in nearly every available space. Everyone had something to express.

The words *Gehen sie weiter hier ist nichts mehr zu Sehen* (Keep going, there is nothing more to see here) had been painted in red. In larger letters of bright blue, *der Beton bekennt seine Schuld* (Even the concrete admits its guilt) was against the backdrop of a drab, brown office building with mismatched stones from bottom to top. Large holes revealed cheap iron-rod reinforcements that had been bent down by tourists so they could cross over for a few minutes. Razor wire had been rolled back in some areas. Reticent visitors merely peered through the holes, too timid to see if it was really safe to take the liberty of walking in. They could have been right. At what point could they actually trust the Eastern guards? No official announcements had been made yet. In any case, they would have seen a desolate wasteland—barren ground with discarded trash everywhere. "Do you believe what you see? Is this rational?" graffiti in English demanded.

Jim and I walked back to the Brandenburg Gate, always the center of all the action, attracting loads of curiosity seekers. We wanted to exchange information with other people to see if we were missing anything. Along the way, we noticed how friendly people were to each other. Most were chipping away furiously at the Wall, waiting for a good-sized fragment to come loose. I had brought a big plastic bag, hoping to make it at least half-full. What an advantage to give friends historical souvenirs that cost nothing and were fine for guys *or* gals. But I would have to drag the "bricks" all the way back home across the Atlantic.

Three Europeans stood on top of the Wall, each taking photos of the surreal sight. Earlier, I had spotted a group of mixed foreigners sitting on the wall in front of the Brandenburg Gate, and I snapped a picture of them. They captured my attention because their faces were racked with the look of disbelief, as if they could not comprehend was what happening. For the most part, they were quiet, just sitting there, absorbing it all. One African man stood on a short ladder, trying to chip off a fat chunk. Residents of the city stood close by, with dazed looks on their faces, observing the drastic change in their city's history unfolding right before their eyes.

You could step up to any person from another country, and if they did not speak your language, you would just make a motion indicating that you wanted to borrow a hammer. Everyone I saw obliged in a welcoming manner. Many nationalities were represented as they lined up against the Wall to help hasten its demolition. We were all on the same mission and relishing every second of it. Sensing a strong feeling of international unity among everyone, I watched as each person in their own way contributed a little something to these historical moments.

Jim and I chipped away at the Wall for over an hour. Pleased to have some genuine relics of the day, we decided to visit the East for a while. Closer to the gate, emboldened by the proximity of Western guards, people did not hesitate to cross over for a short time to see how it looked after a 28-year separation. In the East, we came across a large white bust of Lenin, surrounded by big red flowers, in front of an official Russian building. I snapped a photo, knowing that someday it would be removed. Instantly we were hit with the sight of monotonous buildings, homely cars, and dreary public places, save for the stunning and intricate architecture of yesteryear. We snacked on ordinary meat (or was it?) sandwiches which made us sick later. An East German border guard, handsome enough to be an actor, spoke flawless English. As we conversed with this cordial man and posed for pictures, I could not help but wonder if we had met him a year earlier, would we have run into an evil man, beholden to, and carrying out the orders of, an authoritarian rule? Was he a charmer with a vicious character underneath? Judging by his command of English, he could have been a valuable asset for the Stasi, possibly a spy.

Back on the Western side, we passed an open space with a large, ordinary cross and six enormous sprays of flowers decorated with German flags over a gravesite. In the waning days of the Wall's existence, a young man had attempted to escape to the West when he was cut down by a blast of gunfire. West German guards threw him a first aid kit, but there was nothing else that they could do. Bleeding to death in the wasteland, he was only yards from freedom. Had he waited another month or so, he could have simply strolled across the dirt to liberty. Only 18 years old, he was the very last one to perish at the Wall.

Hoping to feast on *schweinehaxen*, Jim and I entered a rustic-looking pub jammed with patrons. If you love pork, this is the most outrageously good pig meat you could ever dream of eating east of Polynesia. Ham hocks are roasted for hours, while continually basted with beer, giving the outside the consistency of crackling. When ready, the meat is deliciously moist and tender on the inside, and completely crispy on the outside. Served with sauerkraut, salad, and garlic mashed potatoes, topped off with tasty "mom and pop" German wine, is truly divine dining in my book, almost like a religious experience.

In Frankfurt, all the Pan Am crews went to Gert Hitziger's restaurant, the Basler Eck, nicknamed "The gas station." Stickers, logos, and slogans of the world's most beloved airlines covered the walls, giving it a homey feel. Everyone ordered the roast. It was a Pan Am custom to visit his eatery every layover. You could walk into Gert's place any night of the week and see three or four B-747 crews: 60-plus people all wolfing down the same thing. Once we were served, I could hardly carry on a conversation, diving busily into the next bite, forgoing any juicy airline gossip, lost in a world of culinary delight. Gert knew nearly everyone by name, and always "comped" a round of tasty peach schnapps for each table.

Gert even rescued me and two of my crewmembers, Costas and Ingela, when we were attacked by some Turks right outside his restaurant one summer night. They knocked Costas to the ground and hurled an apple, which hit me right in the teeth. While people seated by the window slowly chewed their food and stared blankly at the five-person melee, Gert raced out, challenging the two Turks. He yelled in high German that he was calling the police, hastily writing down their license number. They shrieked at him in Turkish and roared off in their fat BMW.

The intense popularity of the restaurant was also well known at our headquarters on Park Avenue. After several terrorist incidents in Europe during the mid-80s, Pan Am issued a memo discouraging crews from eating there. Management was trying, and rightfully so, to think ahead and warn us. God forbid if a "weird-looking little pineapple" with the pin pulled out had been tossed into the restaurant. They would have wiped out dozens of Pan Amigos in one fell swoop.

Now, with Gert's cuisine only a distant memory, Jim and I were hoping that the Berliners would be able to duplicate his delicious fare, but their version could not compare with his killer chow. We had plenty to talk about, however, as we had both been strongly affected by what we had observed that day.

Bidding Jim good night, I returned to my hotel room and sat on the bed, almost dazed, playing Enya's Irish melodies on my Walkman. Reflecting on the emotional impact the day had brought to us, I began to cry as I played her soothing, spiritual songs again and again. I gazed over at my plastic bag stuffed full of rocks. Now they were pieces of history.

I tapped my memory to revisit the images of my journey to the Berlin Wall in 1969. Then I retraced the steps that Jim and I had taken earlier that day, comparing how the times were strikingly different, contemplating how the citizens' lives would be irrevocably changed *again* when the Wall came down. I imagined the unnecessary, deep lamentation that had taken place, but tried to counter-balance that in my mind by fantasizing about the great joy to come for the families, at the point when East and West would join together to become a united Germany once more.

I was like a little kid who begs to see the same film again and again. Tasting my salty tears which rolled down my cheeks for well over an hour, I played Enya's music late into the night even though I was a little drunk and jet-lagged, too. My stomach growled from the funky East German sandwich as I repeatedly examined our impressions. Images of what we had discovered that day played out in my mind. As an empath, I could "feel" the years of suffering under a police state. The expressions of disbelief on the Berliners' faces were so stark. After having closely observed the people who had flown in from all over the world to be a part of this extraordinary moment, acute images had been painted in my mind, settling there.

I thought about the intense pain that I could understand but had never felt. I know well the anxiety of separation, but not the distress of having been split from my loved ones for 28 solid years. Even though I was a citizen of another land, I went through a catharsis late that night,

THE AMERICAN SECTOR

Zimmerstraße ЕЗЖАЕТЕ ИЗ
АМЕРИКАНСКОГО СЕКТОРА

VOUS SORTEZ
DU SECTEUR AMÉRICAIN

SIE VERLASSEN DEN AMERIKANISCHEN SEKTOR

With French soldiers at Checkpoint Charlie

feeling a sense of fellowship, but most importantly, optimism for the future of our European "cousins." Germany had indeed experienced a profound metamorphosis since that humid summer afternoon in 1969, when a bunch of giggling teenage American girls had crossed the border at Checkpoint Charlie.

Civilian bus intentionally demolished by tanks

5

In the Middle of a Coup
in Moscow

"This just in!" the television blared, "Our sources tell us it appears there has been a takeover of the Politburo in Moscow. President Mikhail Gorbachev is on vacation at his dacha in the Crimea and can't be reached. Details are very sketchy at this moment. We are waiting for more information from our Moscow correspondent. Stay tuned for further developments."

Eric Martin, a fellow purser, owned a house in Queens, New York, where he rented rooms to colleagues. This *pied-a-terre* was a hubbub of crew activity in the summer of 1991. Upstairs, I had been gathering small gifts to put into my tote bag to take to, of all places, Moscow, the next day. "Tania!" Eric yelled from the living room. "Aren't you flying to Russia this month?"

"Yeah, why, Eric?"

He bellowed, "It sure sounds like there has been a coup in Moscow!"

"Whaaat?" I yelled back. "The commies are trying to make a comeback?"

I had the impression that under "Gorby" with his policies of *glasnost* and *perestroika* (policy reform and increased transparency in government) that the days of hardline communism were behind them. Perhaps not.

The country that we had dreaded so much when I was a child, the giant fearsome USSR, was vulnerable to a coup *d'etat*? I was only four when the belligerent President Nikita Khrushchev, referring to capitalist states, yelled to a full-house Kremlin, "We are Bolsheviks . . . whether you like it or not, history is on our side, we will bury you!" which quickly morphed into "We will bury America!"

No wonder school kids were instructed to hide under their desks. I vividly remember my parents watching Khrushchev on TV with a look of terror on their faces. Children almost always emulate the extreme emotions of their parents, so I am quite certain that my little face must have also had a look of contorted horror, as well. At the time, we were living right outside Washington, D.C., where my father had close ties to various senators. If he wanted to verify something officially or off the record, it was easy to do so. Nonetheless, alarmed at Khrushchev's menacing and ominous words, my parents' friends and neighbors understandingly discussed this threat for months afterward. Such incidents, I believe, add to the intrigue that we cook up in our imaginations about a particular place unknown to us, sharply raising our interest.

Additionally, I was named after my tall, blue-eyed, blonde Russian godmother, but not before a battle ensued first. My father Glenn wanted to name me Glenda after him, but my Irish American mother Nike would have none of it. Finally, they settled on Tania, which means "queen of the fairies." My Godmother and I became "Big Tania" and "Little Tania."

In the late fifties, during those heightened days of red communism, my mother was always quick to say that Big Tania, a princess, was a "White Russian." In 1917, when Tsar Nicholas II abdicated the throne and the violent revolution erupted, a knock at the door immediately sent Tania's family fleeing into exile for their lives. Only three or four years old, she had little time to evacuate the country with her royal relatives. Escaping to Paris, the senior prince and princess lived there for many years. Tania moved to America and married John Shields, who befriended my parents long before I came into the world.

Often, before my parents' divorce when I was six, we visited Tania and John's house in the wooded northwest part of Washington for merry "grown-up" parties. Usually, I was the only child attending. Tania always had a dog, which kept me amused while the adults mingled. They owned a black and white television, hot stuff for those days, or I would take a spin in their elevator, quite an uncommon commodity in the 1950s. A cherished collection of hand-painted silk fans, small tiaras, bejeweled necklaces, and other precious artifacts that they had managed to save from Russia were displayed in elaborately decorated cases throughout their home.

Each time we visited, I would rush over to stare at the sentimental memorabilia as if I was seeing it for the very first time. Through a child's eyes, her treasures represented a fairyland, instantly reminding me of the princesses featured in little girls' books, except that this was for *real*. These sparkling royal mementos catapulted my dreams into a fantasy mode. All of this set the stage for my curiosity about Russia.

⌒◎

On the brink of extinction in August of '91, Pan American World Airways only had a few months left until it would be bankrupt altogether, so life with my beloved airline was shifting dramatically. Pan Am had already sold our valuable European routes to Delta. Other airlines were sniffing around our carcass for more lucrative deals, just like buzzards waiting for the end, and we knew it. It was not easy to hold our heads up high and act as if everything was normal when we were continuously being dismembered.

Moscow had been my first choice, and I was delighted to discover that I would be flying four trips to the capital in August. Talk about fate. We had already made one run before the upheaval in Moscow, so I had gotten my Russian feet a bit wet. Plenty of advice came from the senior flight attendants regarding "no-no's."

A non-smoker, I was advised to take cartons of Marlboros, small American souvenirs, T-shirts, M&M's, or trail mix to barter with. Toilet paper and my own towels were added to the list, as those were minimal in the rooms even though our hotel boasted more than a couple of stars. Marlboros could negotiate taxi rides all over Moscow, one pack of cigs at a time. Just step up to the curb and wave them around. Before long, some cabbie would stop and the bargaining would begin. The T-shirts were great for trading, and I acquired dozens of Russian pins—of all types, military and civilian, communist and non-partisan, in return. The trail mix was not only for me because the food in Moscow was so dreadful at the time, but it was also for the KBG lady. Even before my first trip, I intuitively knew to take a bunch of other little items that she might like, including Estee Lauder makeup samples and cosmetic pouches.

More advice: do not take the first-class beluga caviar off the plane. If Customs discovered it, they will be ticked off and ask you a whole bunch of fool questions, holding up the entire crew. When entering most countries, crews sailed through customs like diplomats. A few nations, including Russia, were the exception as they X-rayed our bags and rummaged through our possessions upon arrival, trying to control any competition for their prized caviar. When leaving Moscow, we carefully hid any souvenirs from the flea markets, particularly watches. Otherwise, we could be charged with the offense of not patronizing a government-run store.

An international purser, as any flight attendant knows, has a lot of responsibility, and multi-layered problems race at you from all directions, sometimes catching you off-guard. However, the payoff comes when something that could potentially be a disaster ends up being a golden experience. For this Moscow flight, heading straight into a perilous zone made the outcome of this trip entirely unpredictable.

Pan American World Airways often displayed great bravado in the way they went barreling into situations abroad that were treacherous. Pan Am had a long-standing but low-key relationship with the CIA. It was understood that in times of trouble, the airline would bite the bullet and go in after being advised by intelligence exactly what the circumstances were. They would fly in under hazardous and uncertain conditions, whether a coup, revolution, or humanitarian evacuation.

Pan Am also flew frantic evacuees out of Tehran during the Islamic revolution, staged the last flights out of Chile when General Pinochet violently overthrew President Allende's government, and transported refugees out of Beirut during the factious civil war in Lebanon. In later years, "rescue" flights were dispatched to Liberia and Trinidad after being forewarned by the spooks that there was a high possibility of a coup.

The purser who had worked a flight into Liberia related some of the harrowing details about their arrival at Roberts Field (ROB). Dozens of guerillas with Russian-made AK-47s and hand-held bazookas were prowling through the bush next to the airport. ROB was just about the only place in the world where we disembarked the aircraft and walked directly across the tarmac to our broken-down layover motel, and I mean *motel*. They had hardly arrived at the tattered lodgings when they heard the "pop, pop, pop" sound of gunfire from the wooded area close by. With no phones in any of the rooms, the female purser along with the captain rushed to the front desk to call Pan Am scheduling in New York. Soon they heard their inbound aircraft roar off into the sky. Now, if anything happened, they would be stranded with no way to get out. With her heart in her throat from fear, it seemed as if the scheduling crew would never answer the phone. After all, even in the best of conditions, often you could not get an outside line to another country. Once she heard them pick up the line at the other end, she frantically explained the situation in ROB. She begged them not to put her on hold for fear of being disconnected. The voice at the other end cheerfully said, "Hold on just a minute, please," as the purser pleaded, "No, no, NO! Please DO NOT put me on hold!" As she held the receiver pressed against her ear, listening to total silence, a mysterious man's voice intercepted the hold. "Don't worry, Pan Am," he said with assurance, "It will all be over in 48 hours." Click.

"What? Who is this? Hello, hello?" the purser said. A few seconds later, the scheduling lady came back on and instructed the purser not to let any of the crew leave the motel, as the aircraft would return in two days. Scheduling sounded upbeat. It is certainly easy to feel that way in the safe cocoon of a skyscraper 6,000 miles away.

After several days of a house arrest situation, the crew was super anxious to get out. The motel offered no protection whatsoever, not even a fence around the black mamba and scorpion-infested property. If the rebels didn't get you, the wildlife would. The latest developments of the crisis slipped out a bit at a time. Taking total advantage of the captive consumers, the manager had begun charging $10 for a sandwich (outrageous in Liberia) and $3 each for sodas, no doubt from supplies brought in on *our* plane.

The purser swore for years afterward that the furtive voice on the line that day must have been one of the boys at Langley.

                      ⌒೨

In August 1990, days after Saddam Hussein invaded Kuwait, Pan Am began pouring troops into Saudi Arabia via Cairo. I jokingly told my colleagues, "A Pan Am 747 must have been right on the heels of the Marines, the 82nd Airborne, and the 101st Airborne as the soldiers dropped into Kuwait."

In short, Pan Am would hardly ever turn a "mission" down. The situation in Moscow was viewed as no different.

                      ⌒೨

Our post-coup briefing in the Pan Am crew area of JFK airport was a bit awkward. Engrossed with this compelling international development, the crew was eager to witness the unfolding events up close, but on the other hand, were we being reckless? Who really wants to put their life in danger? How invincible is an airline crew, anyway? Our union vowed to protect any flight attendant from discipline who felt it was too dangerous to go, but only two called in "sick." Obviously, more than a few passengers were spooked as well since the flight had less than 10 percent capacity in the peak summer season.

The particulars of what had been transpiring in Moscow were still scanty at best. The coup was about 24 hours old, so we really had no clear idea what we were getting into. Either way, flight attendants sometimes have this squirrelly habit of looking at the purser as if we are supposed to have all the detailed info of any given situation right at our fingertips. Well, this was not going to be one of those times. Entering the briefing room, the captain introduced himself. He looked grim but had been able to garner more information than we had previously heard from either individuals or on TV.

"I was briefed earlier today. President Gorbachev is still in the Crimea, incommunicado. We don't know his status, or if he is safe. It appears that he is under house arrest. We aren't entirely certain which group staged the coup, but we do know that they are communists. All the radio and TV stations in Moscow have been seized. The TV channels have all been cut off except Channel One, where they are broadcasting an endless stream of commie diatribe every day, aimed at Gorbachev's administration."

Listening to our captain, I remembered hearing once that the expedient way to stage a coup is to usurp all communications, particularly television and radio, simultaneously taking command of all landings and takeoffs at the airport. Seizing control this way makes it difficult for the citizens to gauge exactly how successful the coup has been. This was apparently what they were accomplishing in Moscow.

What the captain said next rattled me, and the rest of the crew as well. Their eyes were becoming larger by the second. Mine, too.

"Intelligence sources have informed us that satellite images indicate the entire perimeter around Moscow airport is dotted with tanks. Certain air traffic is paralyzed, but Pan Am has still decided to go in." He paused. "In the cockpit, we will talk to Prestwick Air Traffic Control and listen to BBC radio as we fly across the Atlantic to get constant updates. We'll let you know of any developments. If things become too dangerous, our alternate landing site will be Helsinki. See you guys on board."

For just a minute there, our skipper reminded me a bit of John Wayne as he strolled out of the crew room.

Bill, an attractive guy on my crew with thick dark hair and an open countenance, was one of those people you like immediately. When I first met him, he had just come off his qualification flight in Miami and was thrilled to begin flying. We hit it off right away on a trip to New York, where I gave him helpful hints about the way things were run at Pan Am, which surely must have saved him at least *some* grief later. Any Pan Amigo would agree—when newly hatched out of training, learning the endless rules and foreign customs could easily overpower you, especially when flying to endless countries on six continents.

Bill was a big plus for the crew once he was on my flight to Russia.

Having attended Moscow University, he spoke Russian fluently and could read Cyrillic. What welcome news. Bill's linguistic abilities would surely help immensely if anything unforeseen cropped up. Every Pan Am flight had at least one speaker of the native language of the destination country to translate, answer questions, and advise the passengers of regulations. Bill volunteered to make the announcements to Moscow.

Anxious to get on board, I wanted to check the passenger manifest to see if I could garner any helpful or intriguing information. It indicated that we had a small delegation made up of five high-ranking Russian military men, not one lower than the rank of colonel, who would be in clipper (business) class together. Four people from our American embassy in Moscow were seated in economy class.

After the meal service, I decided to have a little fun while also trying to secure a safety net for my crew in case Pan Am dropped the ball somehow. Dressing up a nice bottle of champagne in white linen, I grabbed the crew manifest and approached the head diplomat from the US embassy group. Grinning, I introduced myself, asking, "Can I bribe you with a bottle of champagne?"

She asked what she could do. I handed her the crew contact information, asking her to pass it on to American officials in case something untoward happened during our stay in Moscow. In that case, at least there would be a backup list of our names. A friendly lady, she readily agreed, but she was frazzled about locating her colleagues to hear all the details of exactly what had transpired. What would the ramifications be? I thanked her for her time and strolled up to business class to see what the colonels and general were doing.

I introduced myself to the Russian brass. Their fluent English made it easy to converse, and they were quite open about everything they knew up to that point. Returning from a top-level exchange with their American counterparts made up of high-ranking US military officials, they had been welcomed at several bases in the States. Praising their American hosts, they were deeply disappointed that their productive trip had been so abruptly cut short.

As the flight from New York to Moscow takes nine hours, we had plenty of time to chat. We even told jokes. It was good fun to ask them about the various cultural traditions in Russia, as not all of them were from the capital. I figured that I might as well learn something educational along the way. Even though I did not ask, all of them offered their business cards to me and said pointedly that if something went wrong, I could call them. Grateful for their thoughtful offer, I tucked their cards away carefully; so carefully, in fact, that I still have them all to this day.

Our 747 had an uneventful touchdown in Moscow, but as we taxied to the gate, we strained to see if there was any unusual looking military equipment in the airport area. From our standpoint we could not see any. The only thing that initially seemed to be out of place was that the ground agents carried on like people do when they are not only worried, but terribly preoccupied with upsetting thoughts. Their frenetic undercurrent was palpable. Speaking quickly with a sense of urgency, they continually glanced through the windows, looking as if they were ready to duck for cover if they heard any large-arms fire. Even though they were Russians in their own country, it was no picnic for the ground crew, either.

In many ways, international airline employees are like diplomats. Sharing a profound love for what we do, we inherently know that it is essential to get along with each other, regardless of nationality or religion. We have a powerful affinity for our career and potent respect for each other that transcends politics. When an airline or its employees from another country take a hit, such as in a social upheaval, terrorism, or a crash, it affects all of us. It is an overused expression, but we are all truly one giant family. Seeing these young Russians looking so upset made my heart go out to them. By nightfall, who knew? Maybe they would have to run for their lives in exactly the opposite direction from their families and homes.

The depleted load soon disembarked. My new Russian military buddies hastily exited the plane to make some phone calls to get at the heart of the matter. Our captain went into Operations (Ops) for half an hour and gleaned some updated information that had been wired in from New York. The decision had been made for us to fly straight on to Helsinki. We rested there for about six hours. Later that day, we received a call that we were to go back to Russia.

On the bus ride into the city, the streets were eerily quiet, as if in unsettled anticipation of what could happen next. With perplexed looks on their faces, Muscovites watched armored personnel carriers pass by, but the city did not feel in total disarray. In any case, no matter how much Pan Am warned us about potential danger in any given city, good luck trying to keep the crews from delving into whatever that country had to offer.

We could not wait to get to our rooms, dump our stuff and go see what exactly was happening for ourselves. But first, I was going to schmooze a little with the KGB lady, Irena, who was most likely looking for her bribe. This was the way it worked: Arriving from New York all worn out after a nine-hour flight and smelling like "Eau de Boeing" as we used to joke, we would check in at the desk. However, the clerk did not hand you the key, but instead gave you a piece of paper with your name and room number on it. Getting off the elevator at your floor, the KGB person was plopped right there, 24/7. They knew your every move, and for that matter (ahem!) who was dating whom and any peccadilloes, sexual or otherwise. When you left your room to go out, you handed your key to them, and they could snoop willy-nilly through all of your possessions while you were gone. I must admit, though, they never pilfered my things even though I am sure they had a close look.

Irena was there every time we returned to Moscow, always carefully positioned right in front of the purser's room, which was mine. If there were any changes concerning plans or updates with my crew, the Russians figured it would be centered on the purser, the supervisor for the flight. She usually smiled but appeared—or acted—as if she did not speak any English. I sensed that she liked me and was tickled that I had a Russian name.

My austere room had bland walls, homely furniture, ripped towels, meager toilet paper, and no soap. It did, however, have a clear, inviting view of the Russian White House, the government building which serves Russia. Naturally, it became the center of all the action before and after the coup was staged, so in essence, I was located at the 50-yard line for viewing. All I really needed was a good set of binoculars.

As a new visitor to Moscow, I had also been advised to always watch what I said. Even under *glasnost,* you never knew who was listening, and who wants to be interrogated? Realistically, there were still quite a few people out there who remained loyal to the former communist regime. In the bathroom, I spotted a little gizmo that looked like a listening device. Believing that Russians liked to be identified with the epic film *Dr. Zhivago*, I just hummed the melody of "Lara's Theme." That would pass KGB muster, I figured. Well, depending on who was presently in charge.

Luckily, I was going to hang out with Bill, so nothing would be lost in the translation of things. Walking across the bridge towards the Russian White House, we felt the energy of the city begin to shift into a surrealistic mode. At first, it looked as though the masses had been recklessly tossing all kinds of used construction parts in piles around the government building, but then we realized that they were barricades. Nearby, a double-length bus on one of the main streets looked fine on one side, but had been completely torched on the other, entirely blackened by fire. The Muscovites told Bill that it had been deliberately side-swiped by a large tank while jammed with civilians, causing the gas tank to explode. Several people had been killed in the scorching blaze, and dozens more had been severely burned. Piles of colorful bouquets were draped by mourners over the entire length of the burned-out shell in honor and commemoration of those killed.

Bill translated another eyewitness's story. Three young men had been shot dead after one climbed onto a tank to cover the observation slit, preventing the soldier from firing on the crowd. In retaliation, the tank was set afire by onlookers, but the soldiers survived.

One young man had been intentionally mowed down by another tank. I had seen part of that gripping video on the news before we left New York, but now standing on that very spot, I absorbed the stark reality of his death. I wondered what his last thoughts had been. Had he been an activist aware of his possible sacrifice, or a bystander caught up in a violent vortex of political struggle? A big patch of dried dark red blood was on the boulevard where he and his fellow students had fallen. Then I saw something I will never forget. The Muscovites had converted that tragic area into a sizeable shrine. Bunches of summer flowers surrounded the scene lit by candles that had been carefully laid. Small icons, artistically detailed, depicting Mother Mary and Jesus had been lovingly placed. Tributes had been written on solemn cards. People left packs of cigarettes; someone had even left three pieces of fresh ripe fruit—precious rarities. Witnessing the people openly expressing their sorrow without fear in this sacrosanct place moved me deeply.

Nearby, I noticed a hand-written sign in Cyrillic, hanging from a wall overlooking the area. Bill translated: "God Help Us." From a politically atheist society that forbade its citizens to worship freely for decades, it was a courageous expression of deeply-felt genuine emotion.

Reaching the entrance of the Russian White House, we were amazed to see Boris Yeltsin, a prominent politician, emerge, whizzing by in his Zil limousine. I snapped a quick, fuzzy photo, but you can see his silhouette. We really *were* at the 50-yard line. Thanks to Bill, who had a keen intuitive finger on the prevailing pulse of the situation, I finally felt that it was okay to take photos if I was a little sneaky about it.

Hours earlier, in a display of political ferment, Yeltsin had bravely addressed the Russian Parliament and the throngs of people gathered outside. They had been bombarded with thousands of flyers calling for a general strike to demand that President Gorbachev be allowed to address the citizens. Standing tall atop a tank with the backdrop of a giant white, blue, and red flag, Yeltsin urged the military not to be involved in the anti-constitutional coup against Gorbachev. For someone akin to a buffoon who guzzled copious amounts of "spud juice" (vodka) daily and came to work loaded only to goose all his female staffers, the boisterous proletariat had shown he could really rise to the occasion when needed. The conspirators had contemplated arresting Yeltsin during the coup; not doing so may have ruined their scheme. He would later become Russia's first freely elected leader.

As we approached the imposing staircase leading up to the Russian White House, a peasant family enjoyed a humble meal at a picnic table.

Like many others, their curiosity overrode their fear of the ever-present KGB. Wishing to see what was going on first-hand, this family had a ringside seat. A handwritten sign displaying their sentiments hung from the tree above. In Cyrillic, it contained the simple phrase: "We Won." History was unfolding in front of everyone's eyes, no matter where they hailed from.

Strolling in the golden sunset light, I was dying to get over to Saint Basil's in Red Square to see the rare landmark cathedral with its colorful architecture and intricate appointments. Mostly red, it is topped by green-, yellow-, and blue-striped onion domes. Upon first sight, this stunning shrine demands your attention and dominates Red Square from every angle. Inside it is fascinating, with its endless details and alluring aura, reminding me of something from a young girl's fairy tale. Made up of nine small chapels illuminated by intricate chandeliers, it is decorated with colorful icons and paintings of all sizes. Sadly, many of the original artifacts have long since disappeared.

Weary and ravenous, it was time to chow down. Always exploring, the Pan Am crews had discovered a wonderful restaurant, Tren-Mos Bistro, with the best food in town, run by an enterprising young man from New Jersey. An oasis in a city where meat had suspicious ancestry, the grub was delicious, and you would not get sick the next day. There is nothing in the world like running around a 747 when you feel like someone is stirring your guts with a giant wooden spoon. In addition to constantly filling our champagne glasses, the waiters kept topping off our vodka glasses, too, without our requesting it, just as we replenish water glasses in the States. The Moscow twist to being "double fisted drinkers." That night I dove into my lumpy bed, immediately falling into a deep sleep.

The next morning, we returned to Red Square. Rounding the corner, we spotted an elite division of tanks near the world-famous Saint Basil's. Wilting flowers dangled from one tank, reminiscent of the anti-Vietnam war demonstrations at the Pentagon in the late '60s. In defiance of the coup, dozens carried the "new" red, white, and blue Russian flags; the communist red ones with the hammer and sickle were nowhere in sight.

Lenin's tomb, where his body can be viewed through a glass

sarcophagus, is adjacent. People joke about how he could have been stuffed in 1925 and still look pretty good, but perhaps they used a lot of wax. In any case, I would never visit his tomb on principle. We have had more than enough fiends in human history, and I do not need to see how they look either in life or in death.

While still roaming around Red Square, Bill was told that a curfew was going to be imposed that night from 11 p.m. until 5 a.m. The informant added that this could possibly be a sign that an attack on the Russian White House, located directly across from our hotel, could be imminent. If there was going to be any trouble, civilians needed to get out of harm's way. We stepped up our plans so that we could return "home" much earlier just in case it *was not* a rumor.

Back at the hotel, despite the warning of impending trouble, the night was relatively peaceful.

On our last day, we headed over to Arbad Street, the best place in Moscow to buy all types of fun and artsy souvenirs. Every time a European or American hesitated to check out some trinket along the endless line of tables, the Muscovites immediately stopped to see what caught the foreigner's eye, what might seem "hip and trendy" to them. Bill, always outgoing, was having a lively conversation in Russian with the artists, joking and laughing. Sitting on a step, I was taking in the entire scene when I felt someone tickle my ankle bracelet. I have worn one since I was 14; just a gypsy thing, I guess. I was curious to know what this guy was up to. He had been listening to Bill's conversation and realized that we were together. He seemed friendly enough. "Do they really wear gold on their feet in America?" he asked.

I had never thought of it that way, but he was right. As I sheepishly admitted that I guess we did, I began to flash on the numerous ways that people from diverse lands view the customs of others.

I am endlessly intrigued by various degrees of human perception about the things we are exposed to in our lives. When you are born into, and surrounded by, an opulent culture, most unusual inventions or perhaps new ethnic habits are taken in stride. When I have observed foreigners who have grown up in less affluent environments, I am always curious to hear how they describe things as viewed from their individual perspective.

Once, when shown a photo of a large condo building, a Bushman of the Kalahari from a family of nomads studied the structure for a few minutes, saying to the photographer, "Your people live like wingless bees."

Well, if you consider the Kalahari Desert your backyard domain, I can see how a crowded apartment building looks terribly confining to a Bushman. In Mongolia, a middle aged father living in an animal-hide tent became impatient with his son who was begging non-stop for a small TV he had seen in the market. The exasperated father finally exclaimed to his son, "I will NOT buy you the box with the glass face!"

In West Africa, staring at a typical American house with a two-car garage, the tribesman remarked, "Do you really have houses for your transport?"

A word, no doubt, he had learned from the British educational system.

Walking down Gorky Street on our final night, spectacular fireworks suddenly exploded, turning the night sky into a glittering display of light. They were loud, brilliant, and just kept coming. No, this was not the Mall in Washington, D.C., during the July fourth bicentennial celebrations, nor was it a holiday. Itching to know what the celebration was about, Bill asked a group of young people passing by. President Gorbachev had been released from his enforced captivity and had arrived back in Moscow. He looked terribly haggard, unkempt, and simply "freaked out," as we used to say in the sixties. A well-known photo taken that day shows him emerging from his jet. In total disbelief, he looked despondent, as if this had been a real close one.

For the beleaguered Gorby, it had. Fortunately, the opposition soldiers had allowed him to keep a radio tuned in to the BBC airwaves for continual updates on the coup, not to mention his own fate. That was his only legitimate source of information while under house arrest. By the time he returned to Moscow, he looked like someone who had seen their entire life pass right before their eyes with a creepy ending.

Indeed, the fireworks signaled the end of an attempted coup d'état that could very well have changed the course of world history. However, there wasn't too much dancing in the streets. When the full implications of the coup had sunk in, the Muscovites were quite horrified to realize that a handful of disgruntled military men had almost succeeded in steering this enormous country onto a disastrous course.

Even though the coup lasted only three long days, it may have hastened the collapse of the Soviet Union. When one of the conspirators, Boris Pugo, realized that the coup had failed, he fatally shot his wife and then turned the gun on himself. "The commies are a rough bunch, darling," my mother once said during the time when the Reds ruled with an iron fist.

The next day, as I handed my key to Irena, my hotel watchdog, for the last time, I gave her two cans of tuna. She knew it was something special but was not sure exactly what. Bill began to explain in Russian "It is a type of delicious fish that you can fix different ways."

Delighted, with a wide grin on her face, she tucked them away carefully, telling Bill that she would save them for a special occasion. She had never tasted tuna. Turning towards me, she looked me straight in the eye, asking in perfect textbook English, "Will you be bidding for Moscow trips again in September? It has been a real pleasure having your crew here."

Trying to hold back my surprise, I began to speak in airline jargon, "Well, I am fairly junior and will bid for Rio because I have a friend down there, but if I don't hold that line, SVO will be my second choice." True to her position, Irena had understood every single word.

Even though it was the eleventh hour when I "discovered" that she really spoke English after all, we had an understanding. We had never even sat down for an informal chat but shared a mutual admiration. "Irena, thank you for everything," I told her. "This has really been an experience."

"Don't mention it," were her exact words in reply.

Boarding the flight back to New York was frenetic, with everyone anxious to get on, and fast. Most of the Russians had big brown envelopes, which meant that they were emigrating. Having planned the move to America for years, either with their families or to join their relatives, many were not entirely certain that this coup had been squashed for good. Having suffered years of frustrating setbacks, they felt desperately afraid that their carefully laid plans could spin totally out of control and go awry once again. They were cautious and polite, but I could certainly feel their angst coming through.

However, once seated, with all their hands in the air flowing back and forth asking for anything we had, they looked like an ocean full of seaweed.

I shall never forget two of the passengers. One was a tall dark man who looked like a Cossack with a thick bushy mustache curled at the ends. Drawing in his breath, he shouted in a heavy Russian accent "Thank God we are getting out of here!" as I checked his boarding pass at the door. Obviously, someone was not worried that the trip to America might possibly reverse itself and we could remain grounded. I must admit I loved his gusto and candor, and for *everyone's* sake, I also wished that his prediction would come true. It was not unheard of for an aircraft to be impounded if the authorities wanted to assert their dominion over us.

Over Greenland and its ever-present snow-capped mountains, we were serving tea and coffee with sandwiches. The service was rather hectic because the plane was completely stuffed. Additionally, once the Russians realized that they could have more than just one drink, some were asking for three or four. After years of restrictive oppression, being spied upon and ordered about all the time, it was liberating for them to be sampling all these juices, sodas, and tasty snacks from a faraway land. Most were courteous and friendly about it, perhaps because they had respect for *anyone* in a uniform. It was a well-known fact that "flight attendants" on Aeroflot were often KGB agents, so they probably were not sure about the Americans, either.

The second passenger I shall always remember was an attractive young Russian lady. When she rang the call bell, I hate to say it, but my first thoughts were, "What in the hell do they want now? Can't they see we are busy? Everyone is out in the aisle working."

But once I got to this lady's seat, I felt guilty for having had those thoughts. About twenty, with an amiable demeanor, her bright face showed that she was a gentle soul. Perhaps her brown envelope reminded her that her life's hardships were coming to an end. "May I please ask you what that yellow drink is?" she asked in halting English. "It is so sweet and delicious."

Trying to explain that it came from citrus fruit trees grown in Florida, I lost her at the first turn. Racing into the galley, I poured three glasses for her. She was so grateful that I was almost embarrassed. "What is your final destination?" I asked.

"Los Angeles, where my aunt lives," she replied.

"I can tell that you'll be successful in my country, and I sincerely hope that you will be very happy in your new adopted home," I told her.

Sometimes, when I drive through the Russian section of Los Angeles, I think about her and wonder about her life in our country. I am certain she is fine. It takes real courage to leave the only home you have ever known to create an entirely new life in a foreign land over 7,000 miles away. When foreigners escaping oppressive regimes boarded one of our flights, it always reminded me of the traditional "first footing" at Ellis Island.

This airlift of sorts was one of endless dramatic reminders of the unique role Pan Am played on the international stage during times of uncertainty.

Less than ten minutes from landing, a stunning view of the Statue of Liberty came into view as we turned for our final approach into JFK. Sometimes referred to as "The mother of exiles," this light-green lady of freedom and international friendship was glistening in the sun, a hospitable and symbolic sight to those on board. One of her feet stands on chains, characterizing gained freedom. I believe she is the strongest icon in the world that represents liberty from oppression, "I lift my lamp beside the golden door."

I made an announcement to bring the exquisite monument to their attention, and excitement exploded in the cabin as our passengers realized that they had finally reached America. A few minutes later, we touched down at Kennedy Airport. Clapping joyfully, the exuberant Russians hugged each other, or patted the shoulder of their seatmate. Others happily called out to one another from across the aisle. Certain types of human emotion do not need any translation at all.

"Ladies and gentlemen, Pan Am would like to be the first to welcome you to the United States of America!" I announced, almost giddily.

So happy for all of them, I think I was cheering the loudest.

The atmosphere was one of complete joy and made me forget—at least for a while—that I had been in the front row to witness a political event that has gone into the history books.

General Schwarzkopf leading the victory parade in DC

6

Transporting American Troops to Liberate Kuwait

"Tania, do you have any Israeli stamps in your passport? Is your middle name Jewish?" my supervisor in New York urgently asked.

My middle name, von Traeschler, is Bavarian, but I knew exactly why. Pan Am sought crews to fly troops to Dhahran and Al-Jubail, located on the Gulf Coast of the Kingdom of Saudi Arabia, not too far from the Kuwait border. A Jewish name or Israeli stamps in my passport would immediately exclude me from the flights.

Days before, during the sweltering month of August 1991, Saddam Hussein's Iraqi Army had invaded the tiny neighboring country of Kuwait. Pan Am had an agreement with the US government that in times of declared national emergency, they would turn over any of our 38 Boeing 747s requested for US military purposes. The jumbo jets were part of the Civilian Reserve Air Fleet (CRAF) program. Once loaned to the military, these planes could fly personnel or be converted into cargo flights by yanking out all the seats to make room for transporting materiel.

Anxious to go, I hoped I would qualify and not miss out on a valuable experience. I not only relished the exposure of working in some capacity with the military, but I strongly felt that our crews were lending some support to them by making their journey as comfortable as humanly possible.

Six days after the invasion, as part of Operation Desert Shield, the elite 82nd Airborne Division out of Fort Bragg, North Carolina, was the first unit to be deployed to Saudi Arabia to secure the area and its assets, particularly the oil installations of Aramco. Hector Adler, Vice President of In-Flight services at Pan Am, sent a memo to all flight crews.

"Representatives of the United States government have now advised Pan Am that we need to be prepared, if called upon, to comply with our long-standing contractual agreement to the government's CRAF program. In this case, that commitment would require us to supply a certain number of B-747 aircraft and crews to operate transportation missions to and from the Middle East. For those flight attendants who are operating CRAF flights, the company has increased the $100,000 special risk insurance to $200,000 at no cost to the flight attendant. This additional insurance will be in effect while on a trip, including time spent on a layover."

Management was requesting volunteers since our union would protect any flight attendant who felt endangered and refused to go. However, an overwhelming response from so many crews who were willing to fly the missions ensured that the flights always went out fully staffed.

Officials at the Pentagon strategized, burned the midnight oil, and ordered thousands of body bags in anticipation of the predicted onslaught, stoking fear of massive casualties. Newspaper headlines and TV news continually screamed about the sophisticated tanks, armored personnel carriers, and weapons that Hussein had stockpiled from the Russians. Reports in the press claimed that SCUD missiles loaded with poison gas deployed from Iraq could not only reach Israel, but could also destroy the three main cities in Saudi Arabia: Dhahran on the east coast, the capital Riyadh in the middle of the country, and Jeddah on the Red Sea.

My roomie, Kevin Mc Donald, would fly a trip to Dhahran first.

"My God, Kevin, that would be like having enemy missiles aimed at, and capable of, destroying New York, Washington, and LA." Kevin readily agreed, admitting how terrified he'd feel to be under that immediate threat.

Kevin and I met during Pan Am's frenzied flight attendant training program, becoming confidants in a flash. Sharing similar opinions, we also view the world through almost identical lenses. A stunning Black man, Kevin was tall and perfectly proportioned, with glowing skin and refined aristocratic features. Educated in France, he spoke rapid-fire French and Italian, and always dreamed about modeling in Paris or Milan. Laughing, I used to warn him, "Kevin, look out, they worship false gods in the fashion industry," referring to the narcissism.

When not thinking about fashion, however, he relished our global adventures just as all the other Pan Amigos did, flying into Saudi Arabia with an open mind. A teetotaler, Kevin wished that he could have given the soldiers cocktails to make their ride into a war zone more comfortable. A strict no-alcohol policy was enforced for all charters. "We gave them everything they wanted. You couldn't find a tasty morsel left on that plane," he told me. "I wish that we had *more* to give them, they are such remarkable guys."

During the early stages of the build-up, Kevin flew the troops into Cairo to refuel, continuing onto Dhahran. He quickly disembarked, scampering straight across the tarmac to the enormous hangar where they stored supplies. Military equipment arriving from the States was also cataloged there. Among the cargo, I heavily suspect that there may have been a coveted case or two of beer, belly-loaded and smuggled into the country. Any type of liquor is strictly forbidden in Saudi Arabia, and foreigners can expect some real troub—deportation, heavy fines, or perhaps even prison—for "bootlegging" alcohol into the Kingdom.

Wasting no time, Kevin stocked up on souvenir T-shirts for friends which had logos of cartoon dromedaries with the slogan, "I would fly 10,000 miles to smoke a Camel," illustrating caricatures of Saddam Hussein getting his noggin blown off. Kevin chatted with the soldiers who played cards and exchanged stories of their new experiences in Saudi Arabia. Outside, scorpions battled, stingers held high, in a Mid-Eastern version of a cock fight. Soldiers egged them on and made bets on which arachnid would win the duel. Two of the men had already been bitten by large cobras. After the mandatory battery of injections, including anthrax, that each had received, it was ironic that none could prevent poisoning from a cobra's bite.

Others related horror stories of the enormous hairy eight-inch-plus camel spiders, who's oversized fangs can penetrate thick animal skin. The poisonous denizens hunt at night and cause trouble when they try to snuggle into cozy sleeping bags with the troops. Always looking for trouble, the spiders scurry across the sand at up to 10 miles per hour and can even devour scorpions after delivering a poisonous bite in a life-and-death struggle.

After weeks of hearing these stories, my itch was satisfied when I was finally given one of these trips. At the crew lounge, I ran smack into one of my classmates. "Tania, have you signed up for the charters?" she asked. "They are right up your alley, but I have been hearing a lot of stories. Tower Air has removed the American flag from the tails of their 747s by obliterating them with white paint. I don't think that Pan Am is going to spend the money to do that. Our bright blue logo on the tail looks like a bull's eye, especially since we represent America."

She was right. Not long afterward, I spotted a few Tower Air B-747s out on the tarmac with minuscule black letters near the tails, and that was all.

My crew flew commercial to Bangor, Maine, on a small, turbo-prop airplane (aka "weedwhacker") to meet our B-747 carrying troops from the First Cavalry out of Fort Hood, Texas, arriving the next day. Visiting Bangor overnight was fortuitous, as I had close friends there: Catherine, Don, and their son Aaron, whom I had lived with for three years in Northern Virginia. There is nothing like getting paid to party with your close friends. Naturally, they bought some delectable giant Maine lobsters to cook at home. Catherine's parents joined us. Her father had retired from a distinguished and intriguing career working for the CIA in countries as far-flung as Zaire and Cambodia. Curious to know all about Operation Desert Shield, he peppered me with loads of questions about Pan Am's involvement in transporting the military into Saudi Arabia. Once you have been bitten by the bug of international affairs, it becomes a way of life and stays with you always, permeating your soul.

Before each of these military flights, I would slip into a peaceful room for a few minutes of spiritual meditation. To set the tone for the flight in my psyche, I asked the powers that be to make me aware of anything or anyone on board that might require special attention. I envisioned the giant white and blue airliner surrounded by an angelic white light to provide a protective shield for our brave soldiers, along with a fervent prayer that they should return to America safe and sound. I also asked the Almighty that we would have the honor to accompany them when the joyous day arrived to whisk them home.

⌒☉

Cramped into a small room in Bangor's airport, I held a pre-flight briefing.

"As far as I am concerned, we have 425 VIPs on board tonight for our flight to Rome," I began. "Each single soldier is a VIP and should be treated accordingly. As we all know, these courageous young men are putting their lives on the line for us, and I want their flight to be as comfortable as possible. There will be no liquor on any of these flights, but whatever we have on the plane, if they ask for it, give it to them. On day two, from Rome to Dhahran, upon arrival after the soldiers have disembarked, I'd like to take off all the remaining fruit, snacks, and sodas for the military personnel at the hangar."

My crew was more than willing to give all the treats away. We were scheduled to be on the ground for only a couple of hours while they off-loaded all the equipment. On departure, we would take off at a steep angle, heading northwest, flying directly back to Rome. For security reasons, there were absolutely no layovers in Dhahran.

As I held the briefing, I felt deeply moved by just looking around the room at my colleagues. Every flight attendant had purchased decorations for the plane with their own money. Yellow ribbons and flags adorned their lapels. Yards and yards of yellow bunting and streamers had been bought to tape alongside the interior of the aircraft. Once onboard, harvest decorations, yellow flowers, and American flags brightened up the interior. To make the soldiers feel even more welcome, pumpkins to carve on the lengthy trip were placed on the credenza, alongside our long carving knives usually reserved for slicing chateaubriand in first class. This hospitality was typical of the omnipresent Pan Am spirit; always dynamic.

From the onset, it was obvious that this was not going to be an ordinary flight, even for the seniors who had flown for years. I was also relieved that a beautiful senior purser was on the crew. An experienced veteran of Pan Am's emergency airlifts out of Beirut, Vietnam, and Tehran, I could ask her advice if anything untoward arose. You can never have enough intelligent minds in an emergency situation—that is, if they know what in the hell is going on.

Lastly, I encouraged my colleagues to wear something patriotic in place of the uniform if they chose: a flag shirt or sweater, a T-shirt with a patriotic theme, or something similar. My only request was that they should not wear anything too sexy or slinky. Leave the Vickie's Secret stuff at home. I certainly did not want any nonsense that I could not handle.

Walking down Bangor's jetway to board the plane, we spotted the First Cavalry soldiers milling around the entrance chatting. Some casually held M-16 assault rifles. I had to catch my breath for a minute. At first glance, it really took me aback to see weapons on the plane, like the thought of someone smoking a cigarette while fueling a car. Guns and planes just do not mix. Then I looked over those "famous" desert "cammies," the earth-tone uniforms that everyone constantly saw on the news. My generation was so accustomed to seeing troops in green camouflage from the Vietnam era and the Central American operations that the beige ones looked entirely different.

"Good evening, gentlemen! It is good to see you. Are you ready for our flight to Rome?" I asked, shaking the hand of the soldier closest to me.

"Yes, Ma'am!" they replied in unison.

That night, in fact, there were a *lot* of weapons on that plane: at least 850; an M-16 assault rifle and a sidearm for each of the 425 soldiers. And that was not all—genade launchers and machine guns rounded out the arsenal. Most poked out into the aisles.

Something else I observed right away—if you did not have a good sense of humor, you had better develop one fast, because that would fortify you for the extreme challenges that lay ahead. You will be able to survive with a stronger frame of mind if you can laugh about everyday things. On these flights, even with hundreds of troops, they knew each other intimately, including each soldier's fears and phobias. One teenage guy near the back of the plane was petrified of flying. Not long after takeoff, we encountered a bit of turbulence. Soon we started pitching around, enough to disturb the troops who were sleeping. The hate-to-fly soldier clasped his hands over his ears as someone right behind him shouted for all to hear, "OH, NOOO! WE ARE GOING DOWN!"

That was one of many times I wished we had cocktails on the plane. I would have certainly offered to buy the young man a drink to calm his nerves.

As the smell of roast chicken wafted from the galleys, my crew began to decorate the plane, nose to tail. One of my coworkers produced a large poster of "Pam Am's Paris" with a photo of the Eiffel Tower. Signed by all with our sentiments for the soldiers, we presented it to the colonel in charge. Across from my jump seat in first class, there was a pleasant, easygoing Black soldier named Joseph. Hitting it off right away, we told stories and jokes, teasing each other like old friends. Not far below the surface, however, I sensed his fear. Although he was trying hard to be stoic, his nervousness came through in his laughter and diction. His wide eyes darted around the cabin a bit, as if he was already expecting an ugly surprise from the enemy. Then he reclined his seat for a little snooze. Taking one of our handmade posters signed by the entire crew wishing them well, I hiked my uniform skirt to mid-thigh and stepped up onto the armrest. Affixing it to the wall with the sergeant's thousand-mile tape, I jolted Joseph awake. Abruptly rising, he exclaimed, "Oh, my God! I woke up and the only thing I saw was long legs all over me. Have I died and gone to heaven?"

Crossing the Atlantic through a black sky after dinner with all the lights turned off, I asked one soldier if I could borrow his night vision goggles to see how the cabin would look. My vision adjusted quickly. The faint light emanating from the lavatory hallway suddenly brightened up considerably. I could easily understand how you could destroy your vision if you used them in daylight. Outside the window, as the airplane flew at 525 miles per hour, intense friction fought itself as it raced over the wing, reminding me of the electricity you see when flying in thunderstorms. It looked like a tumbleweed plugged into a socket. Inside, I focused on the silhouettes of the soldiers, and could readily distinguish the heat rising from their bodies.

An intimate glimpse of their individual souls made me privy to their life force, emanating from each mortal. I perceived an instant connection with my fellow human beings as I gazed upon their spark of light, privileged to observe the reflection of their vital energy. I have been on a continuous quest in my life to try and understand the common denominator that binds all humans, and in a way, I was witnessing the metaphysical fabric between us, even though we were on diverse spiritual paths. These were the very souls whom I had asked the Almighty to protect and keep safe before each flight.

A pilot once told me that when the plane's cooling system was on the blink, the heat of each person's body became a 1,000-watt lightbulb. Now I was viewing a cabin *full* of 1,000-watt lightbulbs, appearing luminous in the darkened cabin.

While looking over the seats to see how everyone was doing, I thought about how wholesome and dedicated they were. For these men, at least for a time, mankind's second most important instinct was far from their minds. They were busy coping with their preemptive instinct: the need to survive. I could not help but think of the adage, "Is there a man in the house?" Oh, yes, 425 incredible men!

I empathized with the colonel, as well. I could only imagine what was going through his mind—thinking over various maneuver tactics, logistics, anticipating the unexpected, and being in command of, and responsible for, over a thousand troops, just to mention a few things. I had spent some time chatting with him and the chaplain to gain some understanding of what it must be like to manage all that responsibility. Some of his youthful soldiers had traveled out of their home states just once, to report to Fort Hood. Now they were embarking on a journey 8,000 miles away, thrust into a completely unknown situation involving austere customs, foreign languages, and severe climate, in addition to the constant peril. I also imagined if I was an experienced soldier, how I might have disliked somebody in basic training, but as we marched closer to the war zone it would be imperative to change my attitude. Now it would be us against the enemy. As soldiers, we would have to depend on each other for everything, including survival in every sense of the word. The guy whom I had disliked may be the very one who rescued me from catastrophic injury or save my life when I could not save myself.

Infuriated with the Iraqi invasion, some soldiers from my generation, now in their mid-30s, who had fought in Vietnam, had re-enlisted. For someone unfamiliar with the military, I was gathering information about their world, and it was coming swiftly.

Throughout the plane, Pat Benatar's popular song "Hit Me with Your Best Shot" screamed out of endless Walkmen; the tune du jour.

Upon learning that I came from a non-military family, one soldier passed the time by dutifully listing all the ranks in the military on the back of a barf bag. He carefully illustrated their corresponding symbols for my reference. I slipped it into my September 1990 diary, where it has remained ever since.

"Aren't you afraid?" a personable blond guy asked me as we flew over Jordan.

The pilots encouraged the soldiers to visit them throughout the flight, inviting them to sit on the two extra jump seats. Along the way, they eagerly asked each other questions during animated discussions. "I believe in Fate," I replied, "and could get whacked in our back yard in Ozone Park if our neighbors were having a shootout. John Gotti's ("Teflon Don") office is close by. I hear gunshots more often than I'd like to say. I also believe that I won't go a day before I am supposed to."

However, a few hours later, that line of thinking was adjusted significantly. One mustn't be too cavalier, you know; particularly when entering uncharted territory.

Gathering in the aft galley, my crew waited for instructions on how to don a gas mask in the event of a SCUD attack while on the ground in Dhahran. Our instructor was none other than the colonel himself. Each face exuded a look of consternation. Often in our pre-flight briefings, my colleagues might look bored because they had heard it before, but this was strikingly different; a real first. All eyes were fixed intently on the Commanding Officer (CO).

"This is how you don the mask," the colonel said, fidgeting with the awkward equipment that resembled something from a low-budget monster movie. "Be certain to pull this strap back and it will be easier to get over your head. If you wear glasses and can see long distances without them, I suggest that you take them off before donning the mask. They are a bit cumbersome, but speed is essential. I want you to feel comfortable with it, so I'm going to pass the mask around so that each of you becomes familiar with how it works. We may not have sufficient warning if there is an incoming missile," he added.

I felt my eyebrows go up as I looked at the others' faces. I was not the only one. Each of us was weighing every single word coming out of the colonel's mouth.

"If you hear the warning siren signaling a SCUD attack, don your mask immediately. Watch us for signals. Yellow flags will be held aloft as a warning signal, red flags signify imminent danger, and white flags indicate the all-clear. Keep in mind that it'll be difficult to hear each other speak. You might not be able to hear any instructions with the SCUD alert siren screaming. Any questions?"

Even though the entire crew had enthusiastically signed up for this charter, the colonel's briefing had a way of "sobering us up," you might say. His straightforward military-style talk reminded us that we were about to enter a war zone, and if we encountered any type of attack, there was a distinct possibility that it could be each man for himself in the ensuing confusion.

Sitting on my jump seat, I crafted my own version of the arrival announcements. Every time I thought about saying goodbye to our gallant new friends, I felt a tightening in my throat and tears welled up. What could I say other than to wish them well, adding that we would all pray for their safe return? During the last 30 minutes, as we glided over the Persian Gulf and back in for landing, all 425 souls were completely silent. I could only guess what they were thinking. Right below the surface, I could almost smell their fear. The scent of fear is acidic.

The mood lightened up for a few minutes when the tall, lanky sarge asked if he could borrow my hot mike. While grinning at our younger flight attendants, he announced, "Now, listen up men! Take a good, long, last look at these ladies, because they're gonna be the last women you will see for quite some time, 'cause I am going to be your Momma from now on!"

Upon touchdown, after welcoming them and announcing the local time, I added, "Gentlemen, we look forward to the day when we get the welcome call from Crew Scheduling to come pick you up to spirit you back home to America. You are in our hearts and prayers, and we shall never forget you. God bless you and keep you safe. Vaya con Dios."

It was almost impossible for me to keep my voice from cracking with emotion as I said goodbye to them. Even after all these years, I remember those charter flights like they were yesterday. Snapping a photo of them just before they disembarked the plane, one flashed a peace sign at me, but not one of them grinned. Then Joseph winked. With a warm smile, he vigorously shook my hand. "Thank you, Tania, your crew was great. Take good care. We'll never forget you guys, either."

As they left, the sarge was there barking, "Barrels down, butts up, men!" in reference to carrying their M-16s. I grinned as he repeated the words. After the last soldier got off, we quickly rounded up all the goodies in the galley to take to the troops in the hangar. By the time we were finished ransacking the plane, I swear not one candy bar or piece of fruit was left on that 747. Cases of soda were offloaded, too.

I rushed across to the hangar. My thoughts were clicking ahead about the souvenirs I wanted to buy and what we could explore.

"Where are you guys based? Is this your first time on one of these charters?" asked staff sergeant Shelley Ovsak. "What kind of perfume are you wearing?"

I could see why this was a normal question. Entirely surrounded by gobs of testosterone, this feminine gal wanted to engage in some fun girl talk. The hangar was bustling with all kinds of activity. Soldiers lined the perimeter of the large room, sitting on the floor talking while cleaning destructive sand from their M-16s, or relaxing on their equipment for a few winks. Stationed at McGuire AFB, New Jersey, Shelley kept inventory in the hangar of all the materiel arriving from the States. She was also in charge of manifesting the troops for their military flights within the theater. Tall, with pretty hazel eyes and brown hair, she had previously been a model. In this environment, she was worlds away from the modeling and fashion industry, in more ways than one.

In the following months, I flew more unforgettable charters; then January arrived, and war broke out. As I watched CNN for the latest information, I cringed every time I heard the SCUD alert siren go off, especially since I knew people over there. Hearing from Shelley often, I worried about her being in harm's way, because she was well within SCUD range. Unlike Vietnam, we now had detailed—and often immediate—coverage of every aspect of the war. As the news outlets vied for the best stories, their correspondents also risked their lives in reporting them to give us the latest updates.

The night the war broke out, I had the worst nightmare of my life, bar none. I dreamt I was a soldier in Kuwait, and when the colonel asked who in our battalion wanted to guard the village we were in, my hand shot up right away. It was a signal that I was the biggest chickenshit in the world, as our area was relatively safe. Everyone knew that the other towns were treacherous. Surface-to-surface hyper-velocity missiles and detonated grenades rattled entire buildings in a town close by. Land mines had been planted along the roads and we did not have any canine bomb-sniffers. Consumed by profound primal fear, I was being eaten alive. Other soldiers threw me disapproving looks, as it was obvious that I was trying to save myself and not be part of the team's mission. The night sky became white from the bomb blasts. Sirens pierced the air with their ear-splitting screams, making my hair stand on end as I watched the distant horrifying scene of destruction. My blood pressure rose so high from fright that my blood threatened to burst right through my skull from the extreme anxiety. Wham! I abruptly woke up back at home in Virginia.

I bolted vertically straight up in bed. Throughout my body, blood rushed from top to bottom in my vessels at a dizzying pace. Ice water raced through my veins instead of warm blood. An instant, violent headache throbbed from the strain. Even though I immediately realized that I was safe at home, I could not stop the tension nor the rush of "freezing blood" through my veins. My calves cramped up like hell. I struggled to level off, calm down, and control what was happening in my body. Having a difficult time catching my breath, it felt as if someone had hauled off and punched me right in the gut. My heart raced like that of a hunted animal knowing that a predator is about to nail it.

I instantly realized exactly why I saw that vision. Bonding so strongly with the troops, while taking on their energy, I empathized with them from thousands of miles away. I prayed for a long time that night, focusing on a *montage* in my mind's eye, remembering the faces of many of the soldiers we had met, one by one, until I fell asleep.

Thankfully for everyone, the war only lasted a few weeks, but nobody could have predicted that in advance.

Rome—April 1, 1991. I will never forget April Fool's Day, even if I live to be a hundred years old, and perhaps there is that chance, as my maternal grandmother lived to be 109. I just could not wait to fly the 82nd Airborne from Rome back home to Fort Bragg, especially since they were among the first deployed into the Gulf on August 8, 1990. My crew had scoured the flower shops of Rome, and purchased, I swear, every last yellow flower in the Eternal City with their own funds. Proudly wearing their patriotic finery, they were ready for the troops with endless bunches of small flags, welcome home signs, and yellow banners from America.

If you had touched the fuselage of our plane, you would have been electrocuted in short order, the energy was so exuberant and intense. As I boarded the aircraft, I was almost knocked over by the 100,000-watt human power emanating from the soldiers.

"Are you gentlemen ready to go HOME?" I excitedly asked the troops closest to the boarding door, who all energetically yelled their various affirmations. "Welcome to America!"

Once you set foot onto one of our planes, I felt that you were on American soil. Before I could even ask where the CO was sitting, one soldier cheekily called out to me, "Ma'am, I would like to kiss you!"

Next to him, his battle buddy exalted "Go ahead, you are not in Saudi anymore!"

Another one pointed out Lieutenant Colonel Taylor up in First Class. I could always tell right away by their response if the CO was respected or not, just based on their reaction and the enthusiasm, or lack of, as they identified their leader to me. No doubt, this one was most definitely respected.

Introducing myself to the colonel, I asked what time he wanted dinner served and if there were any special requests. Turning to Ron, their chaplain, I invited him to say prayers over the PA. Gracious and polite, they were elated to be going home. And my crew was absolutely thrilled to be part of an operation that would return them to their loved ones after eight months. Everyone aboard felt giddy as our giant bird rushed down the runway and lifted off, leaving Rome behind. The troops burst into spontaneous applause as one yelled, "We're outta here!"

Heading west towards home, we left the bone-dry forbidding desert even further behind us as we soared over a sparkling cobalt-blue sea.

In short, after many months of prayers, it was *the* day that I had envisioned.

Thankful it was not a protracted war, I am certain that each of us gave thanks to the Almighty in our own way. The chaplain related some engaging stories about holding prayer services in the middle of the desert, often in 118-plus-degree weather. Instructed to cover the cross on the front of his helmet, he was advised that he could hold services. Driving way out into the suffocating, barren desert, the chaplain would lower the tailgate of the Humvee to fashion a makeshift altar. The soldiers then held devotion services and communion.

Hearing endless complaints about the military rations, I decided to have some fun on the PA while the galley attendants cooked chicken and lasagna dinners. "Gentlemen, tonight for your delicious dinner we will be serving . . . A-rats, MREs (meals ready to eat), and crackers with water!" A big collective howl went up toward the ceiling.

In the upper deck above First Class, soldiers lined up to visit the cockpit to chat with the pilots, as they relished catching up on stateside news.

"Is it really like they say back home?" one attractive man with clear green eyes and sandy-colored hair asked me.

The minute I looked at his face, I knew that he was from my generation and must have served in Vietnam. "Are they really welcoming us home this time? It certainly wasn't like that when we returned from 'Nam. People spat at us. I took my uniform off at the airport when I reached the States, but they still knew by my haircut that I was a Vet."

I assured him that it would be an entirely different homecoming this time.

Fortunately, Boeing had provided a "welcome home" film that ran two hours, which we played on all the returning flights. Specially made for the troops, it contained the highlights of the Super Bowl and basketball games in addition to various film, TV, and music award shows. It also featured clips from recent popular movies. But most importantly to the passengers and me, it illustrated to the soldiers how America was preparing for their return. Upbeat stories related how millions of yards of yellow ribbons and American flags were being produced. Traditional tree-lined neighborhoods from Middle America, festooned with these decorations blowing in the breeze, characterized the warm welcome.

The highlight of the film was when Whitney Houston sang "The Star-Spangled Banner" accompanied by an orchestra at the Super Bowl. While military personnel held full-sized flags representing each state, an ocean of fans in the stadium waved small American flags to the rhythm of our national anthem. It was just as if she was singing to each of my passengers in a live performance. They felt it, too. Each one's eyes were transfixed on the movie screen, awed by her full-spectrum voice. All activity ceased in the cabin as the crew stopped to watch. When she finished, the sound of robust applause bounced off the walls of the airplane with gusto as if they had heard it live. This well-produced, up-to-speed, tailored documentary was pure Americana, and it garnered their rapt attention.

Since it was April Fool's Day, Colonel Taylor wanted to play a joke on a soldier who was handsome, suave, and self-assured. Plotting our nonsense up in First Class, it felt surreal to be crafting practical jokes with someone who had been devising real war strategies just weeks before. The chaplain was in on it, too. This particular soldier was quite a ladies' man, and had been flirting with a young, beautiful, multi-lingual blonde from our crew, whom he hoped would shell out her contact info by the time we reached New York.

We got her in on it. We cooked up a plan for her to ask the soldier in an enticing way to follow her to the back of the plane. Once there, she pulled him into the aft lavatory, rapidly locking the door, asking him to tell her about himself. After a few minutes, the colonel got up from First Class, walking hurriedly and directly toward that lavatory. He pretended to be super furious, as if something bizarre was happening. The soldiers all sat up ramrod straight as the colonel huffed down the aisle. Many shouted "Make a hole! The colonel is coming in hot!" but with absolutely no idea why he was running through the plane looking so irate.

As he passed through five sections of the jet, each head made an instant 180-degree turn as they craned their necks to see what was going on. Many asked alarmingly, "What's up with the colonel?"

As he reached the bathroom, all could hear the flight attendant inside banging loudly on the door, as if she was trying to escape. The colonel barked, "What in the hell is going on inside there?" calling the soldier's name.

The lavatory door sprung open as the colonel's ultimatum in a loud voice filled the cabin, "What were you doing? I demand an explanation!"

The face of the young Lothario turned bright red. "I swear, colonel, we weren't doing *anything*," he pleaded, "just talking."

Afraid of getting into deep kimchi, he desperately tried to explain in short order that she had invited him in voluntarily. Then he detected a slight smile sneaking across the colonel's face and realized that he had been skunked on April Fool's Day.

Dozens of pillows were tossed back and forth in mock fights while other soldiers played card games or just discussed their war experiences. Our crew chose one lavatory where each one of us kissed the mirror to see if the soldiers in that section could guess which lips belonged to whom. Winners received a First Class amenities bag. In another diversion, we added up all our ages. We asked the soldiers to guess the total on a piece of paper with their seat number. The estimates were collected in pillowcases. The grand prize? The winner would fly a giant American flag through the hatch in the cockpit's ceiling as we rolled up to the gate at JFK airport.

If you work for the airlines and you've never seen that display, you are really missing something. It is one of the most poignant, heart-warming sights I have ever witnessed. It was remarkable to watch the latest arrival, a 747 full of soldiers, airmen, or Marines taxi up to the gate with the jubilant flag-waver braving the four screaming engines to wave Old Glory high above the top of the jumbo jet. Even when I was not working, I would swing by Gate 3 to watch this exuberant, uplifting ritual.

After the contest, news came from the cockpit's scratchy-sounding radio that one of the soldier's wives had given birth two days before. The pilots enthusiastically made the announcement for all to hear. The soldier who had won the "raffle" then invited the new first-time father to go ahead and fly the flag. In an emotional exchange that included congratulatory hugs, they decided to share in this Pan Am tradition.

⌒᎐

On such a glorious day, I was saddened to think that in 45 minutes, I would be saying goodbye to some of the best passengers on the planet, or did I have to? I was not willing to part with my new-found friends so soon, so I approached the colonel. "Sir, my crew is all JFK-based, so we'll be leaving you in New York, where a fresh crew will board to fly you to Fort Bragg. But . . . I feel such a kinship with your men . . ."

Anticipating what I was going to ask, the colonel was already nodding yes. I continued, "I would love to fly off the clock with all of you down to Fort Bragg. I must see everyone's reaction when they are reunited with their loved ones again."

No explanation had been necessary. The colonel knew exactly how I felt.

⌒᎐

As I mentioned in the chapter about Moscow, there is something almost mystical about the Statue of Liberty. All nationalities love her. She is a pale bluish-green, and from ground to torch stands 305 feet high. When the sun shines on her, she can be seen for miles. Exquisitely crafted in superb detail, she is the icon and beacon that confirms the fact that yes, you are not imagining things, you have truly reached America. Often, I have been asked by passengers visiting the States, or desperate refugees fleeing their native land, which side of the plane will be able to see her. You might say that she is the first celebrity that foreigners set eyes upon when arriving in the United States. Once, flying in from Milan, a young Italian boy spotted her, and tugging on his exhausted mother's arm, exclaimed in a loud, Italian-accented voice, "Look, Mama, look! It's *America!*"

Kennedy Air Traffic Control had, purposely, I think, vectored us into New York in such a way that we could view lower Manhattan and this precious symbol of freedom. Fortunate to see her, I made a quick announcement to bring it to everyone's attention. Dozens rushed to the side of the plane overlooking the statue. Jammed with troops craning for a look, I was surprised that we did not fly lopsided. Among the exhilarating whoops and hurrahs, the reality set in that they were finally back in their homeland.

At JFK Airport, the troops disembarked at Gate 3. Walking up the airbridge, they were greeted with raucous jubilation not only from my crew, but the outbound crew as well. Acting as the "Welcoming Committee," they had positioned themselves on both sides of the jetway leading up to the terminal. Clapping and cheering loudly, they shook hands with some and hugged others, welcoming each soldier one by one. This had also become another Pan Am tradition.

In 38 years of flying for nine airlines all over the world, these soldiers were the only passengers who ever made me cry. They were not trying to; they were just being themselves. Sauntering along, some gently touched the wall of the jetway as if they had entered a holy sanctum. Others yelled "ALL RIGHT!" thrusting their fist into the air at their excitement at being home, while some tightly embraced strangers who had come to greet them, as if they were old, trusted friends. Many clutched small American flags as if they were worth a million bucks. A few disembarked, knelt, and kissed the carpet. I continually wiped the tears from my eyes so that my vision would not be blurred. I did not want to miss a single nuance or moment of the soldiers' first sight of home.

As the outbound crew continued to clap, passengers from the surrounding departure gates went out of their way to stop by and welcome the troops. Lines quickly formed at the payphones (yes, we had lots of them in 1991) while some went straight off to sample a taste of American fare: hot dogs or hamburgers with fries. Pan Am provided an entire wall at Gate 3 for the arriving troops to inscribe their names. There was no shortage of eagerness to sign the wall as they jostled to write their comments. Every square inch of that wall, which looked like a mural, was now becoming an impromptu memorial, covered in touching sentiments. Many posed for pictures. The re-boarding announcement for the last leg of their trip saw them back on the big bird in a flash.

Our high-energy passengers' excitement reached a crescendo as we approached home base. As we performed a low fly-by over Fort Bragg, I relished witnessing the bright look on the colonel's and the chaplain's faces. Straining their eyes, they were trying to gauge the size of the welcoming crowd below. Both broke into wide grins as they surveyed the scene. Upon touch down, an uproarious applause filled the cabin as the men shouted greetings. Some slapped high-fives to their neighbors, while others were glued to the windows, straining to see who was there to greet them.

The entire crew bade all of them goodbye as they hurriedly disembarked, but it was not quite over yet. Below on the pavement, the soldiers still had to gather in formation before they were officially released. I asked where the colonel's wife was seated, then grabbed the yellow Roman roses along with yellow streamers and headed across the tarmac to greet her and the joyous relatives.

As I walked directly towards them, I paused for a second to look back at our majestic Pan Am 747, which I have always considered to be the true representation of liberty. She sat there on that gorgeous spring day, gleaming in the sun, just as if she had a human heart, knowing she should be proud, and with good reason. Over the decades, she had airlifted countless passengers and refugees, both military and civilian, out of harm's way and spirited them to freedom. I felt as if I was dreaming as I gazed at her with love and admiration.

My long yellow streamers flapped in the wind as I continued to stroll toward the relatives in the stands. My uniform was weighed down with a few souvenirs from the soldiers: an Army pin with the word "Loyalty," a small flag, and a pin with crossed rifles. The air was permeated with the smell of sweet springtime flowers.

"We would like to extend a special welcome and thank you to Pan Am for bringing our soldiers home safely," the loudspeakers boomed, echoing all around the tarmac.

Overcome by emotion, I felt tears well up. I reached the colonel's wife and gave her the flowers. She heartily thanked me and invited me to join the families. Many relatives approached me, thanking Pan Am for the airlift, telling me their stories. One lady clutched my arm as she tearfully told me how she had gone in for triple-bypass heart surgery and thought she would never see her grandson again. Looking at me intently, she said, "I was afraid that I wouldn't make it long enough to see him return home, and in just a few minutes, I'll be able to hug him again!"

The waterworks washed down my cheeks. A soldier kindly handed me a pink plastic rose, which I have kept to this day.

The order "DISMISSED!" bounced around the base as all 425 soldiers charged in every direction, anxiously hunting for their loved ones. Hundreds of families were there, openly crying tears of joy as they raced towards each other. But one of the saddest scenes I have ever witnessed in all my days happened shortly thereafter. While most of the men had found their relatives, a few soldiers were still looking around again and again, as if there must be at least *one* person who made the effort to come and welcome them home. In an instant I realized that even if you worked in the local deli or barber shop, those soldiers whose families were missing would be so grateful to share their homecoming with just one single person, even if they did not know them well. As I watched the few continually scan the crowd searching, I felt as if someone was squeezing my heart as well as theirs.

Handing my camera to one of the C-5A (the military's largest transport airplane) pilots, I asked him to take a photo of our Pan Am crew on the stairs leading to our 747. As the shutter clicked, we all waved American flags, yellow ribbons, and roses in the springtime sunlight against a bright blue sky. The photo is on the cover of Valerie Lester's *Fasten Your Seatbelts: History and Heroism in the Pan Am Cabin*. It was truly a time to remember. Believe me, every facet of that day is etched in my memory for the rest of my time on this Earth.

Several months later, I was invited by Colonel Daniel Fake of the Big Red One, Fort Riley, Kansas, to the celebratory parade in Washington, D.C. He was another commanding officer whom I had befriended when flying troops back home. While the colonel walked with his men in the procession, I watched from my seat located across from the presidential box. Shortly afterward, General Norman Schwarzkopf led the entire parade on foot past our seats. In a rare display, a phalanx of all the aircraft flown in the war, from helicopters up to the Stealth fighter, dramatically performed low fly-bys to the delight of the crowd. Even my all-time favorite, the mysterious and loyal SR-71 spy plane which reportedly cruises at 100,000 feet altitude, flashed by.

Safe and sound back in America, Shelley Ovsak, the staff sergeant I had befriended in Dhahran, invited me to the ticker tape parade in NYC, her hometown. Bands from the 101st Airborne, "The Screaming Eagles," Fort Campbell, Kentucky, and the First Cavalry, Fort Hood, Texas, my passengers, marched by. We yelled a special welcome home to them. Various aircraft rolled along the parade route, as low fly-bys do not work in a city where some skyscrapers can top 107 floors. Behind us, a Kuwaiti family quietly waved American and Kuwaiti flags, holding a handwritten sign that simply said "Thanks from Kuwait." The parade had a fantasy-like quality to it, as an endless supply of red, white, and blue balloons blanketed the entire scene. The marching dull-colored desert cammies were in sharp contrast to our national colors. Thousands of streamers and confetti were lovingly tossed from the skyscrapers above while the soldiers reveled in the adulation.

Of all the cities in the world, only New York can put on a celebration like that, and we were certainly glad that they did.

⌒◈

Dear Tania,

Thanks for the pictures. They were great. I am still here with my bags packed for another deployment but praying that there won't be one. I hope that you like this 82nd Airborne Christmas card. I'm glad to be here to send it to you! Thank you and Pan Am for bringing us home safely. It's great to be back.

The Chaplain

President Bush approaching limo

7

Wing to Wing with Air Force One

"WARNING!" the large red lettering on the cement screamed. "Restricted Area. It is unlawful to enter this area without permission of the installation commander. USE OF DEADLY FORCE AUTHORIZED."

Oh, I get it . . . authorized to shoot on sight . . . one errant little stroll, and the next thing I know, I could be pleading my case to Saint Peter, I thought, considering the ultimatum. Motion sensors and detection devices abound. Standing on the tarmac, I was just yards away from the hexagonal hangar that houses not only one, but two presidential aircraft, tail numbers 28000 and 29000, both Boeing 747s. Yes, there are two Air Force Ones.

During the waning days of the summer of 1991, I was added to the exclusive White House press charter list. At Andrews Air Force Base, Maryland, I was busy observing everything with intense interest for the first time. Thanks to my supportive supervisor, Ailsa Williams, a beautiful lady from New Zealand, I had finally made the list at the eleventh hour, as our beloved employer Pan Am was going bankrupt. The Secret Service at the White House had completed and approved my background check. Now, in an accompanying aircraft, a Boeing 727, I would be the purser for the crew flying the White House press corps—journalists from ABC, NBC, CNN, CBS, Agence France Press, UPI, Voice of America, and Associated Press. We were scheduled to accompany President George Bush to the United Nations in New York for his annual address to the General Assembly.

Two Air Force Ones, Tails 28000 and 29000

Often when the rigid culture of the military comes into play with à la carte civilians and they must work together, I find it rather amusing. The military lives in a constant environment of rules, regulations, and pecking order, and often there is no excuse for even simple transgressions. Throw a bunch of civilians into the mix as part of the extended presidential party, complete with the Secret Service, A-list visitors, politicos, and all the attendant fanfare, and a definite learning curve crops up for all sides.

Right off the bat, the authorities made certain that I was apprised of key stringent rules, including knowledge of what a "ramp freeze" entailed. Twenty minutes before the president's aircraft comes in for a landing, or for take-off, everything on the runway comes to a full stop. You had better be eye-balling your watch carefully so that you are entirely off the tarmac at the required time, because somehow, I do not think that they ask you a bunch of foolish questions before you get the big blast. You just better know the procedures.

When the president leaves on a trip, both 747s are rolled out of their hangar, stationed side by side. If the president boards one aircraft and there is a mechanical problem that will delay the trip, he simply disembarks and walks to the backup plane. A military cargo aircraft, a Lockheed C-141, loaded with the presidential limousine and other bullet-proof attendant vehicles such as SWAT cars, is dispatched to the destination in advance. In essence, a "mini" fleet of emergency vehicles accompanies the leader of the free world everywhere he flies, whether the destination is domestic or international.

Air Force One has an eclectic team of specialists and professionals. The flight attendants on board are all Air Force personnel, which makes perfect sense. They have passed an exhaustive, vigorous background check. Buzzing around, both inside and outside of the aircraft, are Secret Service agents, who remind me of meerkats, always on the lookout with extra eyes in the back of their heads, scanning the horizon at a full 360 degrees. I could hardly blame them. If I was one, I would wake up every single morning thinking, "By God, if I can help it, nothing catastrophic is going to happen on *my* watch today!"

The stress of the job would have me constantly on the alert, even during my free time. Secret Service agents must be willing to take a bullet for the president. Sharpshooters place themselves in strategic vantage points, gaining a clear overview of the entire operation. Counter-assault marksmen, required to be ubiquitous, also move stealthily around the aircraft when parked. Like an illusion, they are almost invisible.

Among my favorite Air Force personnel were two pleasant but no-nonsense airmen who were "gatekeepers" at the bottom of the stairs leading up to the presidential aircraft. I nicknamed them "sentry bees," as they gently reminded visitors, including endless VIPs, of the rules, usually the one about no cameras on board. I cannot tell you how many times guests would try in vain to talk or bribe them into allowing cameras. "My husband and I raised $20,000 for the president's campaign," one pleaded, unsuccessfully, as they rifled through her purse for any forbidden items.

In addition to all this activity, on every trip I would spot a rigid man in a military uniform walking smartly across the tarmac or down the red-carpeted stairs, always within a few feet of the president. Chained to his wrist, he carried the 40-pound "nuclear football," a briefcase full of codes to launch—God forbid—nuclear missiles in the event of an attack on the US. Armed to protect this exclusive emergency satchel, he was right out of a spy flick, except this time it was *bona fide*. I certainly hoped that he had not had a scream fest with his wife before leaving home that morning.

Observing this uncommon delegation of personnel, I felt a true sense of being in an alternate universe, but for them this was everyday life.

President Bush greeting supporters

"Why in the hell are we running late?" one of the Secret Service agents, a short, wiry fellow barked at me as we stood in the entrance of Pan Am's Boeing 727.

Glancing at my watch, it was three minutes past departure time. All of us had been given a small booklet with a detailed schedule, minute by minute, for each day of the entire trip. Keeping it in my pocket, I knew exactly what to expect throughout the journey.

The magnificent Presidential Boeing 747s, identically painted in two shades of blue with shiny silver running alongside the bottom and white on top, are a sight to behold, especially if you have the rare opportunity to see them parked side by side. Commanding your attention with their noble presence, they are the most pristine aircraft I have ever seen, with their elegant and perfectly matched appointments. Built-in red carpets greet visitors. At the top of the welcome entrance door, the presidential seal is affixed. Presidential seals are also painted below the forward exit doors on each side of the aircraft. A large American flag is painted on the vertical stabilizer. Imposing black lettering on the upper white portion of the aircraft declares, UNITED STATES OF AMERICA. Both aircraft are nearly six stories high and as long as a city block.

Superbly elegant, they are also unique in other ways. They can be continuously refueled in flight through the "bump" on their noses in order to fly steadily for days on end if a national emergency occurs.

Flying up to 45,000 feet altitude, their speed is 650 miles per hour; or perhaps the true maximum speed is classified. Two lower hatch-type doors open in addition to the main exit doors, and the Secret Service can fan out at a moment's notice.

Once aboard, while exploring the airplane's 4,000 square feet, I was instantly elevated to a place that was unparalleled. Since it was my first charter, Colonel Danny Barr, presidential pilot of Air Force One at the time, was giving me a tour. After walking through the main entry door, we made a left and strolled up to the front of the airplane to view the area that would normally be first class. The president's private living quarters, his airborne bedroom, is located there. Beds run along both sides of the aircraft wall, up to the nose. Blankets and pillows were embroidered with the presidential seal. Unusually thick fabric was used to make the blinds, which cover the windows. They are specially designed to completely block out even the brightest sunlight so that the president and the first lady have the best possible undisturbed rest. Each of the nineteen video monitors indicates the current time in Washington, D.C., the local time where you are flying over, and the destination time so you become oriented to the flight plan upon awakening.

On the floor of the presidential bedroom, I was amused to see "Millie's" dish, made of porcelain, also adorned with the golden presidential seal. There was no evidence whatsoever of a "first pooch" on board—no tell-tale muddy paw prints on the beige carpet, no clumps of fur. Once, while George Bush was vice president, I had attended an event up at the Naval Observatory in Washington. An avid animal lover, I noticed a gregarious springer spaniel and called out to her. She ran up to me, and I noticed that her collar was engraved with the name "Mildred K." Just as the canine and I were quickly becoming acquainted, a "man in a dark suit" rapidly approached us with a grimace, "That is the vice president's dog," he snarled.

Now, seven years later, I was on Air Force One, admiring her presidential china.

Millie's effects were not the only possessions that exhibited the presidential seal. Custom designed boxes containing M&Ms had it, along with the president's signature. Matches and napkins also had the detailed seal, along with the words "Aboard Air Force One." In every bathroom, each individual razor had it, as well. If there was any doubt about which aircraft you were traveling on, all you had to do was glance at your seatbelt, which was also embellished with our leader's emblem.

Printed menus with the entrees of the day, along with a list of all the films on board, had been placed on each passenger's seat. Heavy full-sized ovens with electric ranges were featured in the galleys. I guess that weight was not an issue—look at who is footing the bill. On my first visit aboard, they were serving lasagna. Since it had been made from scratch with fresh ingredients, I imagine it may have tasted just a little better than our old pasta casseroles. Who wants the president yelling at you about culinary shortcomings?

In the meeting areas of the aircraft, beige and white telephones sat side by side, about 85 in all. One was a completely secure line for calling anywhere on the planet. Air Force One has an entire airborne office with all the latest accoutrements. In onboard meetings, the closer you sit to the president, the higher you rank in the government.

An emergency operating room is also on the aircraft. When we first walked in, it looked like an empty room with several wide chairs. Colonel Barr explained that they could be pulled together to make an operating table. Dozens of bright fixtures from the ceiling provide ample light for a variety of in-flight medical procedures. Sliding back cabinet doors, crash carts can be effortlessly pulled out. Perfectly placed emergency room equipment, along with an extensive pharmacy, is stored in "camouflage" cupboards. A staff doctor is aboard every flight.

Colonel Barr was hospitable and a really good sport about entertaining continuous guests while the aircraft was on the ground, repeatedly answering the same curious questions. Once, he took my crew upstairs to show us the pilot's in-flight lounge and the elaborate command center with its numerous panels, boasting the most sophisticated airborne equipment on the planet, located behind the cockpit. Among its many functions, it can encrypt the conversations of certain calls for complete privacy and security. Fifty-seven antennas handle the endless flood of signals it receives, providing a secure aerial sanctuary. The president can also be linked up to urgent meetings in the White House Situation Room while in-flight. We grinned when the Secret Service referred to the "Sit Room" in the White House as "the cement mixer."

The command center was enormous with its extensive communication equipment, compared to the much less complex and outdated tail number 26000. A Boeing 707, it was the Air Force One that flew President John F. Kennedy to Dallas on that fateful date, November 22, 1963. Stationed close by was a Pan Am plane, chartered for the press that tragic day. The presidential jet returned to Washington later that afternoon with the slain president's body while a shocked nation, and world reeled in horror.

On the current 747, there are several conference centers of different sizes. A good-sized aft galley occupies the tail section of the plane. Right in front is the section where the press is seated. Just forward of that area, the next cabin holds the Secret Service, a not-so-subtle warning for the press to stay in their designated area. God forbid if any deviant press member made the improper decision to "ambush" the president for an impromptu interview. That action would seal their fate for future invites. They would never fly on Air Force One again. This protocol makes perfect sense. When rules are followed, they are allowed to fly one-way on Air Force One and return on the civilian press charter if they choose.

Colonel Barr even took us down into the belly of the big bird to a portion of the cargo bay. It was spotless. Each spare tire had a custom-made cover protecting it. The walls and floor shone with cleanliness not even seen in the *cabins* of current commercial aircraft. Oh, well, sorry, I just had to say it!

Once on the main deck, I heard voices over the intercom, constantly yelling out angry four-letter words. *What* airplane was I on? To kill some ground time, the Air Force crew was watching the film *Backdraft*, and it was at a pivotal scene where the sparring firefighter brothers were cursing a ruinous fire as they valiantly tried to hose it down.

For decades, Pan American World Airways was considered the unofficial flag carrier of the United States, enjoying a long history of flying alongside Air Force One. As far back as 1943, the Dixie Clipper, a Boeing 314 flying boat, spirited President Franklin Roosevelt from Miami to Casablanca for a wartime meeting with Prime Minister Winston Churchill. Pan Am and agency officials fondly referred to its role as "the chosen instrument."

Attending an 89th Airlift Wing Reunion

In modern times, once the press was aboard the Pan Am aircraft, they would film Air Force One taking off first. Then Pan Am would lift off, and Air Force One would slow down to allow the Pan Am jet to beat it to their destination. This was called an "interchange." Moving ahead, Pan Am landed first so the press could capture Air Force One's approach and touch down on film.

In Pan Am's final months, I worked domestic flights with well-known news personalities such as Ann Compton of ABC News, Jill Dougherty, Mary Tillotson, and Charles Bierbauer of CNN. The days were always drawn-out and challenging but the dog-tired journalists knew the routine intimately and navigated it well.

"Hey, I see a new face on the crew," the tall man said, half teasingly, extending his hand to shake mine. Smiling, he was wearing—you guessed it—a dark suit. "Billy Dale here, nice to meet you, Tania, welcome. They told me you'd be working the flight today."

As director of the White House Travel Office, Mr. Dale coordinated all these charters; quite an endeavor, to say the least. He also had a cool gift for me: a dark blue V-neck sweater, embroidered with lettering, THE WHITE HOUSE. Over the seal with the American eagle it states, "E Pluribus Unum," meaning, "Out of many, one." Like a little kid, I pretended that there was a draft so that I would have an excuse to put it on.

The fiftieth anniversary of the attack on Pearl Harbor, December 7, 1991, was four days away. Certainly, Pan Am would be awarded the contract for our 747 to fly the press to Honolulu to cover the commemoration ceremonies. But it was not meant to be. For decades, we had been in deep financial trouble. Our pay had been cut by 33 percent in a "give back" to help save our company. Our flight attendants' union, the Independent Union of Flight Attendants, had taken a vote to determine if the membership wanted to designate a portion of our $4 million strike fund to pay a top auditing firm to give us an accurate, updated analysis of the exact financial status of our carrier. The answer was overwhelmingly yes, but sadly, it was too little, too late.

On December 3, I was well aware that a court hearing had been scheduled in New York between Pan Am and Delta airlines concerning the sale of our European routes to Delta and our dwindling assets. On Veteran's Day, I had sent a registered letter to Judge Cornelius Blackshear, who was to preside over the case.

> *Your Honor:*
>
> *I implore you to do all you can within your power to try and save our company.*
>
> *We employees love Pan American World Airways deeply and share the most ardent desire for its survival.*
>
> *Tania Anderson, purser, JFK*

That my very last flight with Pan Am would be a White House press charter was somewhat ironic. I had permission to drive directly to Andrews AFB, a 45-minute ride from my home. Our Pan Am 727 took off after Air Force One and flew down to Sarasota, Florida. President Bush went off to visit the Tropicana plant for a few hours. On the next leg, during the flight over to Meridian, Mississippi, White House Chief of Staff John Sununu handed the president his letter of resignation.

The press members on our plane were bursting to get downtown to their bureau to file the breaking story. The second our aircraft touched the blocks, they rushed out in nearly every direction in a mad dash to send their satellite feeds out for the evening news.

As I watched President Bush greet the crowd of well-wishers, I decided to visit Air Force One to see what the fellas were doing. I could sense a pall over the area, but I shook it off, optimist that I am. One of my crew members who had flown these charters for years called after me as I strolled slowly across the tarmac towards tail number 28000. "Tania! Where are you going?"

"I am going to see Air Force One!"

"But you have already seen the other 747, and they're identical inside and out," she yelled.

"I know, I just want to see it anyway," I shouted, adding wistfully, "I want to visit because it might be my last chance. You never know when the party is going to be over."

It was about 1400 hours. The "party," which had been in existence since 1927, was going to last about another ninety minutes, and then it was going to vanish *forever*.

Spending time with the personnel aboard the presidential aircraft provided a welcome respite. Articulate, hospitable, and au courant, they were acutely informed of all current events. Hand-picked for their duties, they provide an optimal experience. We discussed some of their recent passengers and the upcoming trip to Hawaii. They choose crews among themselves, rotating each year. The job is not always "glamorous" either. I could readily see that it was demanding, hard work. Acting as keen diplomats, they had to make sure that certain items did not "walk" off the jet. Let's just be diplomatic and say that some VIPs probably do not deserve that status. They are not always well-mannered or gracious to say the least, and as much as you would like to tell them to go stuff it in no uncertain terms, letting off steam like that could possibly end your Air Force career.

Back on board our Pan Am 727 and still waiting for the press, I was chewing the fat with my colleagues when the captain emerged from the cockpit, pale-faced and dazed. "I guess that's it for us," he stammered. "I've been listening to the radio and Delta has backed out of the agreement to finance Pan Am's South American operation. I bet it was a backroom deal between the lawyers. We are dead. That's it. We are finished."

Like a zombie, I stared at the walls. Perhaps if I scrutinized them long enough, they would provide me with some solace, or at least viable answers. I think they call it "freeze frame" when you enter such deep thought you are not even certain exactly what you are thinking. I loved Pan Am with all my heart, for better or for worse, and now the most prolific pioneer of international commercial aviation ever known was belly-up for good.

Many of us had been hoping right up until the end that a white knight—another airline, or perhaps a successful hotel chain—would partner with us, infusing us with fresh financial blood. We searched for innovative ways to save this institution which had linked scores of countries around the globe since Charles Lindbergh charted the Caribbean routes in 1928. Proud of the richest legacy in commercial aviation, Pan Am had flown the White House press charters for decades. She had made the first flight across the Pacific, the first regular airline flights across the Atlantic, and the first round-the-world flights, going both east and west. She had rescued thousands of evacuees under dire circumstances as their governments were crumbling—in Chile, Beirut, Tehran when the Shah fled into exile, and during the fall of Saigon. She provided vital service to Berlin when it was isolated. During our heyday, frequent fliers had so much faith in Pan Am that we had more than 92,000 reservations for the first flight to the *moon*.

The press boarded our plane at about 4 p.m. Having heard our devastating news, they kindly tried to reassure us that something positive might still save us. "We are really looking forward to seeing you all on the Pearl Harbor trip," Ann Compton said, adding, "Hopefully, in the next few days, there will be a reprieve for Pan Am until you find a permanent financial backer. It would be great if you flew us to Honolulu."

Her colleagues were equally concerned and supportive, which brightened my mood somewhat. Grateful for their kind regard and thoughtful comments, I have not forgotten their graciousness, even after all these years.

When I mentioned that I had seen President Bush waving at our crew while giving us the thumbs up in Meridian, Charles Bierbauer told us that he had smiled and said, "I see the Pan Am girls over there!"

Yes, for the very last time, Mr. President.

Flying back to Andrews AFB seemed to take days, not two hours. Eating a delicious grilled pork chop dinner, I was in a trance, not speaking to anyone for quite some time, as the meat grew cold and tougher by the minute. The sauce gelled.

With one last fond look at our jet, I exited the base for the very last time. I was so preoccupied with my shock, I am surprised that I did not just veer off the road on the way home. With my eyes full of tears, I could not see clearly or navigate the icy winter highway well.

At home, snug in my bed on that December night, I was blessed with a healing dream. In this sensuous dream, I dove into a large pool filled with warm, turquoise-blue water. The tropics were gorgeous, and I could hear parrots and toucans above. It was sunset and the air smelled sweet. I swam underwater for a while. When I came up for air, I felt entirely cleansed, as if my body had been rinsed of all negative vibrations. This tactile feeling helped put my great sorrow at ease.

Early the next morning, I was wedged in a long line inside a bleak office on U Street, a rough section of D.C. While waiting, I contemplated how just the previous day I had been aboard Air Force One, joking with high-ranking military personnel on the most beautiful aircraft in the world, and now, a mere 24 hours later, I was in one of the most dangerous sections of our nation's capital filing for unemployment. It was *unearthly*. At least I was in my own city. Thousands of my colleagues were scattered about in numerous other nations, stranded around the globe, and whose only solace was the mercy of sympathetic carriers to transport them safely back home.

8

Pan Amers Reunited for the Nigerian Hajj

I cannot tell you how long I mourned the death of my, rather, our, cherished Pan American World Airways. It took well over a year. Just three weeks before Christmas we had gone entirely bankrupt. One favorable note was the news report, on the very same day we lost our livelihoods, that correspondent Terry Anderson of the Associated Press had been released in Beirut after six and a half years of captivity. So happy for him, my heart was lifted for his loved ones who had worked tirelessly against difficult odds to secure his release. "At least some people are having a big celebration somewhere, and they certainly deserve it," I thought.

Pan Am's death was shattering. Our beloved colleagues on every continent no doubt suffered from this profound loss. Heartbroken, I also felt overwhelmed. Everyone near and dear to me called afterward, most crying over the phone. Even those who had no connection whatsoever with aviation knew how deeply upset I felt and called with their condolences. Helen Meyers, the kind lady who had taken care of me as a child, implored, "Tania is there anything that I can do for you?"

What could anyone do?

Understanding that there was a big reason for this enormous upheaval in my life, I recited powerful affirmations that my minister, Steve Woods, had taught me to help me stay focused: *I am in complete, total harmony and balance with the Universe, and all the things I set forth from this moment on shall now attract to me that which is perfection.*

As winter approached, my former colleagues fanned out to the four corners of the Earth. In Washington, D.C., the sun always dipped below the horizon at 16:30. The nights were long, but I combated my depression by joining friends at the TGIF restaurant not far from the Pentagon. The regular crowd there was cosmopolitan, right up my alley. Glasses clinked while loud tunes played well into the night as my fave bartender, a mixologist extraordinaire from Ecuador named Wags, concocted potent Long Island iced teas, keeping me properly lubricated to help calm my worries. While chatting with the other barflies from Vietnam, Somalia, Jordan, Puerto Rico, and Ethiopia, I knew deep in my heart that if I could just keep my emotions under control, the main theme of my destiny would emerge again one day: to travel abroad, befriending our fellow human beings who hail from distinct nations.

This eclectic international bar crowd was peppered with "feds" from the various agencies—Defense Intelligence Agency (DIA), the Drug Enforcement Agency (DEA), and the Central Intelligence Agency (CIA) in addition to a good sprinkling of Pentagon personnel. I befriended an FBI agent who was a strong sounding board for me, listening to my moody ruminations. He helped me tremendously through that cathartic time in my life while I expressed my feelings in between cocktails.

During this low period, I gradually "picked up steam" and set about regaining my emotional strength by consistently engaging in varied activities. It was therapeutic for me to be out with upbeat people networking while watching out for any new opportunities to arise. To be surrounded by interesting folks helped me tremendously to heal and stay positive in my outlook. At night, before bed, I would recite these words, also from Steve:

> *I am a divine channel of health, happiness, love, energy, peace, harmony, and prosperity for myself and for all of those around me.*

A real bright spot was that one of our stellar pursers, Mary Lou Ruddy, a 29-year veteran of Pan Am, refused to be sucked into the sorrowful woes that enveloped us after its demise. Instead, she chose to vigorously throw herself into helping the flight attendants from other airlines—namely United and TWA—by co-founding an activist group lovingly named Wings on Washington (WOW), which sought to pass legislation for jobs with assets, requiring international carriers to employ the crews already associated with the routes they had just purchased. Leave it to Pan Amigos to work fervently to help others save their jobs despite our own profound grief.

With support from Senator Ted Kennedy's office, they organized a rally in front of the Department of Labor, with Senator Bob Graham and the Reverend Jesse Jackson as speakers. We got good press coverage. Dressing in my uniform for the first time since the bankruptcy, a friend remarked, "You know you will cry when you hear them speak," to which I replied, "Yes, I know, but it comes with the territory."

Gathering in front of the large marble building, I saw many of my former co-workers. I just loved them all; they never gave up. It was too late for us, but Mary Lou and the others diligently sought to save our colleagues in aviation from our same miserable fate.

Nearly every night, I listened to music in my bedroom until five in the morning while I reminisced over the loss of our great airline and our extraordinary family. I played all my favorites: Enya, Yanni, Phil Collins, Steve Winwood, Bob Marley, A-ha, Pet Shop Boys, and Van Halen. Music speaks to me in a powerful way, telling me stories, showing me images, providing me with advice, and giving me direction. I have always told friends, "As long as they keep cranking out great music, I'll never have to see a therapist!"

Energetic music always inspires me, helping me to pave the way for a new game plan. I hear voices and messages through music. When that happens, my thoughts shift skyward as I move closer toward my goal of being "back on track" again. Then I pull myself together and strategize my next steps in life.

The phone rang frequently, which was a good thing. "Pan Amigos," as we call ourselves, have created the most striking international bond of any group I have ever seen, and certainly of all the defunct airlines. Whoever made up the expression "thick as thieves" must have known some Pan Amigos somewhere along the way. Even to this day, 33 years after our demise, thousands of us are still in touch, spanning the globe. In 2007, we had a reunion in Miami to celebrate the eightieth anniversary of Pan Am's founding. Jerry Cassidy, our chief pilot for the Nigerian Hajj, reminisced. I also came across the B-747 Captain who once had one of my passengers arrested in Frankfurt. After seven hours of erratic and suspicious behavior, the German man yanked his shirt up for our skipper, revealing small, fresh stab wounds across his stomach. That was all the captain needed to see before calling Frankfurt operations to seek assistance when we landed. However long ago they were, we always remember these incidents, and they strengthen the bond between crewmembers.

True to form, at this reunion more than 400 former employees attended. One of the many highlights was a visit to Kelly's Restaurant in Key West, formerly owned by actress Kelly McGillis. The white building with green shutters was the first office of Pan American World Airways, which opened October 28, 1927. Flight Number One taxied down the runway for its inaugural flight to Havana, the very first outbound international air service from the United States. The celebratory festivities got off the ground immediately, a testimony to the strength of this unique aviation family.

Even in its later years, Pan Am employees must have represented nearly every country and territory on the planet. We were always conscious of that fact while relishing our cosmopolitan lifestyle. It was second nature for us to be surrounded by erudite colleagues, many with names you had to pronounce twice to say them correctly. As a purser, I savored one section of the welcome announcements, which certainly set us apart from other airlines: "Ladies and Gentlemen, flight attendants on your flight today are capable of speaking . . ." listing all the languages. "If you are aware of anyone needing help in one of these languages, please contact a flight attendant."

In the house we rented from Eric Martin, Mario was from Argentina, Al from the Philippines, and Barbara from Burma. Kevin, Eric, and I were Americans, but between all of us, we spoke French, Spanish, Italian, Tagalog, German, and Burmese. A favorite Pan Amigo motto encapsulated it all: You call it the world; we call it our *home*.

Consequently, we bonded in unusual ways as we traversed the globe. We resembled a microcosm of the United Nations, except while their staff was snoozing in their cozy beds after a day's work, we were busy flying to six out of seven continents, 24/7. I am smiling as I write this, but I always felt that we played an integral part of what kept the Earth, with all its nations, spinning.

Many Caribbean countries were intensely grateful and loyal to our airline, which had linked them up with the rest of the world long ago in the late 1920s. Pan Am had the faith and the power to help bring them closer to the world community and did so. Passengers from these nations could fly to Miami and then onto Europe, Africa, and Asia. They were terribly sad to see us go under, like the passing of an old and very dear friend. Our airline and these countries shared a long and sentimental history, one which will always be fondly remembered.

As for the former Pan Am employees, our support for each other after the bankruptcy was notably strong; we were constantly in touch. Supportive calls to me also came in from other airlines. Friends from the obsolete Eastern sadly informed me that there had been several suicides since their bankruptcy in January 1991. They told the dark story of one flight attendant who could not even get out of bed for months, despite their pleas for her to seek help. She was deeply depressed over the loss of her airline. They were finally able to bring her around and she eventually healed with the assistance of therapists and devoted friends.

The year 1992 was a blur except for the welcome news that I had been hired by American Airlines. I was grateful to enjoy my benefits again, but the flying was miserable, "bee-bopping" around the US often on six legs a day, which I nicknamed "the hamster wheel." I complained to my Pan Am pals that I could see America in short hops when I had purchased a rusty old trailer and had become wizened, gray, and snarky. I felt like a racehorse that had been slowed down to a trot. "I can't believe that I was queen of the 747 flying all over the world and now at age 40 I'm at the rear of a Super 80 cracking bags of ice," I mused.

Some upbeat news at American was that I had the absolute best supervisor in the world, Tim Bateman. Tall, funny, and super-quick on the draw, everyone adored Tim, and I would wager a guess that wherever he is now, he's loved in a big way. Tim would introduce me to co-workers saying, "Tania used to fly for Pan Am," as if I needed no other credentials. In the early '90s, long before there was a PC in every abode, Tim was already adept with computers. He was kind, understanding, sympathetic, and had a wonderful sense of humor. I loved saying amusing things to him just to hear his laugh. Knowing him certainly took the edge off.

Fortunately, a new adventure was right around the corner, and it involved my old "tribe" in a big way. Thanks to American Airlines' liberal leave policy, I secured four months off in 1993. Free, I was ever-so-ready to explore the world on my own terms again. To make it even sweeter, I planned to join 65 others: pilots, flight engineers, mechanics, load masters, and flight attendants, nearly all of them former Pan Am employees. Back in the fold again, I was reunited with my people.

As we travel the world, most Pan Amers will tell you that if you discover someone you've met who had worked for Pan Am, it is like being reunited with a long-lost cousin who strongly resembles you and shares a similar ideology. Toss these crews in together on an exploration, and you have joyous, non-stop vigorous activity. People who possess this dynamic personality type are really in their element.

This is pure heaven for us.

Well, in Nigeria, it was heaven with some zany frustration built right into it.

One day in March, the welcome call finally came. I had heard about Gunilla Crawford, a beautiful, tall, Swedish Pan Amigo. An instructor living in Miami, she was looking for flight attendants to fly the Nigerian Hajj operation to Saudi Arabia. We hit it off over the phone immediately, joking and laughing like old schoolmates.

I recommended Cicero Fain, and Gunilla hired him. At Pan Am, I had flown with Cicero out of JFK Airport. He was always easygoing, even when a flight was stressful. It is a big bonus for a purser to work with someone like that, and I *never* forgot which ones they were. Conversely, that goes for the eccentric employees, as well—you know, the kooky ones who gave you trouble.

The spirit of adventure runs through the soul of every Pan Amer I have ever befriended. An intrinsic trait of ours; it is in our blood. For us, unusual and exciting experiences "feed the beast" inside and we just cannot get enough. Adventure is our oxygen.

Once a year, a magnificent operation of great magnitude takes place for about 12 weeks. Muslim pilgrims, called Hajjis (men) and Hajjias (women) are flown from countries around the world to the city of Jeddah, the Saudi Arabian port located on the Red Sea. During a four-week period, around the clock, a staggering 2.5 million passengers are transported from more than 100 countries. Performing the Hajj is one of the five requirements of faithful Muslims. From the time they are young children, they are told that one day they will participate in this pilgrimage, so it is a great honor and privilege for them to perform the Hajj: the culmination of a lifetime dream.

Arriving in Jeddah, they are welcomed in a huge edifice that was built as a special reception area. Later they are driven to the primary Holy city of Mecca, where they perform the rites as required by Islam.

A flamboyant leader, Chief Kabo, owned an airline in Nigeria, which he named after himself, Kabo Air. He contracted a US charter airline to transport approximately 38,000 pilgrims from Nigeria to the Kingdom of Saudi Arabia on two Boeing 747s. Each held 480 passengers. Essentially, Chief Kabo was about to become the new temporary employer for 65 airline personnel coming from America. The chief would also make an indelible impression on me.

On the flight to Miami for training, I absorbed the view while flying over the Chesapeake Bay. I happily noted in my diary, "'Ahh, back in the saddle again' as they say out West! Hard to believe that after months of visualizing this I am finally on my way. Oh, *AFRICA*! We are going to have a blast. Why watch *Raiders of the Lost Ark* when you can *be* in it?"

"You must be Tania," Gunilla said, as we hugged each other like old pals. She was, indeed, as lovely as everyone had described, with thick shoulder-length blonde hair and big blue eyes. She loved wearing long flowing skirts and dresses, as did I. We had connected well over the phone, so I felt as if I had known her for ages.

Captain Jerry Cassidy would be our chief pilot. A conscientious man with great integrity, he had that Irish "elf" sense of humor and gab. Our crews were set.

The next day, my boyfriend Jim Burke from my San Diego days drove me to the Pan Am Flight Academy at Miami airport. Just the sight of that sign alongside Pan Am's world-famous logo brought tears to my eyes and a tightening in my throat. I was eager to meet everyone for a "martini afternoon" to discuss our upcoming operation to Nigeria. We also had to review our training and emergency procedures to train the Kabo Air flight attendants in Kaduna before beginning the Hajj trips.

Several suspicious-looking white Lockheed 1011s, totally devoid of markings, sat alongside an MGM-Grand B727 and other planes from yesteryear. As Jim drove past one hangar, I spotted something extraordinary and made a loud animal-like noise. "What is it?" Jim asked, amused at my unnatural tone of voice.

"Oh, I can't believe it, is that for real?" I exclaimed.

Were my eyes deceiving me? I asked him to stop the car.

Parked there before us was not only my favorite type of aircraft, the Boeing 747, but painted on the nose was the eminent name of *Clipper Juan Trippe*, Pan Am's founder. The tail had a one-of-a-kind airline designation: 747PA.

Hello, old girl. God, how I have missed you! This plane had an extremely rich and bountiful history. The second oldest Boeing 747 in the world, she had been in service since 1970. God only knows how many miles this grande dame of airplanes had flown, but I could have nicknamed them "Pluto miles." If only walls could talk, I am certain that we would be enthralled by the endless stories this 747 could tell.

Filled with sentimental thoughts, I looked up at this dignified bird. My eyes welled up with tears again as I scanned her. Then Jim, ever observant, pointed out the lettering on the tail: "Kabo Air." My favorite plane had indeed taken on a different persona.

Flying on one of the world's most senior aircraft was a nostalgic step into the past, but on the other hand, how safe and reliable was she going to be, working 'round the clock every day in and out of West

Africa? After all, she already had tens of thousands of miles under her belt. Even though proud, she was quite elderly, to say the least.

⌒ↄ

As our 747 rolled back from the blocks, motherly Gunilla sat on a baggage cart with friends, flickering their flashlights like fireflies. We returned the sentiments. Vince noted that in a sense, we were about to become like Hajjis (pilgrims) from the upcoming experience. It was a fitting goodbye for our crew.

⌒ↄ

Crossing the Atlantic eastbound under the constellation Orion, a rush of excitement and gratitude washed over me as I repeated another mantra my minister Steve had taught me: *I am in the perfect place in my life and have everything I ever wanted and have achieved harmony in my heart and ideas.*

⌒ↄ

One of the most unusual spectacles I have ever witnessed for a civilian aircraft was when we buzzed Kaduna and all the surrounding villages at a hair-raising low altitude upon our arrival in Africa's most populous nation. While crossing the Atlantic, the pilots had been chuckling as they discussed how we were going to perform some low fly-bys in our 747 over thatched-roof mud huts. This aerial display from our enormous bird was going to officially signal the beginning of the 1993 Hajj operation out of Nigeria.

While announcing our arrival in this dramatic way, we saw plenty of movement on the ground. The contrast of the brightly clad villagers waving at us from their enclaves, enhanced by the backdrop of Nigeria's deep, red-colored earth, made for a brilliant scene. White goats, donkeys, and beige-colored camels bucked, brayed, and fled in all directions at the piercing sound of our high-pitched engines. I do not think that the pilots had enjoyed so much fun in a jet since they had flown F-16s in the military.

"The Whale," as some airline folks refer to the 747, certainly did not have the agility of a single-seat fighter, but we made quite an impression as we crisscrossed the sky at just a thousand feet. We could almost smell goat farts at that altitude.

Most of the villagers had never even been on a plane and were treated to quite a display of flying. Our aeronautical dance must have looked so curious to them. The enormous white Boeing 747 from America was in a sense extending the hand of friendship to our new African hosts from the sky. It was a welcome, friendly sign that Pan Am, as an ambassador of goodwill, had signaled countless times before during its rich and extraordinary history.

The buzzing was typical of the Pan Am spirit. We were "at home" once again.

⚭

From my personal diary, May 5, 1993, Kaduna.

> *I must admit that eighteen months after Pan Am's demise, the "Great Oz" (my pet name for Pan Am) still inspires wonder, for we wouldn't be here today if it wasn't for Pan Am and its giant birds. Every day, as I put on my smart dark-blue Pan Am purser uniform created by the designer Adolfo, I feel as if we have been resurrected from the dead.*

I glanced over at our newly-fashioned uber-skinny Kabo Air manual. Then I looked in the mirror. Pan Am wings pinned to my upper left pocket had seen me safely journey hundreds of times across continents and oceans. Just below was my "In-Flight Purser" pin which reminded me that we would have to keep an eye out so that "souvenirs" would not be swiped. It was a breeze to blissfully wiggle into my old uniform again. Now that I was no longer scarfing down all that delectable, rich first-class food, I had actually lost a couple of pounds. Fighting with my zipper was not a chore. I added the tribal material we had purchased at the market for my scarf. We wanted the passengers to recognize the prints and feel comfortable with us. Continuing my entries, I added:

At the center of every Pan Amer's heart is adventure. It is amazing to me how we were flying low over the grass huts in our jumbo jet, just like the old days. Once again, we have dazzled the local people with our eternal bridge between the local and the universal, our connection to far, far, away places. It still invokes that thrill of 'Africa!' and all the times when Pan Am enchanted me as I embarked on a new adventure or journeyed to a new land. The Clipper camaraderie never quits—just being downstairs telling war stories with the crew and the pit (the cockpit's nickname) in the lounge on our first night here feels like business as usual. The pit has been flying UN soldiers into Zagreb, Yugoslavia, and told us that the Pan Am logos and decals are still up everywhere. The Yugoslavs continually said how much they missed Pan Am.

Making observations about our new "boss," I wrote:

The chief is almost a mystical figure. People constantly kiss his robes. He pays cash for used B-727s here, so brokers do a fast and crazy little tap dance when he comes around. On any given night, throngs of men are lined up outside the gates of his mansion to ask for favors or just cold hard cash. He is somewhat easygoing and has a great sense of humor, but won't hesitate to suddenly commandeer one of his planes to divert the crew to another city.

Bonding with the Kabo Air flight attendants took no time at all. Each crew would have four Americans and ten Nigerians. The day after our arrival, Cicero and I began training the Africans. Gunilla had remained in Miami but relished receiving tidbits and updates from us. That is, when the phones were working.

Although I am not a teacher, I soon figured out who knew what was going on, who was trying to hoodwink us, and which Nigerians I wanted on my crew. I felt for them when we administered the final exam because I have never been a good test taker myself and sometimes nerves get in the way of good common sense. I was glad that everyone passed. Well, *"mas o menos."* (more or less). The females curtsied, one by one, as I handed them the flight attendant manual.

On the last day of training, Cicero and I reminded the Nigerians that we wanted to see our mixed crews work cohesively together. We encouraged the room full of flight attendants to communicate clearly with each other and to ask the Americans if there was anything that they did not understand. Likewise, we requested that they bring to our attention anything important that related to their culture, religion, or Nigerian protocol. We particularly asked that everyone be respectful of the Hajj passengers on every flight. We also pointed out that we wanted our crews to have some fun and enjoy themselves. "Our airline, Pan American World Airways, flew us all over the world," I concluded as Cicero nodded in agreement, "and we love working with people from many different countries. That's why we chose to fly this operation."

Patrick, their Kabo Air supervisor clapped, followed by loud applause from all the others in the room. Feeling so welcomed, it was the highlight of my day. With so many eager flight attendants, I knew that the crews would collaborate well. After all, it was also an experience for them to work with us Westerners. It was essential for the passengers to have a positive experience. Far from being just another plane ride, this was the culmination of a lifetime of dreams and hopes all rolled into one emotional journey.

On my crew, I was going to have Amina, Obi, Kabir, Umar, Doris, and Ibrahim, along with four others. Amina and I had an understanding that took off on day one; we were instantly in sync with each other. In subsequent trips to Nigeria, I always visited her. We enjoyed telling stories to each other just like kids do. Obi was such a character. He loved it when I jokingly called him "Obi-Kenobi." He had a great sense of humor but had this habit of always trying to weasel something out of you. It was funny more than annoying. When we first arrived from the States, we had quite a lot of fruit on board. Once he found out we had big red apples—quite rare in Nigeria—he concocted this story that his throat had become very scratchy, and he just knew that if he had an apple, it would be completely cured.

Kabir was the big snoozer. At the ripe old age of 22, you could find Kabir collapsed on the jump seat at any point of the flight, including boarding. He could have slept through an evacuation. I took photos of him dead asleep right after takeoff. The workday had hardly begun, and we had at least fourteen more hours to go. Once, when I asked him to make the announcements, he proclaimed loudly over the intercom, as they demonstrated the life vests, "This is in case we crash into the Red Sea and get eaten by sharks, but I hope not, *Inshallah* (if God wills)."

Just a small diversion from what it says in the manual. The passengers looked straight ahead as if nothing unusual had been said, while you could clearly hear "Whoops!" being emitted from each of the Americans.

Umar and Doris together were the "Dream Team." They were stoic when things became zany, knew the ropes, and were adept in dealing with passengers who were afraid of the various sounds and clicks a plane makes. And then there was Ibrahim. We connected immediately. A week later, he told me that the first day he went straight home to pray that he'd be chosen for my crew. That was at the *exact* same time I was busy putting together the crew lists and assigning him to mine.

Deep tribal markings, three vertical slices on each cheek, decorated Ibrahim's face. When he was a newborn—only seven days old—they held him down and began splitting his face open with a razor blade. Then some gritty, stinging substance was rubbed into the sliced skin so that the scars would heal in a thicker design. In later years, anyone would be able to identify what tribe he hailed from, indicated by these distinct markings. With 23 brothers and sisters from his father and four wives, he came from a busy family. And you thought that *your* family moved at full tilt! They all resembled each other and got along well. An only child, it was rather difficult for me to imagine sharing a modest bungalow with 23 siblings.

Ibrahim began to teach me Hausa. I wanted to learn some basic words to make the passengers feel more at home. While our aircraft was sitting on the ground, Ibrahim taught me their greeting "*Sa-nun-ka-da-zua.*" Walking over to the open door, I looked down at the local workers on the tarmac, repeating the phrase. I tried to say it in a melodic way, imitating Ibrahim the best I could, while waving to them. Who knows what my American accent sounded like, but they all broke into wide grins, repeating the same words, waving back. I was pleased that they understood. He also taught me how to say "welcome," "come inside," and "sit."

I had some fun things to show Ibrahim, as well. Flying east on our first trip to Jeddah, I invited Ibrahim up to the cockpit where we could see the lights of Khartoum, bright and sparkling. When the pilots turned the lights off, we had a clear and dazzling view. Flying at 35,000 feet altitude over Sudan's desert, we had little interference from any ground lights. I pointed out our bright sister planet Venus to the right of the aircraft's nose, and the Big Dipper to the north. Not long afterwards, we cleared the coast of Sudan and began to fly across the Red Sea, which has a significant meaning for Hausas. They believe that gazing upon the Red Sea during the Hajj will protect them from eye disease. Ibrahim's long-awaited dream of performing the Hajj was now within reach. For him, traveling this route to Saudi Arabia made it sink in that his life-long quest would soon become a reality.

Ibrahim also kept a journal, so I gave him a card with the well-known NASA photo of the Earth showing the African continent. Inside, I wrote: "Ibrahim, I thought that you might like to see how Africa and Saudi Arabia look from space. Great flying with you. Tania."

The Nigerians had at least one good reason to be happy. As part of their employment, they would perform the Hajj themselves, so everyone was eagerly looking forward to that day. In addition, Chief Kabo, who had purchased four vans painted "Kabo Air, Hajj 1993," would gift them to four employees whom he felt had done an outstanding job at the conclusion of the ten weeks. However, layover conditions were less than ideal; indeed, they were cozy, with four flight attendants to a room. Two would share a cramped, bumpy double bed.

Early in the operation, I was busy taking in all the new sights and sounds. I would glance across the tarmac, spot our new colleagues, the Kabo Air flight attendants, walking along, giggling, and joking, feeling so excited to be part of our unusual crew. Occasionally they stopped to look back at our 747 and wave, recognizing that they were now an integral part of the crew that was operating this jumbo aircraft, the largest civilian bird in the sky.

I always loved the film *Out of Africa*, and teaching crews made me remember the scene when Karen Blixen was instructing the Kikuyu tribesmen in Kenya. Everyone bonds more quickly in such circumstances.

Once the doors are opened, the common ground becomes much more apparent, and our mutual goals are more quickly achieved. On nearly every flight, several passengers called the Nigerians aside to tell them how they could see and feel the camaraderie of the mixed crew. That was precisely the perception we wanted.

Africa is alive with color, so when the big wig Nigerian officials walked toward the aircraft wearing their full gambit of colors, I recalled that last touching scene of *The Color Purple*, when the sister from Africa returns after many years to be reunited with the one in America. Their bright robes swayed in the middle of a golden field just before the conclusion of the film. Now in Nigeria, the chiefs, sultans, governors, and other elite walked together with their robes blowing in the gentle breeze, painting a picture of brilliant hues, bringing African color to life for me. Later I learned their individual statuses in Nigerian society when I was introduced to them personally.

One day, Chief Kabo came out to the aircraft accompanied by the usual gaggle of aides and his three brothers to check on how things were progressing. His youngest and favorite brother, Garba, ran Kabo Air's domestic operation. Falalu, another brother, oversaw all the revenue from Kabo Air. With several assistants wearing protective face masks, they counted endless stacks of money in a dusty, dirty, cramped little room at Kano airport. Shiitu, closest to the chief in age, ran Kabo Oil; no easy feat in a country which ranks fifth in the world's oil production. With so much at stake, the company was bedeviled with corruption at every level.

The chief was wearing a cobalt blue traditional robe, called a *babariga*, a tunic with yards of material made of fine muslin cotton hand-embroidered along the edges over loose-fitting trousers. Garba, taller than the chief, was wearing a yellow *babariga* with a matching hat. From the onset I could see that he was quite modest, while the chief obviously ate up all the attention and fanfare. He was somewhat boisterous, but Garba's voice was low and he spoke in quiet tones. A bit stocky, the chief had a wide face, thick moustache, and wire-rimmed glasses. A Rolex watch, the face encrusted with diamonds, was always on his left wrist. Garba was 6'3" tall, with a slender frame and rather thin face. Handsome, with a medium-sized moustache and bright eyes, he had a ready smile. Observant and intelligent, he also took unexpected incidences in his stride, an essential personality trait for anyone conducting business in Nigeria.

The entourage fanned out to "inspect" the interior of our plane. Chief Kabo and Garba were introduced to our Chief Pilot Jerry Cassidy and the check captain, both former Pan Am 747 pilots. Soon, it became apparent that even though the chief did not know jack shit about the technical side of managing this type of operation, he was really bull-headed in his suggestions about how it should be run. In the following days, whether practical or not, all the stops would be pulled out for the Nigerian VIPs, such as the Emir of Katsina.

At 2 a.m., we were unexpectedly called out for our first flight. An English friend often referred to this type of ungodly hour as "at the crack of a sparrow's ass." Linda jarred me out of a dead sleep. "Tania, can you be in the lobby in 45 minutes? We're going back to Jeddah. Vince just knocked at my door."

Linda, a real Pan Am stalwart and Montana ranch girl, had giant bright green eyes and blonde hair. Vince Rossi, also a former Pan Amer, was tall and slender, with blonde hair and deep blue eyes. A New Yorker with a BA in international politics and Middle Eastern civilization from NYU, Vince and Linda instantly bonded despite their polar opposite backgrounds. During the entire Hajj operation, the three of us were almost inseparable.

Bleary-eyed, we met in the lobby within the hour, joined by the Kabo Air flight attendants. At the airport, we waited several hours while they tediously loaded all the passengers' belongings into the cargo hold. Their "luggage" was not packed in suitcases as it is in most other countries. Their possessions were tied up into giant bales, so it was time-consuming for the ground personnel to load them properly. They tossed piles upon piles of bundles on top of one another. I had never seen belongings loaded like that before in *any* country. Passengers dragged along all kinds of local crafts, anything they could think of, to trade for goods while visiting Mecca. This would provide a little income to stay longer in Saudi Arabia if they thought it would be advantageous, even though their visas would have expired and it would be illegal to stay.

One enterprising passenger had brought an entire beehive and had somehow stuffed it all into a circular cooler with a screw top. Dutifully, the ground personnel placed it onto the luggage belt. At the boarding door, I greeted the passengers as they entered. With few clouds in the sky and a nasty odor from garbage, the relentless heat made the air stifling. Suddenly, the cooler containing the beehive tipped and began to roll off the luggage belt. The ground workers quickly tried to catch it, but to no avail. It smashed willy-nilly onto the ground, releasing hundreds upon hundreds of furious bees with a score to settle. Extremely aggravated, they filled the sky, flying every which way while the ground crew ran in every direction for the closest cover they could find.

While honey dripped from the luggage belt and tons of bees buzzed all over the tarmac, one of our male flight attendants sniffed, "Well, there is *nothing* to worry about unless there is a queen bee who they want to fight over."

Fortunately for the passengers, their traditional full-length clothes provided protection. Miraculously, nobody was seriously stung.

In many parts of Nigeria, there is no reason to have a front door to your mud or stucco hut. Some of these villagers had never locked a door. A simple cloth hanging from the top door frame over the entrance would suffice. Who was going to rip them off? After all, they knew everyone else in the village, which included many of their own relatives.

Tribal women carried their luggage in bundles balanced on their heads, as they had done for generations. However, when some reached the bottom of the aircraft, they glared at the top of the staircase as if it led up to Mount Everest. Many of these villagers had never climbed a stairway. If they had never traveled outside of their village, most likely they had not traversed a flight of stairs.

Some Hausa-Fulani women wearing multi-colored clothes dropped down to their knees once they reached the bottom of the plane's staircase, not sure how to navigate them. The guards standing there gently helped, escorting the ladies up to the entrance door approximately eighteen feet off the ground. We greeted them in Arabic or Hausa-Fulani, their tribal language. Arabic words from the Islamic religion are known and spoken throughout the Muslim world, just as Latin was known by many Christians in the past. I greeted the passengers with the salutation, "*As-salamu alaykum*" (peace be upon you), and they heartily returned the greeting with "*Wa alaykumu s-salam*" (peace also be unto you). The word "*haram*" (forbidden) came in really handy. If the passengers were doing something "against the rules" or misbehaving in some way, I would look directly at them and pleasantly say "*haram!*" They immediately got the message.

Ibrahim recited the travel prayer in Arabic over the PA system as we taxied toward our takeoff position. It is a beautiful prayer beseeching Allah to protect all souls on board for their entire journey. Everyone listened silently. Even with 480 pilgrims and 17 crew onboard, all was quiet. The prayer set the tone for the flight.

During the early days of the Hajj, Ibrahim taught me one of my favorite phrases in the world, "*Bismillah ar-Rahman, ar-Raheem,*" which means as you embark upon your journey or project, you do so with Allah's help and blessing. Ever since that time, I have said it often. Even when I am a passenger myself, I recite it when we are on our takeoff roll. I also say it when I start my car.

Women always boarded first and were seated at the back of the plane. Once the women were settled, the men were directed into the aircraft. It took some time to get everyone on board. The tribesmen were restless, but you could hardly blame them, as they were separated from their families; men up front, women seated in the back. After takeoff, they had no idea where to find each other inside the giant bird.

Most of them had never even remotely been in an environment like that, inside a circular steel machine with nearly 500 seats divided into six sections. If you have ever been temporarily lost in a massive parking structure, "Where did we park? P-1 or P-2?" then you know what I mean.

VIPs trailed by their wives and concubines scrambled up the spiral staircase to sit upstairs. During the flights of yesteryear, fashionable first class passengers had mingled there, listening to classical music while sipping champagne and martinis. Now dog-eared, well-worn first-class seats welcomed the sultans and their harems for a dry flight.

Lunch was always served in a brown paper bag and contained a chicken leg, some white rice, and perhaps a boiled egg. Often, I noticed that as the passenger reached for the lunch bag, a digit or two was missing. Although I had seen lepers by the side of the road in India, this was the first time that I had encountered them as passengers. Blinded by the disease, some were dependent upon a younger relative to lead the way for them, even for this journey of a lifetime.

✺

One day, the flight engineer who always smoked a pipe descended the spiral staircase from the cockpit to see how things were—or were not—progressing. He had a crumpled, stuffed brown paper bag which he was clutching as if it contained a block of gold bullion. Well, in a sense, it did. He kept snickering to himself.

"What's up?" I asked, growing more curious by the second.

I could not have guessed in a thousand years, but it sure was not a chix leg. "You'll never believe it," he replied. "There is two hundred K in here!"

"You're kidding me, right? *Two hundred thousand dollars?* Why are you carrying that kind of money around?" I exclaimed, as he opened it up to give me a peek.

Over the years, the Saudis had been ripped off by many airlines. Fed up, they had begun to demand cash for fuel. He said that to gas up, we would have to pay cash for every single trip. "The cockpit is responsible for all this money," he explained. "Or, on second thought, should we take a little side trip together with all this cash? We could have a pretty good time." he joked, winking, while adjusting the pipe in his mouth.

We arrived in Jeddah after a five-hour flight. The Nigerian flight attendants asked the ground personnel if they could go into the terminal area just to explore a little. This was the first time they had ever been in another country. Naturally, they were looking forward to performing the Hajj themselves later on, halfway through the operation. During that same two-week period, we were scheduled to take the aircraft for a "C" check (engine tune-up) while visiting Athens.

As the passengers disembarked, those who spoke English thanked us profusely for the enjoyable flight, adding that in Mecca they would pray that our same crew would fly them back home to Nigeria after their pilgrimage.

⌒◌

"Is there anyone from Pan Am on this plane?" a loud male voice boomed from the entrance door in Jeddah.

Up in the cockpit, I had been yakking with the guys. "Any Pan Amers onboard?"

Zipping down the spiral staircase, I was laughing. "We're all Pan Am people here, except the Nigerians."

"Captain John here," he began, extending his hand to shake mine. "I fly for Kuwait Airways now. We just pulled up to the blocks alongside you. I could not believe my eyes when I looked at your nose and saw *Clipper Juan Trippe* and your tail number 747PA. This is a famous bird in our industry. I used to fly her often. I thought by now she'd be in the boneyard out in Arizona. How is she flying? What on Earth are you guys doing here?"

As John spoke, I was busy studying his face, trying to remember if we had flown together. He had probably been my captain for our multiple European destinations out of New York.

"We are flying for Chief Kabo from Northern Nigeria," I said.

John replied, "That name sounds familiar. I've heard that the flying is rather unorthodox. How has it been?"

"Pretty wild. Something new and unexpected every day," I smiled.

"Yup, that doesn't surprise me," John said, wiping the sweat from his forehead.

Once again, the aircraft's air conditioning was operating at a minimum as the thermometer climbed to 118 degrees outside. "Nice meeting you guys. Have fun."

The pilots forked out thousands of dollars to gas up for the five-hour return trip with only the crew on board. In airline parlance, this is called ferrying. Somewhat like an airborne party without the booze, you could stretch out, raid the galley for treats, read, play cards, or gossip about news from home. Some went up to see the stunning view from the cockpit. Often, I would just look quietly out of the window, taking in the immense African scenery and landscape from above, imagining what lay in store.

The Saudis always provided the crews with delicious food—gourmet salads, shish kabobs, or lamb with basmati rice. Garba, the chief's charming "baby" brother, loved the shrimp with garlic sauce. I always made certain that we had an extra casserole of shrimp for him. He was also becoming a good friend.

"No, no, *no!*" Chief Kabo was yelling as he and his aides ran haphazardly across the tarmac towards our plane in Kano. "Do not take off for Jeddah!" he exclaimed, as his robes flapped in the wind, threatening to trip him.

All fueled up for the flight with everyone on board, we were anxious to go. Looking forward to being airborne within minutes, we could not wait to turn the air conditioning up full tilt to get some relief from the intense heat. As the chief hastily entered the plane, our captain came down the spiral staircase to see what all the commotion was about.

"Captain, the Emir of Katsina is in Kaduna." Catching his breath, he added, "He wants to go to Jeddah right away, this afternoon. You must first go to Kaduna and pick him up, then proceed to Saudi Arabia."

Our captain had an incredulous look on his face. "Chief, you want us to fly to Kaduna *first?* We've just fueled the aircraft for the five-hour non-stop flight to Jeddah. We are rather heavy, and Kaduna is only 35 minutes away, which means that we'll have to defuel. That will hold everyone up for untold hours. We could also miss our slot for the flight."

But the chief was always stubborn, whether he was right or wrong. Most of his employees just completed the tasks demanded of them, however impractical. They were careful not to discuss too loudly how ridiculous his decisions were in case they were overheard. Unfortunately, our captain did not have any options.

As 497 passengers waited on board, the ground personnel attempted to defuel the aircraft with a gizmo that resembled a garden hose. Hours passed while we killed time in the hot, stuffy airplane. Throughout the cabin, the sea of people used their barf bags to fan themselves. In the West, they would have eaten us alive, but in their culture, they have calmly resigned themselves to the numerous inconveniences that occur every day.

Hours later, we finally took off, but our bird was still far too heavy, so we circled. For more than an hour, we dumped loads of fuel on our way to Kaduna. It streamed out of both wing tips. It was a horrible thing to do, but we had no choice. The idea of unnecessarily polluting the air like that is revolting to me. Hitting the ground, we still felt overweight.

The Kabo Air representative who dealt with VIPs hurriedly disembarked, rushing directly towards the VIP lounge. The emir was not there. Frantically, he searched in vain to apologize for our "tardiness." The emir was nowhere to be found. The rep was then casually informed that the impatient emir had grown tired of waiting for us and had returned to his palace.

In a country where the average income is $300 a year, we had just dumped $14,000 worth of fuel in the sky.

We alternated between layovers in Jeddah and three Nigerian cities: Kano, Kaduna, and Sokoto. Each city was individual and unique, so it was fascinating to explore them. Jeddah, nestled next to the Red Sea, was clean and enjoyed sea breezes which helped to relieve some of the heat. The layover hotel was pristine; the entire lobby was made of Italian marble. The staff was also efficient, something that was sorely lacking in Nigerian hotels. It was fun to catch up on all the international news. Another big plus was having electricity 24 hours a day. In Nigeria, when the lights go out, you had no idea for how long. With no candles in the drawer, you just wait in the pitch-black dark like a chump.

Jeddah has some of the best cuisine in the world, imported from all over the globe, including world-class seafood. Foreigners who live there have brought their culinary treats and influence to Saudi Arabia from their numerous countries, so you can find scrumptious dishes from Europe, Asia, and Africa. At any given time, we had at least 60 crew members at the hotel, so we talked the chef into preparing a daily salad bar. We grazed from one end of the buffet to the other, fixing plates with tabouli, dolmas (stuffed grape leaves), feta cheese, baba ghanoush, hummus, marinated eggplant, and fetoosh, not to mention the delicious lamb and beef.

The shopping was incredible. We had an old expression at Pan Am that illustrated how we felt about shopping, and excursions into Jeddah's souk were no different. "Shop 'til you drop. Wear it, don't declare it. The world is my shopping mall!" we chanted as we dragged back endless souvenirs from all over the world, stuffed in luggage decorated with stickers that proclaimed, "If it's not Boeing, I'm not going."

In a Saudi Arabian souk, haggling is a way of life, and you had better learn the skill quickly or you will miss out on some great bargains. It does take a bit of energy, but in the end, it becomes a habit. The payoff is trolling for good bargains and elevating them to even better bargains. In the department stores, you can also negotiate for name-brand French perfume or makeup. Throughout the souk, the air was filled with the scent not only of well-known French and Italian perfumes, but all the exotic oils and fragrances of the East. A plethora of imported silks and spices from all over the world were available. Streets were jammed with every kind of jewelry shop you can imagine. Some even displayed 24-carat gold vests that you could wear over a blouse or dress. The gold was invariably solid 24-carat, and once you had selected the piece you liked, it was weighed for the price. Then the negotiating began. For decades the pricing has been conducted this way, selling it by the pennyweight. Twenty-four-carat masterpieces displayed in the windows are so bright that they reflect onto shoppers' faces with a glow as they admire the collection.

To top all of this off, there was another "nest" of Pan Amigos staying at the same hotel, flying the Hajj for another company. We relished getting together to catch up on how everyone had been since the bankruptcy. I was delighted to come across another former Pan Am purser, Joshua McIntosh. Originally from the Bahamas, Joshua was a gifted linguist, speaking Spanish, Portuguese, and Italian. I first met him in Dr. Bator's office when I was worried about failing Pan Am's comprehensive Spanish exam. He was in the language lab, coaching and helping the newbies with questions. His gentle, nurturing manner put me at ease right away. For months afterwards, I kidded him, saying, "Joshua, I can't see auras, but I'm certain that yours is emerald green," and I meant it.

Gathering in the lobby most afternoons, we enjoyed hot tea and sweets. The reunited crews chatted amiably while cloaked in our *abbayyas*. In Saudi Arabia, the female dress code is extremely strict and requires black robes to be worn over a full set of clothing. Any time a lady left her hotel room, an *abbayya* had to be worn. In a sense, it was as if we were in uniform again. Women are also required to always cover their heads with a scarf, preferably black. Men can wear casual clothes, so while we had *abbayyas* completely covering our street clothes in the blistering 112+ degree heat, men could wear T-shirts and shorts revealing cactus legs, just like home. We loved our little impromptu "crew parties" drinking fresh kiwi juice, strong Arabic coffee, or tea with cardamom while munching on stuffed dates. Alcohol is strictly forbidden in the Kingdom of Saudi Arabia.

Nearby, an intricately designed four-story house with wrap-around balconies close to the corniche (avenue along the beach) had been the resting place for the famed Lawrence of Arabia in between his escapades. We passed by this historical landmark often, studying its architecture, wondering what it must have been like in Lawrence's time. The well-known explorer and linguist, Sir Richard Burton, sponsored by the Royal Geographical Society in the mid-1800s, also passed through Jeddah on his way to Mecca. Dressing like a native, and skillfully speaking fluent Arabic, he traveled without much difficulty.

Near the hotel every morning at 4 a.m., the muezzin (one who makes the call to prayer) climbed to the top of the mosque's minaret and chanted the *azan*, signifying the call to prayer. The chant echoed throughout the streets of Jeddah and out towards the sea.

In our alcohol-free hotel, we were offered all kinds of delicious fruit juices, ranging from mango to pomegranate. They had almost every kind of fresh-squeezed juice you could imagine.

On the other hand, Northern Nigeria, even though Muslim, serves booze. Usually, you could find a paltry selection of whiskies or perhaps vodka. On layovers there, we looked forward to enjoying cold beers and the freedom to wear sundresses. However, the downside was the blackouts, the maids rifling through your things, the malarial mosquito-infested rooms, unreliable air conditioning, and questionable food, like chicken served with some un-plucked feathers. Lack of efficiency and reliability presented even more hassles as rules were made along the way.

Once, they tried to dispatch our aircraft with a full load of passengers and not a scrap of food. As the elfin ground guy began to close the boarding door, I said with some urgency, "What are you doing? We haven't been catered yet."

"Catered" might have been quite a euphemism for 480 brown paper bags, but I was getting madder by the minute. I was not as concerned for my crew as I was for the passengers, whom in some cases had waited several days outside the airport to travel. Our crew would later have meals boarded in Jeddah, but it was certainly not right for the passengers to go without food. Who knew when their last meal was? Maybe 36 hours ago. He persisted. Becoming huffy, I asked Amina to watch the door and not let him close it as I looked for Bello Katune, my favorite passenger. He was buoyant, fun, smart and . . . connected. Bello was the adviser to the Deputy Governor of Sokoto state, Al-Hajji Ahmad Gusau. Quick on the draw, Bello also had a great sense of humor. He had been onboard filming the Hajj as it progressed, and we always had something fun to laugh about and discuss.

I found Bello right away. "What's wrong, Tania?" he asked, seeing that I was upset.

"Bello, who is the highest-ranking person onboard? They are trying to close the last door, and I don't have any food on the plane at all," I said impatiently, hoping that I would not get into a big argument with the ground guy.

"Tania, wait here, I'll bring him to you," Bello replied, rushing up to the first-class section of the plane.

As I waited those few minutes, I had an internal debate about how to address the dignitary. In the Pan Am days, we had an entire section of our manual dedicated to protocol and the proper way to address passengers of a certain station in life, whether cardinals from the Vatican, diplomats, royalty, or Mother Teresa. In New York, Pan Am's representative, Mr. Sho Okagawa, escorted VIPs to the aircraft. If the opportunity arose, I would whisper to him, "How do I address them?"

However, if Sho was not there, I would make a beeline for my manual and flip to that section. This time, it was Bello who whispered in my ear how to address his boss.

"Your excellency, I would like to kindly request your assistance," I began, looking at the striking Fulani man who was the deputy governor of Sokoto state.

His excellency was something else: tall, with honey-brown skin, delicate features, and George Clooney eyelashes fringing eyes that shone. "I know that the passengers have been waiting at least two days for this flight in the holding area of the airport," I said, as Bello listened intently. "It has been so hot the last few days, and as you know, it even rained on these passengers yesterday as they waited. I realize that it has been a long time since they have eaten, and I want the ground crew to provide meals for them before we take off."

"*Inshallah*, I will see what I can do for the passengers. Thank you for bringing this problem to my attention. I agree that we shouldn't leave without any food on board," he said, then added something to Bello in the Hausa-Fulani dialect.

I had already said what I wanted, but I reiterated the words only because I wanted to "scan" this handsome dignitary some more. He had so much light in his eyes, telling me that even if he did not believe in psychic ability, he certainly had a strong natural intuition to understand many things. He could easily have been cast in *Lawrence of Arabia* alongside the stunning and mysterious Omar Sharif. *What a desert fox* I thought. That nickname stuck to him throughout the entire operation among my colleagues who constantly kidded me about the handsome official. They teased me about lusting after a well-known polygamist who already had four wives, as if he was not already busy enough juggling multiple females about in his daily schedule.

With some élan, the deputy governor made it clear to the ground personnel that the crew was not willing to leave without food for the passengers. Moving at break-neck speed for Nigerians, they began running back and forth to the terminal building to see what they could find. Finally, they drove to the market to buy numerous loaves of bread and some marmalade, along with cartons of a "sugar water" drink. At least we had a little something to give them, even though my nose was still out of joint.

There was no shortage of stimuli on the layovers in Nigeria. In addition to Vince and Linda, our crew included several Scandinavians, who stood out with their blonde hair and light eyes. Always attracting curious stares, the locals would say "*Bature,*" meaning "white people," as they looked us over. Some Nigerians had never seen anyone with eyes of any color other than brown, so they moved in to take a closer look, but curiously, never rude. The market bustled with activity as people shopped for food, spices, material for clothes, and cheap Chinese radios. The fruits were usually mangoes, bananas, and oranges.

As we wandered through the market, the smell of eastern oils mixed with the ever-present blast of diesel exhaust from large trucks. Dozens of goats rummaged through discarded plastic bags. You could not help but wonder when you saw "lamb" on the menu if it was really one of these unofficial garbage diggers.

The melodic call to prayer took place five times a day, summoning the faithful to the mosque to worship. Even for people of another faith, the sound stirred our emotions and reminded us, the foreigners, that we were indeed in a land quite different from our own.

My favorite souvenirs to give my friends were snake wallets, which came in a light brown, or blonde-colored crocodile clutch purses. They were a real hit back home in America. Unusual types of animals languished in the market, but "buyer beware," as they were still wild, and could possibly carry a nasty disease of some kind. Large vipers I could not identify slithered about, young chimps and monkeys which had somehow been kidnapped from their mothers played together, along with squawking parrots which had not been trained to speak.

"Tania! Come over here and check this out," a colleague called. "Look at these poor bastards," she said, pointing.

Two spotted hyenas, chained to a stake, were jammed into a small cage together with tiny baskets tied over their muzzles to prevent them from biting. Caked in mud, they stank, and were hunched over with their beady eyes darting about as if they were suspicious of everyone on the planet. Constantly snarling, they were hyperactive and agitated. The spotted carrion-eating carnivores were vastly different from their canine cousins to say the least, but the Nigerians had them for sale, nonetheless. I am sure that they would have made *great* house pets.

Tailors worked on sewing machines outside under large trees, running extension cords to a generator. It was fun to purchase traditional African material then take it to a tailor who would create any design you desired. My favorite tailor was an amiable man named Emmanuel, who kindly taught an ever-present flock of young interns how to sew various fashions. Emmanuel made colorful sundresses that fit me like a glove. Years later, when I met Senator Obama on Capitol Hill for the first time, I wore one of Emmanuel's creations.

If I am ever invited to a special event, an awards show or inaugural ball, rather than buy some expensive evening dress, I would have something custom-made for much less. I would purchase yards of silk from the States, fly to Nigeria, and ask Emmanuel to whip up a one-of-a-kind creation. No need to fret that I would run into another lady at the event wearing the identical evening gown. And I would have money left over to boot.

Although a bit chaotic, the atmosphere felt peaceful to me in northern Nigeria, and the villagers were courteous. We often saw diminutive military men walking in pairs or guarding a government building while brandishing machine guns almost as large as they were. One night, with all of us stuffed into one of Chief Kabo's Hajj vans, we searched in vain for a recommended restaurant; a popular gathering place for Europeans. Our driver stopped to ask one guard standing outside of a government compound for directions. After some discussion in Hausa-Fulani, the guard slid the van's door open, hopping in right next to Vince. He looked friendly enough, but did he have the safety catch in place on the AK-47? It was poking up towards the van's ceiling, and ahead we spotted a series of speed bumps. I glanced at Vince sitting next to me with the whites of my eyes showing. "What if . . .?"

Smiling, he interrupted, "Tania, don't *even* give it the energy."

At the restaurant, the soldier jumped to the ground, promptly jutting his hand out, asking for some *dash*, the Nigerian slang for tip, for having shown us the way. We were just glad that the machine gun had not peeled off a couple of rounds.

"How many bulls do you plan to flag down with that skirt?" our captain joked one morning in the lobby while looking at my billowing scarlet-colored outfit. The locals always seemed to enjoy observing what the *bature* were doing. One young man, observing that my olive skin was a bit darker than that of my colleagues, noted, "I have noticed that your skin is darker than the others. Why is this? What tribe are you?"

Amused by his boldness, I replied, "My mother was from the Irish tribe, and my father was from the Catalonian tribe in Spain. My mother was light-skinned with blue eyes, and my father was dark with brown eyes."

"So, you are mixed tribes?" he asked, comparing my answer to his understanding of the 44 main tribes in Nigeria.

"Most Americans are of mixed tribes whether they admit it or not," I assured him.

As anyone who flies knows, crews always ask everyone to fasten their seatbelts. What many people do not understand is that if the plane is roaring along the runway and must halt suddenly, or even abort a take-off, your body still moves at that speed, pitching forward. In Kano one day, "all zipped up and ready to go," we taxied along the tarmac and moved into position for our take-off roll. The pilot gunned up the engines, released the brake, and let her rip. We began to roar down the runway. Fortunately, the flight attendants had completed their safety checks and were buckled up. As the aircraft raced down the blacktop, the pilots were horrified to see a group of about eight people run directly across our path up ahead, followed by dozens more. At our speed, almost 180 miles per hour, the giant bird could wipe them out in no time. The locals had spotted two dozen large garbage bags which had been taken off our inbound flight. Thinking they might contain valuables or food of any salvageable kind, they risked their safety, and their lives, to go rip them open.

Once in motion, it was difficult to stop the heavy aircraft. The pilots slammed on the brakes so violently that passengers could not prevent themselves from hitting the seats in front of them. As I caught my breath along with everyone else, the loadmaster shouted down the spiral staircase what they had just seen from the cockpit. The people on the tarmac continued to wrestle with the newly discovered "goodies," apparently unaware that our large aircraft had just aborted its take-off roll. My crew raced down the aisles to ensure that no passengers had been injured, or to reassure them if they appeared frightened. We were all greatly relieved that no one either on the ground or in the aircraft was hurt, thanks to our pilot's adept flying skills.

Our only other incident during the operation occurred in Jeddah. It happened as we were leaving for Sokoto. I was seated on the first class jump seat with a coworker facing aft. Just after takeoff at 180 knots, we heard a *ka-boom*! I immediately looked out the window and certainly did not like what I saw.

Instantly, I gasped, covering my mouth. My colleague had been looking in another direction. "What, Tania?"

My reply sounded as if it came from a five-year-old. "*Fire!*" I shrieked, straining to keep my voice low, trying hard to see what exactly was transpiring.

What I did not realize until seconds later was that the fire was not on our side of the aircraft, but on the *other* side, engine number four. In an instant, it had flared up so high that the reflection on engine number two, right next to us, made looked as if it had originated there.

A shrill cry came from the upper deck. Seconds later, a piercing alarm emanated from the cockpit as the fire warning system signaled impending danger.

The loadmaster immediately rushed out, yelling downstairs that an engine was ablaze. The pilots were busy fighting the fire, flying the jet, and communicating with the Jeddah tower, advising them of our emergency status, all at once. They were way overloaded.

"We're going right back in," he barked, with eyebrows furrowed. "We had a fire in engine number four, but it looks as if it has been extinguished. I'll let you know right away if the captain wants to implement any procedures. I think he is too busy to make any announcements right now" he added, sprinting back up to the cockpit.

Making an "all call," I advised my crew of what had happened and asked them to be ready for any instructions from either the pilot or me. They had to stay put in their jump seats until further directives.

The co-pilot and the flight engineer fought the fire while the captain flew the plane. Engine number four was then shut down. Jeddah tower had been notified that we required emergency clearance to land immediately.

Other aircraft were instructed by the tower to hold their landings while we turned around and made our approach. We had crawled up to a low altitude and were now going to land weighed down with an aircraft full of fuel, crowded with passengers, and heavy luggage on the remaining three engines. It was rather a hard landing, but I am certain that had another captain been flying, it could have been a slammer. Fire trucks surrounded our plane and sprayed us with foam to prevent any further outbreaks of fire. Ten of our eighteen tires had to be replaced. The friction and heat caused by the weight of the plane upon landing had badly damaged them. Nobody was hurt. In fact, to our astonishment, many of the passengers had slept through the entire episode, thinking we had already landed in Nigeria! In a way, I could understand. Exhausted, they had been exposed to extreme temperatures: 112 degrees-plus every day, with little respite from the sun. Most had not been provided with white umbrellas, which come in handy to avoid sunburn, or even worse, sunstroke. Many were dehydrated or had food poisoning because they were unaccustomed to the rich cuisine from anywhere outside of their home villages.

Relieved that everyone was safe, we asked the passengers to disembark. The wait for the next flight out would be hours. Later that day, our pilots ferried the aircraft to London on three engines to have the obliterated one replaced.

As a treat for the kids, many of us had taken bags of candy to Nigeria. One sunny afternoon I was surveying hundreds of passengers below from the boarding door who appeared to be more upscale. I spotted two beautiful sisters dressed in frilly white party dresses, which reminded me of the one that my father bought me for my confirmation when I was eleven. I rummaged around in my bag for the candy and went downstairs.

"*Say Noh, Bar Kah*?" (Hello, how are you?) I asked the pretty girls as I handed them the candy bars. "*Mon go Day*" (We thank you) they replied, ever so politely, while bowing their heads a bit. They scampered off to show their parents what the *baturia* (white woman) had given them. Right behind them was a young boy, about seven years old. As I held out my hand to give him some treats, his eyes grew to twice their normal size. He screamed loudly, made an immediate U-turn, leaping away from me to much hearty laughter from onlookers. Bello, watching from close by, sported a wide grin.

"Bello, why is he so afraid of me?" I asked.

"Tania, I hate to tell you this, but his parents have taught him to be afraid of white people, that they are devils," Bello chuckled. "Please don't be offended."

"Bello, I've had people run away from me for a myriad of reasons before, but never because I was white," I joked.

My colleague Linda had the biggest green eyes you ever saw, complemented by thick blondish hair. During the ten weeks of this assignment, we spent all our time together, from Nigeria to Jeddah, Athens to Mykonos. She always laughed and said in a phony thick accent, "Tonight we drink. But first, we must *dance*!"

She was right when she made the remark that we were "cut from the same cloth," as we dove into all the same activities. We had both loved Pan Am so deeply.

One afternoon while we were helping the women at the back of the plane, one lady sat down with her baby boy on her back. It was obvious that he had never seen light eyes. Even though terrified of Linda's green eyes, he could not stop glaring at her, either. He would stare at her for a while, then let out a loud squeal and tuck his head into his mother's shoulder. It reminded me of watching scary movies when we were young. We could not wait to watch *Chiller* together on Saturday nights. If it was a really good show, we were afraid of watching, but if the story line was compelling enough, we could not take our eyes away from it, either. He repeated the staring and screaming nearly the entire five-hour flight. His mother occasionally laughed, but she could not convince him that we were not "devils."

Ibrahim made sense of it all: "Tania, to us, blue or green eyes look just like cat's eyes," he explained, apologetically.

Often, at the end of an eighteen-hour flying day, keeping your eyes open becomes increasingly difficult. On one such occasion, we were flying east towards Chad when I made myself a cup of hot tea and sat down on my jump seat, waiting for the caffeine to kick in. As I tried to read a magazine, my out-of-control eyes just ran off the page. Hindatu, a beautiful young Fulani lady, was seated across from me. She began to ask me the particulars of the flight, and I was happy to converse with her. In the Pan Am days before planes had TV monitors illustrating the flight's route, the captain would come downstairs and post a map of the world with our flight plan for that day. Passengers would then be able to see all the particulars: altitude, speed, certain landmarks, and projected landing time.

She spoke perfect English and had flawless skin with a round face and inquisitive eyes. She looked somewhat stoic to me, as if she had already experienced difficult things in life but had handled them well. A bright yellow headscarf complimented her complexion. Married for about four years, her husband, whom she adored, was busy shopping for wife number two. While he was out scouting around, she kept their home in order while hoping that he'd find someone she could *also* share her life with. Naturally, he prowled around the market, a bustling stew of activity. He had readily consented for Hindatu to go on the Hajj with her female cousin, who was seated next to her. After months of courting numerous women, (and probably some mixin' and matchin' if you ask me) her husband brought home a viable prospect. He was looking for Hindatu's approval, even though he was free to make any decision he wished. Hindatu described the young lady. They had gotten along immediately, much to the hubby's relief. It must be nice to have a peaceful household and not have *two* wives mad at you and each other. The new bride, whom she would share her home with, was educated and had a good sense of humor. Deciding to give her consent, she felt that his next choice might not be as good. "I will treat her as a sister," she confided to me. "She will become a part of my immediate family," she said in a quiet voice of resignation.

At the end of another long 28-hour day, we returned to Kano empty. We were all punchy but not snarky. I poked my head into the cockpit after we blocked in to see the pilots and flight engineer all cackling at some joke. It was heart-warming to observe their deep friendship, as they had flown together for years across the globe in every type of situation. As we came to a complete stop after this exhausting day, we noticed that the only two sets of stairs in the airport were being used by another airliner.

The B-747's doors are eighteen feet off the ground, so staircases are required for boarding and disembarking. Our crew had to disembark down through avionics under the first-class section, and then through a hatch located over the nose wheel. Our flight attendants were wearing skirts. Noticing that we were going to come crawling down over the nose wheel, the Nigerian ground personnel rushed over to "help" us. They were completely in our way, not helping at all. They carefully positioned themselves to get an eyeful of the white girl's thighs as we descended the plane through the hatch.

Halfway through the Hajj operation, our American crew flew one of the 747s to Athens for a ten-day rest while the Nigerians performed the long-awaited Hajj. We could not have been in more diverse environments. While they were praying at one of the Earth's holiest sites, we were enjoying belly dancers in Athens and chartering yachts to cruise the beaches in Mykonos.

However, while the Americans and Nigerians were separated, each often wondered how the other group was faring. I could only envision the thrill for our fellow workers as they saw the minarets of the Al-Haram Mosque in Mecca for the very first time while entering the state of Ihram (purity). As they joined over two million other pilgrims of nearly every nationality on the planet walking around the Kaaba, we were exploring the Acropolis and other historical sites in Athens. I instinctively knew that we were praying for each other from many miles, and many cultures, away.

Vince, Linda, our pilots, and eight others took the ferry over to Mykonos to spend a few days. We stayed in a modest hotel but could still reach the beaches quickly by scooter. Our hotel was traditional Greek, so every night all the Europeans and Americans ate and drank while feigning the "Zorba the Greek" dance. I have always loved that style. Hardly anybody is left out. You just dance around the room with your arms on the shoulders of the people on either side of you, kicking up your heels. Just scan the other patrons to see who looks either fetching or lonely, and when you swing around to that side, you just scoop them up. It is an energetic dance, and nobody gives a damn if you are not a good dancer as long as you do not yank the entire chain down with a misstep.

Renting several scooters, we formed a caravan to explore. We chartered a small yacht to go to the other side of the island, taking picnic lunches and drinks. The sea captain took us to a semi-private lagoon that was right out of a travel brochure. Large rocks were scattered about in the water, with small "cliffs" that you could climb to make a dive into the lagoon. The water ranged from turquoise blue to emerald green, depending on what part you were in and how the sun was shining on it. The water temperature was perfect, and we splashed in it for quite some time.

After a couple of hours, our boat captain set course for Paradise Beach, where many Europeans go to relax in the sun. The beach was wide and unspoiled, although busy with many sunbathers, with or without clothes. Several large yachts with impressive footage were anchored offshore. We glided up closer to the beach.

"It's the land of jugs and jewels!" exclaimed Richard, a Pan Amigo surveying the scene. "I'm going to go check it out. Who's coming with me?"

Watching one of the pilots playfully goosing a female colleague getting off the boat, his eyebrows went up as he advised, "Oh, no, be careful, skipper. You are falling into the Pan Am snake pit of love."

As everyone jumped into the shallow water, I stayed on board to finish my sandwich. Fondly remembering the Pan Amigo connections that brought me to this experience, I wore my "White House Press charter" T-shirt. With illustrations of both Boeing 747s flying side-by-side, it read "Pan Am and Air Force One, thanks for the memories."

Linda soon returned to tell me that I should really cruise the peeps. She was right. The beach presented some real "eye candy" for us, regardless of your persuasion. Mischief got the better of me and I peeled off my top just as our pilot was coming up for air, instantly chucking. "What do we have here?"

I thought what the hell, might as well join the locals instead of ogling them. I loved the freedom and felt right at home. Five of our pilots posed with a topless Tania on the beach, the polar opposite of decorum in our next destination. The weather was perfect that day. Most sunbathers had a golden tan or were beginning to peel, aka "the gecko look." At a nearby café, I remained topless as we devoured Greek salads, moussaka casserole, souvlaki, and tzatziki, washed down with either grappa or beer. It was ethereal compared to the exhaust-filled dirt streets of Kaduna. Live Greek music wafted from the terraces, decorated with arbors covered with plump red and green grapes. The sweeping view of the sparkling sea dazzled our eyes. You instantly realize why visitors come from all over the world to visit the Greek islands. Each island has its own unique atmosphere, energy, and characteristics. It was really difficult to leave. We had absorbed Mykonos into our souls.

Riding the ferry back to Athens with Linda and Vince at the stern, we silently watched the harbor of Mykonos fade from view into the peacock-blue horizon. I stared at it for a long time to etch the view permanently into my mind. If I kept a strong connection with the ambiance of the Greek islands, I felt I would return many times. I told Vince that I felt like a migrating hummingbird leaving behind a reservoir of our memorable visit, which I would be able to draw upon later as a resource when I became depressed for any reason. Everyone else was super quiet as well, almost upset at leaving such a gorgeous place.

With the engine overhaul completed in Athens, we were ready to ferry our plane to Jeddah for the second part of the Hajj. Then we would begin to transport the Nigerians back home. Our aircraft took off with just our crew on board, all seated together in the front section. Hardly anyone said a word. Everyone spotted Mykonos as we flew above it, like saying goodbye to a cherished lover. Greece had elevated all our spirits.

Soon we were cruising above the Nile valley with patches of green stretching miles to the east and west of the river; truly the "life of Egypt." Beyond the emerald-colored crops and papyrus, the desert stretched to where the earth meets the sky. From an aerial perspective, one can easily see how precious the Nile is to the survival of this populous nation, now 112 million people strong. The sun had set. As if right on cue, the full moon rose over the Sinai Peninsula to cast a silver glow over this ancient country.

Under the luminescence of this lovely moon, we landed in Jeddah. Now in Saudi Arabia, I retrieved my *abbayya*, the black robe that was de rigueur in the kingdom. Pulling it over my street clothes, I fished for my dark headscarf. My bright blue scarf from Greece would be frowned upon by the *Mutawa* (religious police). Who wants to be hassled?

As we disembarked, looking beyond the lights of the airport, I knew that my dear friend Maamoun Zahid, whom I had not seen since our Millfield days in '69, was out there somewhere. *No matter where he is in this city, I will find him*, I thought. The ground staff handed me newspapers and magazines which had been flown in from Nigeria for the chief. As our van pulled up to our hotel, I noticed a rather large African man wearing an impeccable dark-blue pin-striped suit like those purchased from Bond Street in London. As I struggled with all my purchases from Greece, he greeted me. "Tania, I see that you have the reading material I requested from Nigeria," he said.

Taken aback, and a bit embarrassed, I realized that it was Chief Kabo. He looked so entirely different dressed in Western clothes that I had not recognized him. Shame on me, but I must admit he looked worlds apart in Western finery. I had only seen him in brightly colored *babarigas* since we had arrived from the States. Perhaps it was "culture shock" in reverse.

With Chief Kabo on one of his 11 planes

Bounding across the tarmac towards our plane, the Nigerian flight attendants dashed up the boarding staircase, with *Zamzam* (holy water from Mecca) in hand. Even though we had loved our Greek trip so much, I had an intense desire to hear what their journey had meant to them. Each one had cut their hair to signify their pilgrimage. Many displayed one gold tooth fitted neatly over their own natural one. They also had new titles: *Hajji* for men and *Hajjia* for women. After the Hajj, pilgrims are addressed as *Al-Hajji* or *Al-Hajjia* in front of their name. About 25 of them were jammed into first class, all speaking at once and relating their experiences, so excited that they did not know which story to tell first. Their faces shone with light, and their smiles were so intense that they lit up the entire cabin.

Then I found Ibrahim. "Hajji Ibrahim, how was your pilgrimage?" I asked, hugging him.

The females squealed with delight in such a way that I realized I had done something wrong. "Tania, you are not supposed to touch the males," they advised me through their giggles, but even though I had made an inadvertent faux pas, my action actually enhanced all the excitement. They certainly knew me well enough to know that I would never intentionally do something that was *haram* (forbidden).

"Tania, in Mecca, I prayed to Allah that you would embrace Islam," he said, smiling. At a loss for words to describe his complex experience, he added, "I was *seriously* impressed with everything we did while on the pilgrimage."

Ibrahim, like the others, had been overwhelmed by the experience. They had been grouped with other Nigerians and had walked around the Kaaba the obligatory seven times while continually praying. He had kissed the black stone encased in solid silver that is revered by Muslims because it is sacred in their eyes. They believe that this stone was brought from heaven by the Archangel Gabriel.

The Kaaba is covered in a black cloth, called *Kiswah*, every inch of it embellished with calligraphy in Arabic, embroidered with solid 24-carat gold wire. It is replaced yearly. Once I had the honor to see these artisans meticulously and painstakingly embroidering the cloth when they were flown to the States in a cultural exchange by the Embassy of Saudi Arabia. I have not seen anything similar anywhere else. The thick entrance door to the Kaaba is made of solid 24-carat gold, illustrated with a detailed Islamic design. It stands approximately seven feet high and is intensely bright. You can readily see why men fell in love with gold when it was first discovered.

The Hajj has a unifying significance that brings pilgrims from all over the world to worship together at Mecca. The Nigerians had joined more than two million other pilgrims, all wearing pure white garments, to epitomize a sense of unity. This also removes elaborate clothes from the wealthy and creates a sense of equality. Despite the intense heat, they were able to visit all the required sites. Ibrahim and the others had taken part in Eid-al-Adha, where an animal is offered to commemorate Abraham's sacrifice. Afterwards, a major feast is enjoyed by all.

A big believer in the human aura and the "vibes" we all send out, I have often thought about the energy in Jeddah, a 90-minute drive from Mecca. Five times a day, millions of worshippers from all over the globe face Mecca, offering prayers. Jeddah was a remarkable place to live, close to one of the holiest sites on earth, receiving angelic blessings five times a day.

Vince and I had a long conversation about it. We shared similar impressions of the world and believed many of the same visions in the spiritual realm. We discussed how before each flight we were consciously surrounding the aircraft with positive thoughts and white light energy. We visualized the entire aircraft bathed in heavenly white light and discovered that both of us had made similar prayers and visualizations during the Gulf War, asking for the soldiers to have a safe journey.

Vince always said a special prayer for passengers who might need assistance so that they would come to our attention. Often the flights were frenzied, and our concentration may have been taken away from some soul who needed help. Perhaps they were anxious, afraid, or confused. Our Nigerian crew represented a dozen tribes, so they often translated any concerns to us. On every flight, at least several pilgrims were quite ill from debilitating, unidentified illnesses or disease.

Once I was asked by the ground crew in Jeddah to clear a seat in the front zone for a seriously ill passenger. It was so difficult for them to move him up the stairs. They kept pushing the obese man forward to avoid everyone cascading backward all at once. When I tried to move a passenger to reserve a seat for the disabled man, the passenger sitting there refused, even though our flights did not have assigned seating. It was ridiculous for him to be territorial; his was an economy seat in the old first-class section, but he made it clear that he was not about to move. I glanced down the stairs at the sick Hajji battling desperately to make his way up. The sight of him struggling so broke my heart. I lost my cool.

"I am not asking you; I am *telling* you!" I shouted. "If you don't get out of that seat right away, I will call the authorities, and you know what that means. There are other seats available, and my colleague will show you where they are."

He certainly understood what I meant concerning the authorities. He rapidly gathered his belongings because he knew that if he was taken into custody, many months could pass before he saw his sweet homeland again. His loved ones would have no idea how to contact him, or even begin to speculate about what had happened to him.

The sick man, huffing and puffing, entered the doorway aided by his helpers, but just barely. Rather young, perhaps mid-thirties, he was exhausted and debilitated. His right leg was blown up like a blimp from toe to thigh. He grimaced and groaned from acute pain. He did not have a shoe or sandal on that foot because it was so bloated. As he collapsed into the seat, Linda fanned him with a safety information folder. Was it elephantiasis? Visiting Venezuela in 1951, my mother had been so shocked the first time she saw a patient. I knew by her description what it looked like. Sadly, I had also seen similar cases in the children asking for alms at Agra near the famed Taj Mahal. As his helpers straightened out their shirts, the man caught his breath. Linda handed him a glass of ice-cold water. "Hajji, would you like some water?" she asked.

Despite his condition, she brought a smile to his face as she acknowledged his new status in the Muslim world.

‿౨

"Yes, this is the home of Maamoun Zahid," the friendly lady's voice said. I wondered if I had the correct residence. Had I found him that easily after 23 years? "We have a photo of him at Millfield on our wall."

I gasped. I had indeed found one of my oldest and dearest friends. "I'm his wife Mona, and I'll tell him when he comes home that you called. He'll be so happy to see you again after all these years. Perhaps we can get together for dinner."

Hanging up, I fell backwards onto the pillows laughing. I was thrilled that after so long I had found my close confidant. Additionally, what amused me was how kind and friendly Mona sounded on the phone. Just try and call an old friend who you knew when you were fourteen and speak to his wife, telling her that you want to see her husband after all these years. Her voice will instantly change, and she will ask, "Who is this? Where do you know him from, *exactly*?"

Then she will enter the contemplation stage where she will debate whether she should tell her spouse at all. Now, in the age of computer research, single and not-so-single boomers are looking up former paramours, so this happens more and more frequently. Maamoun and I had always been platonic friends, but at the time Mona did not know that.

Wednesday, June 8, 1993. I just got off the phone with Maamoun's wife Mona, I wrote in my diary. *I can't believe I've found my good friend after a solid 23 years!* I excitedly wrote. *"It'll be so much fun to catch up and find out how he has been doing all this time. I can't wait to ask him who he is still in touch with from Millfield.*

Pulling my *abbayya* over my clothes, I happily recounted how my mother reacted when I returned from Millfield relating all the stories of my experiences which always had something to do with Maamoun. In 1967, possible war was brewing between Yemen and Saudi Arabia, so he was late returning to school. Calling from London, I had lamented to Mom, "If Maamoun doesn't come back to Millfield this year, I just have no idea what I'll do." I had said it in a plaintive voice, as sensitive teenagers do when they feel their lives are spinning out of control. During the holidays in the States, my mother imitated my crooning. Lifting her head up towards the ceiling, she called out, "Moon, Moooon!" using his nickname. She was fascinated by our enduring friendship that had transcended our polar-opposite cultures.

The phone rang. It was Maamoun. I was hearing his voice for the first time since 1970. "Tania, how are you? Welcome to the Kingdom!" he said, excitedly. "Can you come for dinner tonight? We will pick you up at six. We'll talk about old memories and make new ones," he added, his voice sounding the same after all this time.

"I can't wait to see you and meet Mona," I enthused.

The white sedan pulled into the hotel's driveway. I hurriedly ran out to greet them, making a beeline straight for Maamoun. Knowing I wanted to embrace him, he laughed, heading me off at the pass, just in time. "Tania! You can't touch me in public, but you can hug my wife."

Smiling broadly, I gave his beautiful, chic wife a welcome hug.

Seated in the front of the car next to Maamoun, I studied his face intently as he spoke. He is 6 feet 3 inches tall, with a medium build and golden-brown complexion. The eyelashes, yes, the eyelashes! He always had long, curly eyelashes in school and they were *still* there. I was elated to be in their company as we reminisced all about our school days with our eclectic, international friends.

Mona was the dream wife for him. From Cairo, she was a cardiologist hailing from a family full of successful physicians. She attended medical school in England and Scotland. If I had such a trying time ingratiating myself into the culture of Great Britain, I could only imagine how difficult it had been for her, being from Egypt. Mona spoke perfect English with an English accent, a consummate cosmopolitan beauty who keenly understood both Eastern and Western cultures. Their young sons, Ahmed and Ameen, already spoke flawless English and alternated between answering their parents in English and classic Arabic.

Intricate Oriental carpets placed over white marble floors greeted us at their home. The scent of foreign spices filled the air along with the fragrance of our Western perfumes. A delicious traditional seafood dinner was being prepared for us. Maamoun played my old favorite song from school, "Where Do You Go to My Lovely?" by Peter Starsted. I was astonished that he remembered. I find it remarkable how individuals can sometimes recall certain miniscule details of their lives. I believe that it has to do with the impression, whether positive or negative, that a particular period has on our lives. Maamoun and I had so much catching up to do, as we had shared many of the same friends. It was easy for us to recall the fascinating personalities we had known.

After dinner we discussed our teenage years. We spoke about the young royals from Ethiopia, Thailand, Saudi Arabia, Romania, the Emirates, and Brunei, whom we had befriended and spent our free time with at Millfield. I noticed a large photo of King Fahd with another Saudi man in traditional robes. Anticipating my question, Maamoun said, "That is my father in the photo. He sits with the king."

Between Millfield and Pan Am, it seemed as if my world was becoming smaller and smaller by the minute, but that was a *good* thing.

"How many times have you been to the Kingdom that you didn't call us?" Maamoun asked, in a mocked scolding.

"Pan Am had a daily flight between New York and Dhahran which I worked a few times. Then I made some trips to bring American troops into Dhahran in 1990, and out again after the war ended. So finally, I am here, in your hometown of Jeddah after all this time, Maamoun," I added. "I just can't believe that I am sitting here with you, it is surrealistic."

"Just like me you love adventure, Tania, and the international lifestyle. You haven't changed that much. Your soul and spirit are still very much the same."

Giving each other a big hug, we headed out into the night for the ride back to my hotel. Our friendship was right back on track, just as if it had only been a week since I had last seen him. Maamoun and Mona will be my close friends always.

The Hajj operation was in its final days, and the exhaustion was beginning to show on everyone's face. It felt like we had devoured everything in sight at a smorgasbord, gorging ourselves, so now it was time to go home, regroup, and take some papaya tablets. I needed time to reflect and digest all that we had experienced.

After three solid months in Jeddah, enjoying a marble villa with a private pool priced at $2,500 a night, I imagine that the chief had just about had his fill, as well. The squad of houseboys, chauffeurs, and bodyguards whom he had brought with him were also frantically running around, trying to get some last-minute deals for gifts to give families or sweethearts back home. The final bill presented to the Chief for utilizing the villa during the Hajj had reached about $225,000 . . . plus some extras.

In one last ritual to signify the end of the pilgrimage, the chief arranged for seven head of cattle to be sacrificed.

A large flatbed truck was precariously backed into the hotel's entrance. An army of bellmen were loading dozens of boxes containing TVs, VCRs, radios, and boom boxes onto the truck, as quality electronic items are difficult to find in Nigeria. Chief Kabo was flying the massive load back home. Soon the mountain of goods would be hauled to the airport for the baggage handlers to load into the cargo hold.

Upstairs, the chief was about ready to find out something he did not want to hear—the extra aircraft which had been scheduled to transport all this *shit* was already in Kano, positioned to return the next morning for America.

Andrew, the ground coordinator, an affable Englishman with a great sense of humor, was red-faced in anticipation of delivering the bad news to the chief. It was not Andrew's fault the earlier flight had been given the go-ahead to leave, but he could possibly be lambasted, nonetheless. Unfortunately, somebody must take the heat in these situations, whether it is their fault or not.

"Tania, has anyone seen the chief?" Andrew asked. "Is he in the coffee shop? I have some bad news for him. The plane which was scheduled to take all his private cargo back home has already been dispatched. In fact, it is sitting on the tarmac in Kano as we speak."

As he searched for the chief's familiar figure, his eyes narrowed. "Oh, God, now I see him. He's in there, having tea and chatting with some first-time heavy-hitter Hajjis. Wish me luck," he said as he briskly walked towards the coffee shop.

I stayed a respectful distance away, even though I was dying to hear the conversation. Like a genie with different personas, the chief had switched back into an elaborate bright yellow *babariga,* appearing ready to return to his sphere of influence in Nigeria. He stood up when Andrew reached his table to hear the latest developments. The chief began waving his hands about, as he often did. Andrew's body language showed he was trying to break the news gently. It was hard to see if Chief Kabo was angry or not, but just when I thought Andrew was going to get cooked, I saw the chief fumble with his robes and hand Andrew a fat envelope. He bowed his head slightly, shook his boss's hand, and rushed back out. With the luck of the leprechauns, Andrew had caught him in a good mood. "What happened?" I asked, so curious.

"The chief must want to transport his stuff badly," Andrew sighed. "He just handed me $50,000 cash to arrange for the aircraft to come back from Kano just to pick up all his gifts and luggage. I've got to run and make the arrangements, Tania. You know how things go. It might take me several days to get that plane back here, delaying its departure to Miami for your home-bound trip. See you tomorrow."

Upstairs under my door was a note from our captain. It was addressed to each of the American gals. "You're invited to my room at 6 p.m. Let's have a small debriefing with you lovely ladies." I was pretty sure that the skipper, even with his prolific connections, had not come up with any moonshine.

Room service had delivered a selection of fresh-squeezed fruit juices for us. "Come in ladies," he began, bowing as if he was a manservant at Topkapi. "I have something for each of you," he said, smiling. "Camels from the souk, but you can fit them into your purse rather than your pickup."

Each of us opened a beautiful box containing a 24-carat gold chain with a solid gold camel dangling from it. That was the perfect gesture from our skipper; a memento of our adventure that spanned three very individual countries. "What about the boys?" Linda teased, as we heartily thanked him.

"The boys ain't getting anything," he said, smiling towards Vince, who was sipping Arabic coffee, watching our reactions to the gold camels.

Our operation was ending, and it was difficult for the captain to see its completion. Although very fit, he was 59 years old, and by law, had to retire at 60. Naturally, he had sentimental and melancholy feelings that his sparkling career, which had taken him on endless adventures to every corner of the Earth, would soon become part of his past.

"I wanted to invite you tonight just to say how incredible this entire twelve weeks has been, including all the wild stuff. There's still much work to be done and I know that you are aware that the craziness may not be over. In fact, I don't think it is over until we reach American shores," he said, taking a sip of pomegranate juice.

"To give you an example, last year there was a real imbroglio with the last plane to leave Nigeria. The flight plan had been submitted to Kano tower, the cargo doors were closed, and the stairs had been pulled. A few managers from a Lebanese charter company were on board, ready to fly back to the States. Just as they were beginning to wonder what the holdup was, a tower guy with a thick accent stated that their flight plan had not been approved. You can imagine their reaction. Astonished, the veteran pilots asked what could possibly be wrong. As the radio crackled, the Air Traffic Control man casually mentioned that there would be a

$10,000 dollar 'takeoff' fee. Was the crew living in a cartoon? "What take-off fee?" they demanded.

The voice shot back, "If you don't pay the take-off fee of $10,000.00, we'll shoot your plane's tires out," the voice from the tower bellowed. Just who in the hell was talking to them, making that outrageous demand?

"So *now* you tell us," Linda teased.

Vince looked serious. He did not find it funny at all. It would be so easy for them to demand the same this year. "What was the outcome?" Vince asked, studying his face for any leading clues.

"The two Lebanese managers went ballistic as their Middle Eastern tempers flared. "Those thieving sons-of-bitches! I've had more than enough of this for one season!" one inadvertently screamed into the pilot's ear. "We'll show *them* what is going on!" the other yelled, "I am going to pin their ears back!" They hurriedly disembarked from the aircraft through the hatch and ran across the tarmac. The sun had just set, but as they reached the top of the stairway to the air traffic control tower, those in the cockpit could see their silhouettes shifting back and forth as they engaged in a pitch-black battle. They were much bigger than the tribesmen, and the Nigerians soon realized that they had stretched their luck, and asking price, too far. The view of the punch-up in the tower was right out of a Gary Larson cartoon," our pilot added.

"The two Lebanese guys came rip-snortin' across the runway, hastily boarding the aircraft yelling "Let's get out of here!" We scared the stuffing out of them, and after what we just did, I think we have enough time to get out of Dodge!" He added, "They cleared Nigerian airspace in double time, and never heard about the incident again." Our captain paused. "You guys already know this, but I just want you to be aware of everything as we wrap this operation up. Thanks, you have been a fantastic crew."

Two days later, both of our 747s were at Jeddah airport. The first one was packed with passengers and cargo, ready to return to Nigeria. The last one was ours, brought back by Andrew, with only 25 passengers on board, all seated in first class. After takeoff, I fished out a dusty old travel video showing Miami and the Keys, playing it for the Hajjis. They continually smiled as they watched scenes of bathing beauties on white sand beaches, scuba divers, sleek Ferraris, bars, killer yachts, nightclubs, and beachside cabanas. They knew that this was the world we hailed from. Even so, I felt that we communicated well.

Beyond the 25 passengers in first class was a super-abundance of cargo. Endless boxes and equipment had been haphazardly thrown into the seats, on the floor, in the aisles, wherever they would fit. Rope nets that are used on ships had been thrown over all the boxes from nose to tail. What a mess! As a purser, I did not know whether to laugh or scream. With severe turbulence, all this nonsense could become airborne missiles. Even a large man could get whacked by them. At least after all this trouble, the chief's personal cargo would be safely delivered to Nigeria. However, I never found out what happened to the balance of his $50,000.

⁌

It was difficult to say goodbye to all the Nigerians whom we had worked with, especially Ibrahim. "I showed your photos to my family," he told me, "They wanted to hear everything about you and the others. I had so many things to describe to them about the Hajj. One night they had a party for me, and all my cousins came. We had a wonderful time. Now everyone calls me Hajji Ibrahim," he added proudly.

I pulled out a small box containing a pair of amethyst earrings I had bought in Athens. "I noticed that you don't really have an eye for any of the Nigerian ladies on our crew," I said, "But as soon as you meet that someone special, perhaps you would like to give her these."

He opened the box and broke into a wide grin. "Tania, these are beautiful. *Na go Day*. Thank you so very much. I will keep them close to my heart for that certain lady.

"I'm going to miss all the Americans. I feel like I have known this crew for years." Ibrahim continued, "I liked the captains, too. They were brave when we had the fire." Leaning in towards me, he whispered, "They are really nice guys, but you know the pilot doesn't fly the plane. It is really Allah who flies the plane."

That was the last thing Ibrahim ever said to me.

Nobody comes back from the Hajj the same, regardless of their nationality or religion. There are just too many elements involved not to change you in one way or another. I strongly felt that we had encountered old souls in three distinct nations. We had what I call "cosmo camaraderie" as we all meshed and worked hard to be certain that the operation went as smoothly as possible. We had crossed some type of threshold by living and working with the Nigerians. I found out more about myself, learning to view the Americans through African eyes. All this while making new friends, both with co-workers and passengers, in previously uncharted territory.

I joked with Linda, "I think we need to be debriefed in Wiesbaden, Germany, before returning home," referring to what an extraordinary experience we had just been through.

You always return to your homeland a changed person, hopefully for the better. My guardian angel Ishmael channeling through my friend Steve once said that it is like a horse who drinks from a stream. The benefit may not be immediate, but it is there, and will serve its purpose at a future date. Feeling so pensive on that very last flight back to Miami, I just wanted to take it easy and slowly recall all the new friends, old friends, images, smells, sounds, laughter, and the deep impressions of our trip while we chased the sun across the Atlantic.

"WELCOME HOME, PAN AMIGOS!" the large sheet exclaimed. Gunilla was holding it aloft outside the Miami customs area, but she dropped it every time another crew member came out so she could run to hug them. Then she would spot someone else emerge, perhaps a mechanic or loadmaster, and rush back to her post to hold it high again for them to see. We were quite giddy at a nearby hotel to celebrate our homecoming. We had "re-entered the Earth's atmosphere" as I like to say any time we return from a prolonged adventure.

Soon Gunilla's suite was jammed, everyone vying for her attention as we related our zany stories. The "tribe" had been reunited, and the tales could have been snatched out of any Pan Am history book. We had kept the dream alive.

Days later, Steve gave me a reading. Sequoia, one of my guardian angels, came through right away. I was so anxious to hear what he thought of our journey.

"Tania, you came across many people you knew from former lives. That is why you bonded so quickly and so strongly with them, feeling as if you had known them forever. Many of you recognized the light in the others, as old souls do."

He delighted me with what he said next. "Tania, you have unfinished business in Nigeria, you already know that. You also understand and feel that you have a strong connection with that part of the world," he added.

"You just went *home* again," Sequoia whispered.

We had crossed the continent of Africa 28 times.

⤺

Hajji Ibrahim Maidunama
1968-1994

Six months after we returned to America, a dreadful accident occurred. Late one night, Ibrahim was riding his motorcycle along an unlit country road on the high plains of central Nigeria near Jos.

In pure blackness, except for a car's headlights and the brilliant stars above, Ibrahim swerved his motorcycle in a desperate attempt to avoid the oncoming vehicle, but it was too late. He was hit head-on and killed instantly.

He was a dear friend and colleague who taught me many things about his language and culture.

I shall miss him always.

⤺

With Groom Cicero on his wedding day

9

A Traditional African Wedding and Owambay

While our crews crisscrossed the skies above the Nigerian landscape during the Hajj, a romance had been quietly blossoming in Kaduna. Cicero, my friend from Pan Am, had met Amina, the daughter of Alhajji Ibrahim Nok, a prominent chieftain from the ancient village of Nok. She worked reception of our hotel, and a courtship flourished.

"Tania! I'll look to the sky and pray for the sight of your aircraft!" my friend Bello blurted out over the crackling sound of the phone line as I informed him that I planned to attend their January wedding as a surprise.

My first visit to Nigeria since the Hajj one year prior, I knew that it would be a truly unique ethnic experience now that I had friends there. I flew to London and spent a few days with Vince, Linda, and other Pan Amigos, now on an assignment for Tajikistan, before proceeding onto Kano.

Nigeria had an unreliable phone system with no phone books and certainly no 411. When I told my Hausa friends that you could dial 411 and get info about anyone in the US, they burst out laughing, thinking I was pulling their legs. "What's so funny?" I asked in a quizzical way.

"Madame, that is *not* possible, how does such a thing exist? How do they keep the records straight?"

In lieu of 411, I must compliment the Nigerians and say that they have perfected their own "phone tree" *without* phones. News travels just fine by word of mouth, thank you. When I wanted to relay a message to someone, I would plant the seed with certain individuals and the news then traveled at the speed of sound. Nigerians readily enjoy, just as Americans do, being "in the know."

I was really looking forward to surprising Cicero by "sneaking" into Nigeria to attend his wedding celebration, but somehow the word had leaked out and was already circulating around that *Baturia* (white woman) was arriving from London any day now.

Upon arrival and navigating my way through Customs, I asked one of the drivers to locate Bello Katune, my favorite passenger from the Hajj. A jubilant and breathless Bello welcomed me with a warm hug. Men and women are not really supposed to touch each other in public, but this was an exception because everyone knew about the impending wedding. "*Sah-nun-kah-da-zooah!*" he greeted me with.

I repeated the words to the delight of curious onlookers, amused to hear my funky accent in Hausa-Fulani.

Our taxi was so beaten up and rusted you could see the road pass under your feet through a large hole. No matter. I was safe, happy, and glad to be back in my adopted African home, also in plenty of time to join the pre-nuptials. Bello and I had so much to catch up on while driving to MD Hassan's house. We had not seen each other for over six months, so we were busy discussing all that had transpired since the Hajj.

Dodging numerous goats eating days-old food from discarded plastic bags, we finally reached MD's house, which he shared with just one wife but . . . ten children. And another one was on the way. MD Hassan was Chief Kabo's right-hand man and confidante at Kabo Air, handling all his business affairs. He was genuinely friendly, had a wonderful sense of humor, and a great command of English. Regardless of what was going on in the world, we always began by teasing each other like old friends do.

He loved to chew the kola nut, which tastes bitter but gives you an espresso-type buzz throughout the day. It also eventually paints your teeth red, just like the betel nuts in India. A large gap between his front teeth was revealed when he grinned. He always wore the traditional robes, but not in flashy colors. On the other hand, Bello owned such a diverse *babariga* collection that it was probably one of his most valuable assets.

About 5'6" and a bit overweight, he always gave me a welcome bear hug. This time, upon my return to his country, he picked me up, swung me around like they do in films, and planted me back down on the carpet. "I'm so glad to see you!" he gushed.

Delighted, I laughed, "I always told you that I would return. I'm here again, isn't that wonderful?"

Sitting down to some hot tea, his children came in a few at a time. It was hard to keep up with all the faces and names. Imagine ten energetic children in a modest abode. Their English was good and they were polite and charming; well brought up.

While Bello and I sipped tea, MD produced a lovely lady's formal garment. "What is this, MD?" I asked, curiously.

"This is our gift to you, a traditional dress to wear at Cicero and Amina's wedding. It has some extra material that can be fashioned into a hat of some kind. What do you think?"

"I love it!" I exclaimed. "What do Nigerians call this dress?"

"A boo-boo" Bello told me.

Now it was my turn to have some fun. "A *boo-boo*? Do you know what that means in the West? It is the word that kids use when they make a mistake." It is amusing how certain things have such different meanings in the world.

It was a deep taupe color with long wide sleeves and gold metallic embroidery around all the edges. I pulled a gold belt out of my bag to fox it up a bit since it went straight down to my ankles and had no shape. "What are you doing?" Bello said, sounding upset. "You can't do that, you will take it *completely* out the fashion!" he exclaimed, waving his hands in the air.

I assured him that I would wear it as they do customarily. I changed back into my drab and dark woolen clothes that I had worn from London, now looking odd and out of place. We headed off to Chief Kabo's exquisite "villa."

"Madame has returned to Nigeria!" the chief happily exclaimed, formally shaking my hand as I entered the living room with Bello and MD. This was the first of many times in Nigeria that I was the only Westerner, only lady, only white person, and only Christian in the gathering, but I truly felt right at home in this atmosphere. Brought up by my father after my parents' divorce, I used to eavesdrop on his business conversations with his male colleagues from the balcony overlooking the living room in our Tudor-style house. Over the years, it became second nature for me to be surrounded by men discussing business. In this case, it was the business of aviation, my business, and definitely the chief's—he owned eleven commercial aircraft, including some former Pan Am jets.

Grabbing the landline, the chief said, "Let's call Garba!" in his melodious accent.

Garba, the youngest and most handsome of the four brothers, ran Kabo Air. We met during the Hajj when he was flying to Saudi Arabia. Unpretentious in a land of enormous, battling egos, the gentle Garba had a modest demeanor.

I whispered to Bello, "Why is the chief calling his junior brother?"

Bello looked surprised. "You don't know? Garba really likes you. Now that you are here, I bet you that he'll be up on the first plane in the morning from Lagos!"

And indeed, he was. It was a wonderful thing because Garba, the perfect host, intrinsically knew the ropes around Nigeria. A natural diplomat, he was widely popular and deeply admired. He inherently knew that I would need a sharp liaison to deal with the cultural ethos I would encounter in his country now that I was on my own. He kept the facts straight, always making certain I had someone with me for protection, although it was always low-key.

One night, when we hastily left the house to join friends for a much-anticipated evening, he said "Don't worry," referring to the fact that he had given his bodyguard the night off.

Before he started the car, he showed me a firearm that was straight out of a 007 film. It looked like an object d'art made of sterling silver that had just been polished. It would look right at home on display at the Spy Museum in D.C.

Garba is a good judge of character, an essential quality for any businessman in Nigeria, where they try to swindle you at every turn, especially if you come from a prominent family. When Cicero and I used slang expressions, little escaped Garba's understanding.

We traveled to Kaduna to meet Cicero and his fiancée, Amina. Rather quiet, she was intelligent with a great command of English.

Ebony-complexioned like her father, the chief of Nok, she had fine features and looked stunning in any color she chose to wear. Cicero and I had flown to Europe together on many trips for Pan Am. Shortly after it went bankrupt, I ran into him at a mall near my home in Northern Virginia. *Fate is such a funny thing.* I had spotted him through the window of a small café. What if I had simply been looking in the other direction as he passed by? He would have never met his future wife, because not long afterwards, when the Nigerian Hajj came up, I called him to join us.

A few days after my arrival, Amina's Aunt Salamatu held a pre-wedding ladies' luncheon on the large patio surrounding her home. About 45 ladies attended, including my friend, Amina Garba, who had been on my crew. A large buffet with Nigerian specialties was complemented by various types of sweets, with juice to drink. A local traditional band played while dancers performed. We all settled in to eat and enjoy the entertainment while discussing the upcoming nuptials.

"Bello," I said, "I thought you said that this was a ladies' luncheon, for women only."

"Well, it is," he said with a sneaky little smile, "I'll leave shortly."

But he stayed on for some time. I could hardly blame him, as the scene was really "cruisey." What better place to be on the prowl for a new girlfriend, or wife number two, than a pre-wedding party with young, upper-crust fetching African ladies parading around in their finest?

After Bello left, I witnessed something heart-wrenching and unusual that I had never seen before in any country. The low-key din of simple instruments playing outside the gates wafted in while the wedding musicians took a break. A crowd of local impoverished tribespeople had been gathering quietly. Because there were many guests and few tables, we just put our plates down on the ground to be collected by Auntie's servers when we finished our meal. Her main house boy went over to the gate to let the unfortunate people inside. Many were middle aged and blind, being led by young children. A great tragedy is that Nigeria has the world's highest incidence of river blindness, so you see frequently see blind people.

These additional guests joined us, assuming humble postures as they entered in an orderly line. Most of them smiled as they carried an empty bowl. The wedding band began to play again as the people went from chair to chair, helping themselves to any leftover chicken and rice, Nigeria's national dish. Very courteous with each other and so quiet, they were almost invisible, and completely honest. In a country where you must sprout eyeballs in the back of your head to be on constant alert, this tranquil scene was the exact opposite. The house boys dutifully collected the leftover food from the buffet and divided it up among the visitors. All of this transpired in a respectful way, and they patted their hearts in thanks, also giving the special wave with the thumb through the fist that Hausa/Fulani's show as gratitude.

The next day, our wedding party settled into a caravan of eight cars to drive to Amina's home village several hours away. Most of the cars were punched-out Peugeots. I was sitting in the front seat of the bridal car, which held Amina and her closest friends. The driver was furiously chewing on kola nuts and the faster he chewed, the more we sped—way too fast on a road filled with potholes, renegade goats, and the occasional lopsided, top-heavy overstuffed pickup truck that had flipped onto its side. In a gentle way, I reminded the driver that we wanted to arrive at the wedding in one piece. God forbid if something had happened, because hospitals are quite rough and may not use sterilized needles, not to mention what other practices. The driver, in his mid-twenties, grinned, displaying a perfectly shaped set of red teeth. Ah, that kola nut working its cosmetic wonders again.

We pulled up to Amina's family's house in Nok Village. Chief Ibrahim Nok and Amina's stepmom, Hajjia Hauwa Nok, his wife number two, welcomed us. I say "wife number two" because in Northern Nigeria it is an accepted practice to introduce ladies that way. The pecking order begins with the first wife the man married and works its way down. When introducing the children, you will often hear, "This is Omar, son of wife number three," etc., which also places the offspring in order.

Inside their home, several goatskin rugs covered the floor. Numerous photos on the wall showed the diminutive chief with various well-known African leaders, including President Nelson Mandela. It was a relaxed picture showing a happy occasion. I studied it for a while. In a thousand moons I could have never imagined that four years later, I would also meet the celebrated president at a special ceremony on Capitol Hill.

Chief Nok and I hit it off right away, talking about all the places we had visited. He soon made me promise that I would look out for Amina once she relocated with Cicero as newlyweds. America is an enormous place, and she would not have the extensive contacts and protection there that her family had in Nigeria.

Outside in the village square, under an enormous tree, the women strained to see the foreign white woman dressed in a traditional *boo-boo* who had come many miles for the civil ceremony. Even though Nok has historical significance, few outsiders visit, so they marveled at the group of wedding guests from abroad.

Unknown to me at the time, my close friend Amina Garba had fashioned the extra material of my *boo-boo* into a hat that expressed a political statement, so that piqued the villagers' curiosity. They take the material and duplicate the favorite hat design of the First Lady they admire the most. Amina had created a "Miriam Bambagida" hat for me, and the villagers recognized the signal. Without even realizing it, I was already making a strong political statement in Africa's most populated nation—perhaps not a wise idea.

After an informal meal of rice and a piece of fatty meat served with a pungent ginger root drink, we walked to the small building where the marriage ceremony would be held. The ginger drink taught me in short order to always carry a bottle of mineral water. I was so thirsty from the trip that when Bello handed me the drink, I took a gulp and just about choked. It is extremely sharp tasting and difficult to ingest unless you are accustomed to drinking it.

Friends and relatives of the wedding couple gathered into the cramped room for the nuptials. All eyes were on Amina as she entered with her father, joining Cicero in the front row. She wore a feminine yellow *boo-boo*, lovingly embroidered in detail around the edges with a pale-yellow chiffon scarf over her face. Cicero looked splendid in his sky blue *Babariga,* a real natural. He could have easily been mistaken for a Hausa. Dressed in their national costumes on their wedding day, we temporarily became part of the Hausa/Fulani tribe and felt so welcome in Nok Village.

The simple ceremony was conducted in English and Hausa by the *malam* (priest) so everyone could understand. Amina looked lovingly at Cicero as he agreed to be her faithful husband. With standing room only, the local kids outside were all pressed against the bars across the windows, jostling for a better view. After all, this was the village chief's daughter getting married, and to a foreigner, no less. Aunties pressed tissues against their cheeks. Relatives stood up one by one to express their sentiments toward the couple, praising Amina and welcoming Cicero to the family. The vows were repeated in both languages and gold rings were exchanged as flashes went off.

We all filed outside. Caught up in all the rituals, I think that Bello was almost as excited as Cicero. "Well, you did *it*!" Bello enthused, clapping Cicero on the back.

I held back, trying to absorb all the features of this colorful display. I loved watching everyone interact in this ethnic scene as their traditional robes swayed in the calm breeze. Even our driver wore a bright turquoise *babariga*. He could easily have been mistaken for a wedding guest, and at one point, he was.

We jumped into our cars for the ride back to Kaduna to attend the big *owambay* (reception) for the newlyweds.

Arriving at Amina's cousins' house, we were joined by dozens more guests, including some United Nations diplomats. As brides do in the West, Amina had changed her clothes. Now she was wearing a shiny white and pink *boo-boo* with an elaborate headdress in bright pink—the color of love. With her dark complexion and bright red lipstick, she looked gorgeous, as a bride should, especially when she is marrying my good friend.

I sat with Garba, and every time he got up to greet someone, he asked me to watch his Sprite. Curious as to why he wanted to preserve it so carefully, I took a sniff and *voila*! It was fine French champagne. Forget that old "I don't drink" stuff, pour me some bubbly. It had been a unique day.

The northern Nigerians have a custom I have never seen. The bride and the groom invite all their former lovers to the wedding reception. No doubt this would cause quite a stir at weddings in the West. The former paramours in most cases already knew each other. However, as they paraded around like peacocks, they were also making observations on who else might have unsuspectingly been in the picture. Everyone

Cicero, Amina, Garba and me

was lavishly dressed, and these grand images of color reminded me of an ethnic *haute couture* fashion show. Amina's bridesmaids, all wearing matching orange, gold, and white *boo-boos* were absolutely convinced that if I had flown all the way from Washington, D.C., I most certainly must have had an affair with Cicero, and he was showing me off, as well. Not so, Amina assured them, as she knew that Cicero and I were just friends, but they did not buy it. Like a mating ritual, this was just another Hausa custom.

The lively band's ethnic tunes screamed over the loudspeakers, and they were entertaining to watch. A dozen twiggy dancers shook their butts at 90 miles per hour to the music, never taking a break. Most certainly, when the time came to congratulate the bride and groom with cash gifts, they were not going *anywhere*. In a flashy display, guests took turns approaching the dancing bride and groom, peeling off endless naira (Nigerian) notes. In the West, we might quietly give a check to the wedding couple in a discreet envelope, but not in Nigeria, where there is a type of friendly competition to see who comes up with the most greenbacks. And when certain guests present hard foreign currency, the stakes are raised considerably.

Garba took my hand and led me out to the dance floor. After a couple of full-tilt dances and a slow one, he moved in the direction of the wedding couple, who were now swaying to the beat. He reached into his pockets and pulled out one $20 bill at a time, showering Amina and Cicero with cash. Average Nigerians—drivers, houseboys, tailors, or maids—make about $25 a month. Imagine watching someone pulling out your entire month's salary, repeatedly. It would make your head spin.

Unfortunately, Cicero and Amina had not arranged for one of their trusted friends to collect the wedding money as they danced. Seizing a rare opportunity, the band began to play frenetically, and the dancers wiggled so fast that I thought some hips might become dislocated. They fanned out faster than the eye could move and quickly mopped up fistfuls of cash while dozens of wedding guests talked, drank, ate, and tapped to the beat, unaware of the heist. So many guests were jammed together that the hired dancers could readily move around like slinky pickpockets.

Garba told me later he had given Cicero and Amina $800, nearly three years' salary in Nigeria, but most of it disappeared into the ethers that starry night.

A few days later, my colleague Amina Garba came by the Durbar Hotel to visit, bringing a cotton scarf as a gift from her family. She invited me to meet her relatives, and we passed through the market on the way. Some stalls sold hand-decorated material by the meter while others had blonde crocodile clutch purses and snakeskin sandals for sale. The large cage which had previously held the grey parrot was now empty. African Greys learn words quickly; the well-trained Alex in America was one of them. Nobody had the patience to teach the Nigerian bird some Hausa, so he imitated all the delightful sounds that the children made when they frolicked close by. Other than occasional bickering from the local shop owners, that was all he had ever heard. Fortunately for the bird, a nice young couple from Germany rescued him one day. Now I am certain that he is somewhere in Germany with a decent vocabulary in high *Deutsche*, richly peppered with the exuberant sounds of young African children at play.

I was greeted warmly at Amina Garba's house which, like many houses in Nigeria, had no doors, just a curtain over the entrance. Inside, Amina's mother and the other three wives were present. One was busy breastfeeding. All of them were bulky women. In some parts of Nigeria, even if they are not wealthy, young women purposely gain weight because it gives the impression that they are "living opulently." Amina was no exception. At only 24, her size had ballooned. Once, looking at a photo of me, she exclaimed, "Tania! You look FAT!" I smiled, "Amina, in my country that is *not* a compliment."

But to her, it was. She could never understand why Westerners want to look whippet-thin and scrawny with bones protruding.

Roosters, hens, and chicks strolled at will, pecking at the faded living room carpet for discarded seeds. Goat bells rattled just outside the door while they munched on shrunken weeds. After the introductions, we sipped Fantas. Her family was so open and hospitable, the kind of people who would readily offer you the last tasty treat in the fridge. They were anxious to hear about life in America.

When I travel abroad, I always feel as if I not only represent my company and myself, but also my country. I strive to be gracious and diplomatic to citizens of other lands. Through an endless barrage of films and TV shows, the whole world knows us, or thinks they do. However, I always want to hear about their lives, trying to understand how America is viewed from their perspective.

Back at the hotel with Amina, I was packing my things in double time because I did not want to be charged for a late checkout. "Why are you in such a rush?" she asked.

"Because I don't want to be billed for another day," I replied.

"You have nothing to worry about. Everyone here knows that you are the chief's guest. And besides, the chief bought this hotel this morning."

"He did what, Amina?" I asked.

"He added this hotel to his others. The contract was signed earlier today," she replied.

Indeed, the chief had added the Durbar Hotel to his growing "empire." With no shortage of assets, the chief owned Kabo Air, two health clinics, and homes in several Nigerian cities in addition to residences in London and Miami. The profitable Kabo Oil Company produced sweet crude which has better quality than Middle Eastern oil.

One day when I wanted to cash the 80,000 naira ($1,000) check the chief had given me, the hotel clerk assured me that the bank would not give me any grief because he owned that, too. As I waited in the bank manager's office, a miniscule man strained to wheel in my entire bank balance, stacked up about thigh-high, banded in crumpled 1,000-naira stacks, for my approval. As the wide-eyed clerk looked on, the manager then counted out my 80,000-naira cash in tons of fresh notes. I kept about $20 for pocket money and signed the receipt. The new stacks of money were added to the growing pile, as the frail man wheeled it all back to the vault for, I hoped, safekeeping.

The chief treasured his fleet of cars, mostly Mercedes, with license plate numbers from "Jarma 1" up to "Jarma 7," affixed to the new boxy Mercedes SUV. I had never seen one before, neither in Europe nor the States. Everyone knew that the cars belonged to Chief Kabo. Jarman Kano, meaning "warrior of Kano," was a title bestowed to him from the emir. The chief's close friends and associates called him Jarma for short.

At Lagos Airport one day, the chief was in the mood for some real fun. Due to fly the "red eye" to his home in London that evening, he suddenly asked the British Airways agent, "Madame, how many first class seats are available for tonight's flight?"

She had twelve seats left. Waving his hands about, he said, "Let me have all of them."

His main bodyguard smiled broadly, and with permission from the chief, quickly left to inform eleven fortunate employees of the surprise trip. With his diverse entourage made up of house boys, drivers, and Kabo Air workers, all thirteen boarded the flight for London. First class was now completely full. Most were wearing colorful but simple *babarigas* made of paper-thin cotton and sandals. It was November in foggy, drizzling London.

Once, pleased with a superb job that Shehu, one of his house boys, had done, the chief impetuously rushed into his living room. With a wide smile, he presented the astonished house boy with the keys to one of his Mercedes cars, valued at around $65,000. Shehu was the envy of all the workers at the villa from then on. Thrilled to have the gleaming black Mercedes, he took friends for fun jaunts around Kano every day. Others were given a deluxe lift to work, as there was no organized public transportation. Already popular before the automotive windfall, attractive girls were nearly lined up for his attention. Soon, a peculiar noise rattled under the hood, and Shehu reluctantly took it to the mechanic. The good news? It was not anything serious, but the bad news was the cost to get it fixed would be prohibitive on his meager salary.

Hesitant to return the luxurious gift to the chief for fear of appearing ungrateful, Shehu finally listened to his friends' good advice and approached his employer. Understanding that it was an unrealistic gift, the chief gave him a somewhat battered Toyota, but one that had low mileage and would be dependable for years to come.

Chief Kabo then turned his attention to building a 30-room hotel near his guest villa. Construction was coming along nicely. They were using durable materials, the floor plan was practical, and the chief was especially proud of the gymnasium, boasting top-of-the-line equipment imported from Europe. The shiny machines were the latest for getting a great workout. The gym was kept under strict lock and key for obvious reasons. A phone line was connected to the hotel, but idiotically, only one single guest could speak at a time. The line would then be busy if anyone else called, even for an emergency.

The Chief proudly showed me the $15,000 generator imported from Italy, which would jump-start the electricity about seven seconds after the power went out. "Brownouts" are common in Nigeria. Not far from the equator, the sun usually sets around six p.m. If you lose power, you are trapped in total darkness, sometimes for a few minutes, sometimes for hours, so the generator was a welcome addition to the hotel. It always came on like clockwork after an outage. One night we lost the lights and I counted to 20 but the generator still had not kicked in. My first thought was that after spending $15,000, I certainly hoped the chief had not been ripped off. With no candles, we just stood in the dark hallway conversing.

This time, I decided to investigate. The general manager (GM) of the hotel had the personality of an electric eel. He was nasty with most the employees, whom he considered inferior; something I detested. But when the chief came around, he quickly changed gears, quickly transitioning to symbolic idol-worship. He kept bowing towards the chief and bending over to show his availability to fulfill any request at a moment's notice. Leaning over and constantly fluffing the chief's robes, he was the *uber* lackey. I loved to imitate all his baloney when he was not around, to the sheer delight of the hotel employees, most of whom I knew by name. I had them all in stitches, imitating the way wealthy people walk in Nigeria. I stuck my snout up in the air, positioning my hands behind the body as they did, and walking with a flow, puffing out to make myself appear taller. If I happened to be wearing a billowing skirt, I exaggerated the moves by flapping the material. Those kids needed a break, and I loved to try and make them laugh. Nigerians of any tribe rarely lack a sense of humor.

Everyone knew the chief's schedule, as their lives revolved around it. If he was in town, you had better be on your toes, but the minute he went on a trip, everyone slacked off for a well-deserved rest. On one of these occasions, the GM became a schemer in the chief's absence.

During the blackout, I banged on the GM's door. He knew that he was not exactly one of my favorites, but by now I had Nigerian allies all over the place: hotel staff, Kabo Air employees, and the house boys. "Madame?" he asked, answering the door.

He had obviously been sleeping. It was so dark in the hall I could hardly see. We had now been without electricity for five hours; no a/c, nothing. Giving him the benefit of the doubt, I asked, "GM, do you have any idea why the electricity has been off for so long? Is there anything wrong with the generator?"

I explained that the chief had shown it to me, and knowing that it was new, I wondered if it was defective. It that was true, we needed to tell the chief upon his return so that the Italians could send him a replacement for the $15,000 machine.

Now that I look back on it, his answer was comical. Sensing that I knew what was going on around Kano, he fessed up right away, even though I had approached him in a non-accusatory way. It would not do any good to hoodwink me because I would figure it out, anyway. No doubt he knew how close I was to the chief.

"I was a bit low on naira," he began.

"Yes, and?" I inquired.

"I siphoned the diesel fuel out of the generator, took it to the market, and got some money for it," he explained.

"You did *what?*" I asked. "Do you seriously mean to tell me that first, you took advantage of the chief's absence, second, you took something that didn't belong to you, and now you have deprived the entire hotel of electricity?"

Looking ashamed and fidgeting with his robe, he replied, "Well, I didn't think I would get caught. I didn't expect us to lose power this evening. My plan was to replace the fuel before the chief got back from London."

Not only was this guy the biggest kowtower in Kano, but now he had deprived at least 30 hotel guests of their lights and much-needed air conditioning. The nerve! "So, GM, can you get us some fuel tonight?"

"No, Madame, there won't be anyone at the market."

So, everyone retired until the morning when the fuel was hastily replaced. One had to wonder what other tricks he had up his sleeve, but for the time being, I felt that he would be watching his step.

My rascal Kai

10

My Chimpanzee Roommate

"Where is the kiddo?" demanded the chief as I followed him into the Sultan's Suite of his new hotel in Kano.

On the veranda was a collection of kids' toys—a cheap plastic tricycle, some balls, a tiny swing hanging from the ceiling. Surely the chief was not annoyed with someone's innocent little kid, was he? "Does anyone know where Daisy is?" he asked the house boys.

"She's downstairs, chief," but I did not hear any child-like sounds.

I followed him downstairs and instantly saw one of my biggest critter wishes of all time sitting right there on the carpet, playing with two male housekeepers.

Daisy was not a spoiled child; she was a spoiled *chimp*! And a young one at that, about two years old. From my childhood, I had always had two big "critter" dreams—one, to swim with dolphins in the open sea, and second, to play with a chimp. Yasser once took me to the East Coast of the Sinai Peninsula in Egypt to frolic with wild dolphins in the Red Sea. Now I was about to realize the second dream, to party with a chimp. In the States, they always seem to be either in zoos or sadly locked away in small cages for research, so it was almost impossible to interact with one in an uncontrolled environment.

The chief instinctively knew that I was a real animal lover, and I was going to have her all to myself. The housekeepers were super glad too, because she was more than just a handful, getting into everything like young kids do. But she also added another dimension to the "terrible twos," as you could never tell her "no" concerning *anything*.

Naturally, I wanted to pet her, but an inner voice said, "not so fast." I sat down next to her but did not touch her for ten minutes. Off the top of my head, I tried to recall anything that I had ever heard about simians. They have eight times the strength of humans, so I planned to proceed carefully. I just observed her while sending her loving vibes in the process. Finally, I took one of her small hands and gently flipped it over. Just like me, she had long fingers, long nails (no polish yet), and all the lines for a good palm reading. Her palm also had a lengthy lifeline like mine, thanks no doubt to my maternal grandmother, Mildred, who lived to be a staggering 109 years old.

Daisy and I bonded immediately. She blew me away. I could never take my eyes off her, just as if she was my little kid. The old expression "more fun than a barrel of monkeys" rang so true. But I certainly did not need a barrel, as Daisy had plenty of energy all rolled up into one neat package. She was a darling and I would bet anyone cold, hard cash that she instinctively knew it, too. I quickly nicknamed her "Kai." This Hausa word has no literal translation in English, but the closest would be to express surprise. When my Hausa friends spoke in their native language, I often heard sentences punctuated with the word "kai," so I asked what it meant. If someone hears either good or bad news, the general acknowlegment will contain the word "kai." No question, the young chimp had many surprises coming my way, so the nickname seemed appropriate.

Once I was all settled into the suite, Kai was a great diversion for another reason. The satellite hook-up had not been installed, so I was deprived of cable news, but Kai easily filled in that void. In a way, *she* became the news. Every night I put Kai out to snooze on the veranda, where she slept peacefully. Every morning, the houseboy brought me toast, African coffee, and fruit for breakfast while Kai watched with her face pressed hard against the glass, pleading for me to let her in. You would have thought that I was sitting amidst a banana plantation the way she looked at me so plaintively. She was never restrained in any way, so once I let her in, she owned the place, and ran around berserk until she got either bored or tired. She was not always so hyperactive, but I had no way of determining her energy level for the day until she was already inside; too late for me. My camera was always at the ready,

I never wanted to miss a shot. She was indeed a "walking photo op."

Only once did she bite me, or more accurately, "time stamp" my hand, although it drew a little blood. She had gone for the phone and was yanking the cord out of the wall. If she succeeded, it could have been weeks before it could be fixed. Reaching over, I carefully took it from her. No matter, she was in charge and at some level knew it. She bit me at lightning speed in between the thumb and forefinger, then took off down the hallway. Even though I am not a mother, I did what parents sometimes do—I gave her "the freeze" for the rest of the day, no playing whatsoever. She soon got the message. After all, I was her new buddy, and not a bad one at that, constantly giving her attention. While I read the newspaper, she just sat next to me on the sofa making soft noises like a young child.

Kai really needed a good mentor. As I discovered later, she came from a traumatized past, just as many human children do. Up in a tree among the thick jungle of the Yankari Reserve, she had been on her mother's back when poachers had shot her mother dead. Falling from the tree, the tiny Kai was instantly an orphan. Sometime later, while undergoing a health checkup, the vet observed on the x-rays that she had shrapnel embedded in her collarbone area from the horrific incident. At the market, the chief's people saw her and brought her to the hotel where she would be safe.

At night, taking a cue from humans, and not necessarily simians, she would grab several blankets, making a nest along with some stuffed toys. It would not be long before she fell asleep. During the day, I was grateful that she had a keen sense of the perimeters of the hotel compound when I took her outside. God forbid she decided to go over the wall, barreling towards the busy street, but she never did. Somehow Kai sensed that it was beyond her realm of safety.

She did climb the mango tree one day, right next to the wall, shitting with abandon as she ascended the tree. I watched her closely as she stayed near the top for some time, just looking at the view, I guess. As she came back down the trunk of the tree, she had obviously forgotten her earlier transgression. She began to slip left and right, like coasting down a greasy pole. She looked so terribly annoyed. Her screwed-up face had the expression of disgust as if someone had played a bad practical joke on her. She began to take the stuff off her feet with her hands but quickly discovered that that was not the solution. Stinky and fed up, her face bunched up in frustration, she jumped off the branch onto the pavement with ease, gladly skipping the remainder of the slippery trunk, then proceeded to wipe the caca from her hands onto the sidewalk.

Soon, I was walking around the compound with her riding on my hip. One of the houseboys, quite entertained by the simian hitchhiker, called to me from across the courtyard. "Madame, she likes you so much because you are white!"

Now it was my turn to laugh. "Come on you guys, she likes me because I am sympathetic and understanding to her."

She was a great passenger, as well. I really enjoyed her company and having fun with her. However, when I grew tired of the piggybacking, it was difficult to get her *off*. Once again, it was going to be on her terms. "What to do?" as the Brits say. I asked the house boy to get some bananas. That would do it, I figured. But when he came back down, he did a goofy thing and handed the bananas straight to Kai. "Don't do *that!*" I protested, "I will *never* get her off me!"

Taking a large banana, I tossed it some feet away. Reluctantly climbing down, she scurried over to get it.

Two months later, the hotel officially opened and Kai had to be sent away. She had become such an integral part of my daily life that it was so difficult to let her go. The Chief had found a marvelous reserve owned by an American couple in Southern Nigeria. Kai was taken there and given a complete physical upon "check-in." Reassured that she did not have HIV or any other disease, I flashed back on the day she bit my hand and felt relieved. She passed her physical with flying colors. She also had plenty of creatures to romp with, including the couple's retriever and two other male chimps her age whom she was introduced to on her first day.

Sadly, I said goodbye to my exhilarating friend with a gentle back rub. I missed her terribly, and the new guests in the hotel were no consolation. Her antics had kept me endlessly amused, and now there was a large void in my everyday routine.

True to her nature and her exposure to humans, on her first night at the reserve, the male chimps settled in on tree branches for the night's rest. Kai, on the other hand, went around collecting her blankets and stuffed toys. Choosing a favorite branch, she climbed upward. She then arranged a little nest for herself before settling in for a fitful sleep, just as she had always done on my veranda.

11

Visiting a Leper Colony

Chief Kabo had cooked up another surprise for me. He was about to offer me a job with his airline, Kabo Air. One day there was a vigorous knock at my door.

"Madame, what are your plans? How long will you be in Nigeria?" he asked.

"Jarma, I'm traveling up to Sokoto for a few days to meet with the sultan's brother Maazu. Then I'm scheduled to fly back to Cairo."

"How would you like to work for Kabo Air?" he asked. "The crews already know you from the Hajj, and you could even bring one of your colleagues to Nigeria. I'll pay both of you to train my employees."

My thoughts zoomed into overdrive, but I did not have to think much before saying yes.

The compensation part cropped up. The chief suggested payment in a combination of naira and dollars, but I insisted the entire salary be in greenbacks, the American kind. "What salary are you expecting?" Jarma asked.

"Three thousand dollars a month," I replied, without hesitation.

"That's a high salary," he said.

Nothing like negotiating over a few thousand bucks with someone whose income is over $20 mil a year. "Jarma, you must know that $3,000 is what we got paid during the Hajj," I added.

"All right, three thousand it is, but don't tell anyone the amount."

I could certainly understand the secrecy. The Kabo Air pilots would be furious if they found out. Their approximate monthly salary was only $750 by comparison.

My mind began to race with all kinds of exciting thoughts. I could not wait to get back to Cairo to tell my boyfriend Yasser all the details and to invite him to Kano. But first I had to travel to Sokoto. Ever since flying there for the Hajj, I had contemplated building a small shelter for the lepers. They are almost completely overlooked by authorities and everyone else. Living together in a wooded compound outside of town, they are shunned from the entire population.

MD Hassan introduced me to his architect, Chinidou, who created some blueprints for me in double time. He understood exactly what I wanted, remarkably drafting my ideas into the blueprints. Bello then arranged for me to meet the Emir of Sokoto's younger brother, Al-Hajji Maazu Abu Bakar. My plan was to try and talk Maazu into getting his brother the sultan to donate the land for my shelter.

Sokoto in the northwest is oppressively dusty and hot with deep, red-colored earth that can be seen from the sky. As part of sub-Saharan Africa, it sometimes suffers from great sandstorms. Referred to as "Harmattan," the unfortunate winds blast dusty particles into villages, which can cause asthmatic attacks.

On my first day there, I was fortunate to be introduced to a kind missionary couple from New Zealand named Robin and Sean, who specialized in treating leprosy. A handsome couple with blonde hair and blue eyes, they had two fetching young children with the same coloring, a boy and a girl, born in Nigeria. With all the things that could go wrong, I really admired this couple for taking the chance of bearing children in a place that could possibly have a serious shortage of *anything* that might be needed. The children had completely grown up in Africa. It was charming to see them converse, interact, and play with all the little Hausa-Fulani kids in their dialect; so blonde by dark-skinned children. These well-adjusted kids were unique in a place where most people had never seen either blue or green eyes.

The next day, Robin and Sean drove me to the leper compound, explaining the basics of leprosy along the way. I wanted to see how shelters were run in Nigeria. It was much nicer than the one I later visited near Kano. Tall trees surrounded the compound, keeping it somewhat cool, a real advantage in the oppressive desert heat. The lepers raised animals to eat and tended an organic vegetable garden. Living in sizeable grass huts, their community appeared to be a society within a society, not a bad one at that, considering the circumstances.

However, two things upset me—the severe shortage of medical personnel and the chronic lack of equipment. The examining room had broken glass all over the floor from used slides, and the microscope had been dropped and was inoperable. Both the slides and microscope were essential for detecting the bacillus that lepers have. Patients' records were strewn all over. Without diagnosis, there was a good chance that some people living there did not have leprosy. Overwhelmed, the few medical staff members were just dealing the best they could with the little they had. Nobody could be treated properly without even basic equipment. These people were the forgotten ones.

Many children of the patients were free of the disease but, still isolated from the world, ran and hid, played tag, and carried on with all the games that kids play everywhere. You would have thought they did not have a care in the world. Robin and Sean examined the disenfranchised lepers as they patiently stood in line out in the garden. They had such tremendous heartfelt respect for the lepers. Even with a bit of a language barrier, the patients instinctively knew that the New Zealanders were doing everything within their power to improve their health and the general situation on the compound.

It was a great respite to join Robin and Sean at their place for dinner. Willowy trees surrounded their home and a well in the garden provided "fresh" water. A large porch with comfortable chairs beckoned you to enjoy the view, but you had to brave the aggressive mosquitoes. Dinner was a delicious stew. I was amazed at how Robin, like a wizard, could fix such tasty food with the limited supplies in Sokoto. She had it down to a science. They produced a bottle of vodka, quite a rarity in that part of the country. We laughed as Sean poured us drinks.

"Where in the hell did you guys find a bottle of vodka in Sokoto?" I asked, wasting no time in taking a sip of the vodka tonic.

"One learns quickly to hoard supplies," Sean replied.

"We've actually had it for quite some time, and just drag it with us to the next place for special occasions," Robin added.

Pretty soon their destination would be Christchurch, New Zealand. Robin was expecting again, and it was time to head back home. As I congratulated her, she said they were both wondering how their children would adjust in New Zealand. They had spent their entire young lives in Nigeria, having adopted all the customs known to the Hausas. It would be fascinating to discover how they would settle down in the land of their ancestors.

It was wonderful getting to know Sean and Robin during my days in Sokoto, and I treasured our time together. It was just as if we had grown up in the same neighborhood. There is a special type of camaraderie that "ex-pats" develop when far away from their homelands. The Nigerians were also pleased that they had brought the white people together with our concern for the lepers. Bidding my kind hosts goodbye, I rode back to the hotel to prepare to meet with Maazu, the sultan's brother, the next morning.

☙

Bello picked me up and gave me a briefing on the way. "He's quite religious," Bello began, "but he's a good man, and popular. He doesn't mind being the younger brother of the sultan." Bello winked. "The sultan gets a lot of attention you know, Tania."

In northern Nigeria, the emir, sultan, and certain chiefs rule the roost. They have the power to change laws with the mere signature of a document, wielding an incredible domain that stretches way back into Nigeria's history when Kano was located on the main trading route between West and East Africa.

Bello told me that Maazu always wore white. "Do you have any other pointers, Bello? Should I call him 'your excellency?'"

"No, Tania, you can call him Maazu. It'll be fine, both of you will get along well."

I was ushered into Maazu's office and, true to form, he was wearing a white cotton muslin *riga* trimmed in gold. He stood up to shake my hand, and I decided to be a little formal, addressing him as Al-Hajji (a pilgrim who has made more than one trip to the Hajj) Maazu. He liked my greeting. It immediately established respect and an understanding of their culture. Clutching the blueprints for the shelter, I was anxious for him to see them.

"One day my dream is to build a shelter for the lepers here in Sokoto in honor of my parents and godmother," I began.

Maazu wondered what a godmother is to Christians, so I explained that Elva had been my parents' close friend. As I settled in, I wanted him to know that I had done my homework and had already visited the leper shelter where Robin and Sean treated the patients. "Is that place not good enough for the people?" Maazu inquired, looking a bit puzzled.

It was essential for me to be diplomatic. Even though the compound left much to be desired, I had to be careful how I expressed my thoughts. Describing how the patients raise their own animals for food in a peaceful atmosphere, I then made him aware of the equipment that needed replacing. I also explained that at whatever point my shelter was built, it would also have an outpatient clinic to service the people. Who wants to spend time in a medical facility if they do not have to?

Maazu carefully unrolled the blueprints to "Nikelva Glenn." The name was derived from the three most important people in my life—my mother Nike, my godmother Elva, and my father Glenn, who are all long gone.

Before they were completely unrolled, he said, "Tania, I must ask . . ."

My first thought was "Oh, no, I've blown something!"

Maazu was choosing his words cautiously. He was not quite certain how to phrase his sentence for fear of insulting me, as I realized a few moments later. "When you open this shelter, as you call it, you aren't going to . . ." Maazu was searching for the correct words, even though his command of English was excellent. Getting right to the point, he belted out, "Well, you won't bring in a group of Christian missionaries to try and convert our people, will you?"

Throwing my head back, I laughed out loud. This was not about converting people; it was about healing them. Maazu looked relieved but also curious as to why I found that so funny. "Maazu," I said, still smiling, "if you unroll the entire sheet, you will see that I have instructed the architect to include a mosque right in the structure!"

A look came over his face that I will never forget. As I pointed to the mosque area, light from the desk seemed to go straight up to

Maazu's face as it brightened up with a luminous glow. In that instant, he realized that *baturia* at least had *some* idea of the Hausa culture. We had connected.

Maazu assured me that he would speak to the sultan about donating the land, while recommending me. Before we parted, Maazu had one more question. "Tania, how long are you going to be in Sokoto?" he asked.

"I must get back to Kano to fly to Cairo later this week. Why, Maazu?" I asked.

"Oh, I was just going to ask you if you would like to join me tomorrow for a road trip to Niger, our neighboring country. I have some friends up there and I would like for you to come. You would have the opportunity to meet some real interesting people."

"Thank you for the nice invitation, Maazu, but I really must get back to Kano," I said.

"That's too bad," he replied, sounding disappointed.

I gratefully thanked him for his time. It had been a productive meeting, but I knew that if I had accepted his offer to visit Niger, I might very well have come back quite a different girl than when I had left. When you visit unusual places, you really must develop a heightened awareness, especially when traveling alone in Africa.

Besides, I had the joyful duty of thinking about how I was going to surprise Yasser when I returned to Cairo, where I would invite him to join me in working for the chief.

༼ༀ༽

12

"High Tea" with the Emir's Wife Gogo

The ride back to Kano took hours. Without organized public transportation, you go to the car park in the center of town and ask which car is headed in your direction. Locating a station wagon, I waited several hours. When the ninth person appeared, we finally left, jammed in like refugees, cheek to jowl.

The stench of petrol hit our nostrils and I wondered if the driver, an ordinary guy just trying to make a living, had spilled some as he was gassing up. Not so. A large plastic container of gas sloshed back and forth right behind my head as we belted along the bumpy road. It was directly under the hot midday sun beaming straight down through the back window. "Don't even think . . ." I decided.

What should have been a four-hour drive dragged on for six, although not entirely a mundane journey. The car stopped so that the men could get out, face east towards Mecca, and pray, while the ladies wandered about to chat with the locals while drinking Cokes. A group of five Fulani girls approached us, imaginatively dressed as if they were just leaving for a special event. Two of them had their hair meticulously fashioned into neat, creative cornrows decorated with beads. They looked shy, but reluctantly agreed to a photo. Wearing everyday customary clothes, they could have easily graced any United Nations reception by our standards.

More tribespeople came along, all staring at me. Located halfway between Sokoto and Kano, they were not accustomed to seeing

Caucasians. A passenger from our car translated for me. "What are you looking at?" she asked them in Fulani.

"*Baturia* (white woman)," they replied.

"Why do you keep staring at her?" she asked, "Haven't you seen a white woman before?"

The tallest lady stepped forward to get a closer look. "Not in about a year," was her answer.

"Then, take one last look and scram!" said the passenger.

I giggled as I felt the scrutiny—like a bug in a bug box, perhaps.

A giant falling star with a long trail cascaded down through the midnight-blue sky. I called it to the attention of my fellow passengers. A big believer in signs, I knew that something positive was about to happen.

Back in Kano, I returned to my favorite restaurant. La Locanda was run by a tall, slender Filipina lady whose hair was blue-black and so long that she could sit on it. Esperanza, or SP for short, had married a Nigerian man, and they had two children. Now they had gone their separate ways. She was happy to remain in Kano to be with her kids. Remembering her restaurant from our Hajj visit three years earlier, I dined there often. It was a retreat for ex-pats and a 20-minute walk from the hotel. I never felt creepy about walking down that road alone, even on a moonless night when it was pitch black. The atmosphere was peaceful, and nobody ever bothered me.

One day SP asked me if I would like to have tea at the palace with the Emir of Kano's second wife, Hajjia Amina, fondly called Gogo. I did not hesitate a second before saying I would love to go. Gogo's own grandfather had been the Emir of Katsina, so she was from nobility herself. The Emir had enjoyed all the accoutrements of the title and position, which included four wives and a staggering 82 concubines, all vying for his attention.

Our taxi dropped us off in front of the palace. The formal greeting party was there: dozens of official guards, all dressed in their customary robes of green and red topped off with large turbans. When spotting a cluster of these guards anywhere in the North, it always signals that the emir is either arriving or leaving. But I was really surprised by what I saw next. When I had heard "emir's palace," I had assumed that it would be an elegant marble edifice. The compound was extensive, but the buildings had all been constructed out of irregular *mud brick*. The entire area was something from the pages of the *National Geographic*, which you might see in Mali or even more remote African places. The site was ancient, so in its own unique way, it was interesting to explore for its cultural import.

Our sandals slapped on the stones leading up to Gogo's house. The garden was full of lush bushes, tropical flowers, and even cotton plants you could pick. A lithe house girl answered the door, but Gogo was right behind her, anxious to welcome us inside. Her face was full of light, with finely chiseled features and dancing eyes. I instantly knew that she was very intuitive. She hugged SP. When I greeted her as "Hajjia Amina," she asked me to call her Gogo, which endeared her to me right away.

As we drank sweet tea and sampled various pastries, she poured out a good portion of her life story. I was transfixed. I already knew that one day I would write a book, but if only I had carried a tape recorder with me that afternoon. With so many fascinating stories to tell, she clearly wanted to engage in some animated conversation. For just three women, we were a rather eclectic trio: the psychic Gogo from an ancient royal African family who had accepted her fate; the hard-working SP, half a world away from her island home in the Pacific; and me, discovering this multi-faceted land called Nigeria.

Gogo continually laughed as she told us her own story, and I was right alongside the journey with her. When she was six, some high official at a palace party asked her what she wanted to be when she grew up. Without missing a beat, she astonished the adults by declaring that she wanted to be a *nun*. Imagine their reaction to that statement coming from a youngster of a well-established, traditional Muslim royal family in the '50s. When pressed for details, the little girl could not recall where she had conceived the idea.

Later she decided that she wanted to be a flight attendant for Nigerian Airways, no matter what. A gregarious soul, she was hoping to explore the world on her own terms, just as airline people do. She knew well that I would be tickled by that, and truly enjoyed telling her story. However, her dreams were cut way too short. Becoming serious, she told us about how when she turned 18, her life changed drastically.

That year, the teenaged Amina was abruptly informed that she would marry her cousin, the emir. At 48 years old, he was 30 years her senior and already had one wife. Her dreams of traveling the world and attending university were crushed in an instant. Realizing that her future would be completely out of her control, she burst out crying, devastated at hearing the proclamation. A favorite female cousin tried hard to comfort her. With an arm around her shoulder she said, "Amina, you have always wanted to perform the Hajj. Now that you'll be marrying the emir, you can go to the Kingdom as often as you like, a remarkable gift," which helped to brighten her spirits.

Her own mother had been betrothed at the tender age of five. Gogo told us with resignation, "We were all born here on the palace grounds. We will live our entire lives here and will die here."

She was about 48 years old, and she had lived in the palace compound for three decades. For the previous two years, according to their tradition, she had not even been beyond the gate of her own garden.

Despite her situation, she made the best of her fate. Outgoing, clever, and innovative, she engaged in a practice that was most unusual considering her elevated status in Kano. She arranged for the palace drivers to pick up underprivileged ladies from a nearby village and bring them to the palace. There, she taught them practical skills—weaving baskets, making bags, creating small fashionable items—learning things to help them earn an income. They were served sweets and hot tea while also engaging in conversation with Gogo; quite a treat under any circumstances.

Once the emir walked in unannounced, and the women, completely taken aback, jumped to their feet. Some gave him the special Hausa wave, and a few pulled their scarves closer to their faces, looking down at the floor in humility. Others were more verbal, greeting his excellency in Hausa. Incredibly, these naïve village women had been unexpectedly thrust into the presence of someone who, by American measure, would have the total power of a senator, governor, and bishop all rolled into one.

Gogo told us that many of the ladies remarked that they felt "led" to visit her at the palace. She was a dear; a most unusual soul caught up in restrictive circumstances. She was also gifted psychically, which was clear to me from the onset. She animatedly described how she "traveled" in her dreams to other nations. She "observed" faraway places, a comfort to her since she could not tour the globe as she had once fervently dreamed.

Hmmm, Gogo was astral traveling all over the world! I have always called it "the cheapest way to explore." She "saw" things in other lands which she remembered the next day. She also visualized having fun with the guests who came to visit her. I am sure that is what the ladies meant when they confided how they felt so intensely drawn to Gogo at the palace. I believe that they were picking up on her external "vibes."

With long hours to fill, she watched a lot of TV, telling us how much she admired Oprah. She loved to listen and learn from Oprah's diverse and fascinating guests. She always relished seeing what Oprah's subject du jour was. Smiling, I said, "Gogo, I'm certain that Oprah would love to get ahold of *you*!" We laughed, knowing that Gogo's story would make an extraordinary interview.

Pleased to discover that I had been studying Islam at the mosque two blocks away from my home in Virginia, she admitted that she had been curious about Christianity since she was a little girl. Over the years she always looked for the similarities, not the differences, between our two religions, just like me.

Because Gogo was part of Nigeria's royal family, I mentioned some of the princes and princesses I had known, understanding that she would readily be able to identify with them. She was so much fun to converse with, I just wanted to delight her with some connections which I felt she would relate to. If she had not had such a restricted life, I am certain that she would have been gallivanting around the world, meeting the royal families of other countries in Europe and the Middle East. The aristocracy from various nations easily become acquainted as they belong to an especially exclusive club. On an international "circuit," many members of royal families continually come across each other in the world's coveted and exclusive locales. They have so much in common, whether they are rulers, figureheads, or in exile.

We discussed my school, Millfield, where the brothers Prince Turki Ibn Saud and Prince Mashour Ibn Saud from Saudi Arabia had studied. Crown Prince Mahidol Vajiralongkorn of Thailand, now His Majesty King Rama X, was my classmate our first year. Princess Sihin Asfa-Wossen and her sister, Princess Mary Asfa-Wossen of Ethiopia, were also in our circle of friends. Prince Turki and I had reconnected just a few months earlier for the first time in 27 years. We had so much to catch up on, as we had shared many of the same friends from Africa and the Middle East. Our reunion had been so memorable, as they always are with old friends. I told Gogo how Prince Turki had described performing the Hajj and how elated he was to have worshipped from *inside* the Holy Kaaba.

I have remained in touch with the gracious Asfa-Wossen princesses since school. The last time I saw their father, the crown prince, was at their home in Virginia shortly before his passing. I had asked Sihin if it was all right to hug him goodbye, not wanting to breach any kind of protocol. With a slight nod and smile from her, I gave him a long warm hug. I was so glad that I did because I would never see him again.

Gogo was a time traveler and soaked up stories from other nations. She listened intently as I recalled meeting Mother Teresa at her home in Calcutta. I also described my journey to Medjugorje in Bosnia, a powerful site for Christians. Visionaries believe in the miracles there, where Mother Mary reportedly appeared in 1981. Gogo was glad to hear that former President Jimmy Carter had an acute interest in Nigeria. Several projects at his foundation in Atlanta are dedicated to eradicating malaria, guinea worm, and river blindness. I had spoken with him at an event in Washington, D.C., and readily saw the sincerity in his eyes as he described the foundation's work.

I described to her the lively and colorful Kashmiris, whom we flew out of New Delhi to Saudi Arabia to perform the Hajj. Speaking about Jerusalem, I told her about Khaleel, a kind Palestinian Muslim who took me to the Dome of the Rock at the Al Aqsa Mosque. I related that story to her because that mosque is the third holiest place in Islam after those in Mecca and Medina.

Inside the mosque, I had placed my hands on the rock that fell back to Earth as the prophet Mohammed (Peace be upon Him) ascended to heaven. I could feel rays of intense white light energy fanning out all over the globe. Judging by the intent look on her face as I told the story, I saw that Gogo and I had connected powerfully on all levels. I also knew that she would like to hear about Jebel Musa (Moses's Mountain) in the middle of the Sinai Peninsula, where Yasser had taken me earlier that summer. It is a holy place to both Muslims and Christians, where the faithful of both religions come together in harmony. It takes hours to climb all the way to the top of the rocky mountain. At dawn, everyone watches the sun rise over the desert. This is the exact spot where scholars believe that Moses (Musa) received the Ten Commandments. I sincerely hope that Gogo will visit one day. Being so enlightened, she would enjoy Jebel Musa immensely.

I was certain that if Gogo had not been so confined, she would have experienced a life of exploration like mine. If she could not go out into the world, I was certainly hoping to bring a slice to her.

Nearing sundown and getting close to prayer time, we prepared to leave. Walking into the garden, I imagined how amazing it would be to bring Yasser to meet Gogo, a true African royal. I was anxious for him to enjoy Nigeria with all its facets and wanted to introduce it to him head-on. He was Muslim as well, so now he would see how West African Muslims lived differently from Egyptians.

"Gogo, may I ask you something?" I began.

"Why, of course, Tania, what is it?"

"Well, my friend will be coming from Egypt soon to join me here in Nigeria to work for Jarma. Could I bring them by to visit you? I would just love that."

Gogo, with that ever-pleasant look on her face, replied, "Why, of course, Tania, I would love to meet her. You can bring her anytime you like."

"Oh, it is not a lady, Gogo, it is my boyfriend Yasser," I said.

Laughing at my innocence and ignorance of the palace rules, Gogo informed me in a gentle voice, "Tania, I can't entertain men of any kind, other than the emir, in my house, not even my own relatives. Once a man, even a cousin or nephew, turns 18, they are prohibited from visiting me here. I have several young male relatives whom I haven't seen since they turned 18. I miss them terribly, but this is our custom."

Hugging us goodbye, the incandescent Gogo escorted us to the gate leading from her garden to the palace grounds. "This is as far as I can go," she sighed. Then brightening up a little, she added, "Oh, Tania, you are most welcome to visit me any time you wish."

Counting our 12k!

13

Reunited with Yasser

On the flight to visit Yasser in Cairo, while over southern Libya, I reminisced about the first time I met him. I clearly remembered Easter Sunday, 1995, when our crew flew from Karachi, Pakistan, back to Jeddah, Saudi Arabia. Those roundtrips took 22 hours, beginning with a 4 a.m. pick-up in the lobby. Reaching Karachi, we always raced off the plane to spend our earnings in Duty Free. Having the tastes of a gypsy woman, I prowled the endless boutiques, admiring the brightly-colored national costumes called *shalwar kameez*. In the late '60s, when I lived in England, I would have grabbed the entire rack. As it is, I own nine of them in a riot of color. The detailed jewelry, endless silk clothes, cobra shoes, wallets and belts, onyx chess sets—nothing escaped our scrutiny. We dragged it *all* onboard our Boeing 747.

My roomie Donna purchased a full-sized trunk inlaid with brass, then hired two brawny Pakistani men to carry it on board. They hoisted it up the skinny spiral staircase to the upper deck then secured it with seat belts. If we had encountered turbulence, and it had gone flying, any object in its path would have been smashed, human or not. That heirloom trunk was so solid it will outlast any of us. Looking around, I even found a suitable present for Chief Kabo. That is how I became acquainted with Yasser. What unique gift do you give to someone whose annual income is more than $20 million? Why, a 75-rupee ($2.50) gift, of course.

I do not think anybody ever gave the chief anything. In most countries, I have observed that people just assume that the wealthy already have everything they need. In addition, these tightwads, or "cling-ons" as I call them, often sit back when the restaurant bill arrives, a non-verbal message that they are expecting to be treated to dinner. That body language annoys me. The wealthy love gifts and being remembered as much as anyone else.

"Do you know what that says in Arabic?" Yasser asked in a soft voice, leaning in to take a closer look at the hand-carved onyx. "It says *Mashallah*."

I had no idea of the meaning. He explained that the word is used to invoke God's protection when expressing admiration for somebody or something. If I visited someone's beautifully decorated home, I could say "*Mashallah*" to them as a compliment.

In the meantime, the 6'4" attractive Egyptian was engaging my curiosity. Yasser was one of our translators. We flew to Turkey, India, Pakistan, Egypt, and Sudan in addition to many other nations, so native speakers were an essential part of our crew. They were invaluable to us, not only in assisting with the languages, but also in explaining the various regional customs. We naturally worked well with them, as they were a great asset. They also lived in our compound in Jeddah, Saudi Arabia, so we knew them on a personal level.

Yasser always stood out among the crew with an approachable demeanor, and the passengers often stopped him to ask questions. His voice had a well-polished tone over the PA when he read the travel prayer in Arabic to our 480 passengers. Always looking forward to hearing it, I never grew tired of the verbal presentation Yasser made, asking Allah to bless the passengers and crew on board, and their loved ones.

I had been admiring the chief's gift when Yasser joined me on the jump seat. He had bought the same onyx carving for himself. We discovered how we both love adventure and traveling to unusual places, so there was plenty to discuss. Yasser is also Piscean, so we shared similar energies, attractions, and dislikes, too.

His brown eyes kept twinkling at me as we laughed and joked about various things, while I thought *he couldn't possibly be interested in me, but it certainly feels like he is flirting big time.* The reason? Yasser was 28 years old. I was 43; a fifteen-year difference. I could not imagine that he saw me as a potential girlfriend, but he did.

In the weeks that followed our relationship deepened, as we visited many out-of-the-way places. Things did not have to be discussed between us; they were just understood. Mediums refer to this as "vibrating on the same frequency."

Now, flying from Kano to Cairo, I was really looking forward to this new experience of having Yasser come to Nigeria. That is, if I could talk him into it.

⌒୭

Cairo Airport was bustling and raucous as always. Itching to get out of the noise and into the car to tell Yasser about Chief Kabo's offer I gushed, "Yasser, you'll never guess what!" I was hellbent on a mission to persuade him, even if he was reluctant. "I've told you about Chief Kabo, right? Well, he has offered me a job to train his crews, and I can bring a colleague. I'd love for you to join me. Yasser, it'll be such an experience! I know so many people now and have a much better sense of what's going on. What do you say?"

He hesitated. "Tania, I'm not quite sure."

We climbed four flights of stairs to the flat where his mother and three sisters were waiting to give me welcome hugs. As we sipped Cokes and munched on sweet cookies, they asked about Nigeria. There was so much to say about the journey, but I was almost in sales pitch mode. It would be so much more fun if Yasser came to Nigeria. Besides, he would be paid extremely well. His mother asked about the salary.

"Three thousand dollars a month," I replied.

Politely and silently, they looked at each other in a non-believing way, like they *wished* I was telling the truth. The wages were sky-high by their standards for a flight attendant, so it seemed as if I was stretching the facts. In Cairo, a *doctor's* beginning salary was 1,500 Egyptian pounds ($300). "The chief and I agreed on $3,000 a month because that is what we were paid during the Hajj," I assured them.

⌒୭

"Come on, Mohammed! Please drive a little faster," I said to my driver, "I want to see Yasser get off the plane!"

At Kano airport in Nigeria, I ran up to the highest deck so that I would be able to spot Yasser the minute he disembarked the Egypt Air jet. For this special occasion, I had selected a deep purple flowing silk dress to wear with a gold metallic belt and gold sandals to match. Each passenger took forever to get off. Finally, he emerged into the sunlit doorway, wearing a crisp pale green jacket with beige trousers. At his height, my handsome Egyptian was easy to spot. The Nigerian experience was about to test his flexibility, as well.

We stayed in the hotel where I had babysat Kai, located a few minutes walk from the chief's spacious guest villa. Run by a staff of 30 employees, I had befriended most of them, but Isaac and Titus were my favorites. I could not have foreseen how valuable their friendship would prove to be later. They had the pulse on what was happening at the guest villa; knowledge that would be extremely helpful to us in the coming months.

⌒ෙ

"I'm from Egypt, but I'm also an African," the dashing Yasser began as we introduced ourselves to Chief Kabo's 65 flight attendants in the training classroom.

Every Nigerian gal in that room fell in love with him the instant they heard those words. It is unusual to hear someone from North Africa refer to themselves as African. Usually, they will call themselves Egyptian or Arab. It was a complement to our fellow flight attendants, which they immediately recognized. His graciousness to them made him irresistible. They were so impressed with Yasser, in fact, a few of them made strong advances toward him, as if I was invisible. Olive-skinned, tall, and affable, he captivated their imaginations. They wiggled their hips and flashed their eyes at him when they figured I would not notice.

The time came for Yasser to meet Chief Kabo, and a Mercedes arrived to pick us up. The chief could be moody, but as he greeted us, I was relieved to see that he was not testy. Yasser and the chief hit it off right away as Yasser described his life in Cairo and how we had met while flying together. It was time for prayer, and the chief asked Yasser to join about ten of them in the living room to pray together on the large Persian carpet. Taking off his shoes, he entered the salon. I was relieved to see that this was going to work out on all fronts, or so it appeared at the time.

We then flew down to Garba's office at the airport in Lagos so that they could meet. The office was constantly humming with multiple projects all taking place at once. Someone was always over in the corner, facing Mecca, praying on a small Oriental carpet. Without unions, whenever there was any trouble at work, everyone headed directly for Garba's office. Cranky passengers always found his office. His duties also concerned salaries and ground transportation. The chief got all the kudos and back-slapping, but in my view, Garba was the glue that held the entire airline together.

Despite all the activity, Garba jumped to his feet to give Yasser a hearty welcome. They chatted while I wandered outside to buy a *Hello* magazine. Lagos airport has minimal fences surrounding the runways. People of all kinds just wander in to see either what services they can provide, or simply to "case the joint," observing who, or what, appears to be vulnerable. "Security" was rapidly going downhill at the airport.

One day, a jumbo jet was taxiing for takeoff position to fly back to Europe when the pilots noticed an indicator light was on, signaling that one of the cargo bay doors was open. They notified the tower, who scanned the belly of the aircraft through strong binoculars. The light was correct. The cargo bay was open, all right. A handful of enterprising thieves in a Jeep was driving underneath the belly of the plane as it taxied along, trying in vain to unload and rip off anything from the cargo area that was not completely nailed down. Just the thought of the screaming engines would be enough to dissuade most people, but not these guys, who were giving it their best shot. The jet stopped abruptly, and the bandits zipped off empty-handed to escape the oncoming airport security SUVs.

A few weeks later, a Boeing 727, flown by one of Kabo Air's competitors, took off from Port Harcourt en route to Lagos, tragically crashing into the swamp. All on board were killed, including 12 tribal chieftains. Chief Kabo then asked me to visit the US Embassy in Lagos.

My 'mission' was to convince them that all of Kabo Air's jets were safe, and that our envoys should make his airline their first choice. American diplomats were driving from Lagos to Abuja, Nigeria's capital, to avoid flying. The poor quality of the accident-prone roads made it treacherous, and along the entire route, well-armed thugs were watching out for well-to-do foreigners who were juicy targets.

As I entered the hallway of our American Embassy laden with photos of our leaders, it felt strange to be "out of the bush." I had embraced the culture of the Northerners more than I had realized, and this experience highlighted that contrast for me. I was re-entering my own environment, to speak with my own people, particularly the number three man after the ambassador. Articulate with a slight build, he reminded me of my first cousin, who is also an envoy. I had always referred to these types as "stiff suits" or "preppies," and he was no exception.

Knowing the chief's airline well, I had prepared some useful notes, just in case he asked me something unexpected. I could not blame the diplomat, as it was his duty to ask some hard questions. My best line of defense was that Kabo Air's pilots had been trained in the States at the US Airways facilities. The aircraft were ferried to America for engine overhauls, and as a supervisor, I was flying on them nearly every day myself while instructing the flight attendants.

At the conclusion of the meeting, I asked, "Certainly flying from Lagos to Abuja is much safer than driving, wouldn't you agree?"

Just the thought of being ambushed on the road by renegade bandits was horrifying to me. He assured me that he would relay our discussion to the ambassador. "Chief will be quite pleased," I thought.

I went downstairs to get a quick greasy American snack from the cafeteria. Many of my countrymen were in there, rapidly conversing. The acoustics were awful; everyone sounded like squawking parrots in a small cage. The place was understandably crawling with Drug Enforcement Agency (DEA) agents, one of whom I ran into at a bar some months later back in D.C. I was now observing Americans from an objective point of view. They were in a rush, and they were loud. You had to forgive them, though. Lagos is a difficult place to live; a "hardship" post as the diplomatic corps refers to it. You must be constantly on the alert for carjackings or just plain pickpocketing. Taxis often lack air conditioning, and with the windows down, you must continually monitor what is going on all around the car or you could get hit out of nowhere. It was time to return north, and I took the next flight back to Kano to join Yasser.

Life was simple for us in Kano. Every morning like clockwork, Mohammed our driver took us to the airport to board a flight to supervise the crew. After work, we would swing by to visit Nigerian friends or rent some grainy old VHS tapes to play in our room with our favorite housekeeper Suley, front desk clerk Abdul, and Natania, the engineer. Often Yasser visited the mosque to worship.

A month passed. The time was coming for him to return to Cairo to have his eyes operated on and renovate his condo. This was also when my friendship with the chief's houseboys really saved me from a real tango with him. Chief Kabo had been traveling abroad and owed Yasser and me together almost $12,000. I hate to ask for money, even when it is owed to me, but I desperately needed to send some back to the States for my mortgage payment. Feeling subdued, I walked down the road to the guest villa. The house boys knew what I had come for, and the urgency of it all.

"Madame," Isaac said, intercepting me so that nobody would hear, "this is a very bad day to ask the chief for your salary."

My heart sank. "Why, Isaac?" I asked him.

"The Malam (Muslim priest) was here today, and he made the chief furious," Isaac said.

"Why on Earth would Chief get mad at the Malam?" I inquired, so curiously.

"He suggested that the chief retire early and give up all of his companies."

The chief blew up at the Malam for even daring to suggest that. Then, unceremoniously kicking the religious leader out of the house, he went around screaming at anyone who got in the way. If I had approached him about my salary, I would have walked straight into a horseshoe ambush. Not only that, if the chief was moody, he could later try to link my request with the events of that day, looking for an excuse not to pay us. So grateful to Isaac for the valuable advice, I made myself scarce and slipped right out of there.

The chief relished having a gaggle of people greet him at the airport anytime he returned from abroad, so all the houseboys and airline employees gathered right on the tarmac to bid him a hearty welcome. Nigerian officials allowed the chief to disembark the aircraft when arriving from any foreign destination and to walk straight across the tarmac to his boxy Mercedes SUV, completely circumventing customs. It was amusing to watch because every single time he was the first one off, heading straight for his SUV. Dozens of European passengers naturally followed him, and the officials went crazy, frantically trying to rope in all the foreigners to steer them towards customs inside the airport, where employees were panting to snoop through all their valuables.

Yasser and I went along, clapping and cheering as if he was some type of returning hero. "*Jarma! Sa-nune-kah-dah-zoo-ah!*" I exclaimed, as if he was a victorious conqueror.

Leaning over, he whispered, smiling, "Madame, I have your money. I wanted to get it from London so that there wouldn't be any counterfeit dollars in there," he added, handing me a rumpled brown paper bag.

Gratefully accepting it, I could not *wait* until Yasser and I returned to the hotel so that we could count it all.

We carefully laid the rumpled stacks of $100 bills out on the bed. "It's all here," Yasser happily declared, "Twelve thousand dollars!"

I could not resist taking a photo of him sprawled on the bed with dozens of hundred-dollar bills. He looked like he was enjoying life on the strip in Las Vegas, not Kano, Nigeria.

The day arrived for Yasser to return to Egypt. I was really bummed about his departure, but it was best for him. I was also distressed about getting the funds safely out of the country. It is almost impossible to wire money out of Nigeria due to fraud, so he was going to hand-carry the entire amount of $12,000 in his briefcase, then wire my portion to my bank account. I tried hard to keep creepy feelings at bay as we approached Kano airport, fearful that the authorities would try to confiscate all our funds, which could easily have happened. They relish going through every section of your bags, and I would have had a coronary right on the spot if they had rifled through his briefcase and found the twelve thousand bucks.

My "protection" against this happening was Mohamed, Jarma's chief counsel. He was honest, smart, dependable, and funny. He was always asking me out for a date. Once Mohamed lamented, "Why did I not meet you before Yasser? It is Kismet, I guess."

However, his friendship came through in a dramatic way. A handsome man, he was someone you could call on when things spun out of control, which in Nigeria was frequently. He stepped right up to the plate when I asked him to accompany us to the airport. Everything went smoothly, thank God. While they looked at Yasser's other bags, they did not seem to care about the briefcase. I breathed a huge sigh of relief. Mohamed was a well-respected attorney, so we sailed right through the "inspection." Yasser gave me a goodbye kiss on the cheek.

Mohamed and I watched the Egypt Air jet take off toward the east until it disappeared into the pale blue sky.

The hotel was now completely silent. I sat alone on the bed, already missing Yasser. I watched *Gone with the Wind*, and then the disappointing sequel, drinking an entire bottle of cheap-tasting French red wine. I was wearing a blue dress covered in hieroglyphics that he loved. He had always complimented me in Jeddah when I wore it. Feeling a bit weepy, I rinsed off all my makeup. It was a quiet night except for the songs of tropical birds outside my window. The days were getting shorter. More surprises lay ahead, and not all of them good.

If only you could see these gold walls!

14

Magnificent Palace in Maiduguri

One Friday, returning from Port Harcourt, I decided to swing by Garba's office in Lagos to check in. As usual, the crowded office was swirling with activity, but Garba, as always, made time for me. I was probably the only one in there who was not malcontent about something. Several men prayed quietly in the corner.

"Tania, do you have any plans this weekend?" he asked.

I knew he had something cool up his sleeve just by the way he was looking at me. Garba and I share similar views on life, so we readily enjoy the same type of people and activities. "No, Garba," I answered, "*Ina Labari*? (What's up?)"

"My friends Bana and Bakura are back from Zurich, and you are welcome to visit their palace over the weekend."

I sure liked the way this was sounding. He continued, "Unfortunately, I can't go as I would love to see the look on your face as you walk through their home. I will arrange for you to take our first flight up tomorrow to Maiduguri. Bana will meet you at the airport, and they will put you up in their hotel tomorrow night."

I gushed, "Garba, that sounds incredible!"

How exciting to visit this dreamy palace. Garba had previously described this opulent residence to me. With all he had been exposed to, if he was impressed with it, I knew that I was not going to be disappointed.

At my stepfather Archie's urging, I had registered my name with the US Embassy after meeting with the envoy. "Tan, I'm afraid that someone will take a pot shot at the chief one day and you will be in the way," he warned.

Even though I was comfortable moving around the country unescorted at times, I knew in my heart that Archie was right. However, I felt secure flying to Maiduguri alone, away from frenzied Lagos. The North was more tranquil, so I felt safer, not like I had to be on the alert all the time.

Up in dusty Maiduguri, near the border with Chad, Bana picked me up in an everyday Toyota and drove me to the hotel. Wearing a babariga of light green, he was modest, easy to talk to, and a close friend of Garba's. We spoke of our mutual friends. I think he was flattered by how much I liked Nigeria. We set a time for my pickup the next morning.

The hotel staff was friendly and knowledgeable. Right out of the mid-1970s, my room had deep shag funky pink carpet and a bumpy double-sized bed with track lighting running around the bottom . . . just like the emergency lighting system on a plane. Elvis would have felt right at home. I sat outside on the balcony mentally reviewing all that had transpired since I had arrived in Nigeria. I listened to Yanni, which fit in exactly with the peaceful scene, as I gazed at Orion, my favorite constellation. The sky was filled with stars. I felt at home in Maiduguri already.

Bana came by early and the friendly captain who had piloted my flight the previous day had weaseled his way into joining us. I asked Bana if it would be all right to take photos, thinking that if this place is as elaborate as described, nobody back home would believe me unless I had proof. The answer was yes.

As is customary, we took our shoes off before entering, arranging them in a neat row. Inside the foyer, we were greeted with a massive light pink, hand-blown Venetian glass chandelier, with color-coordinated mirrors along the walls. The staircase split into two parts which ran down, from top to bottom, on both sides of the enormous entrance hall. What an ideal place for a wedding. I could just see the bride making her entrance at the top to greet the guests before descending the palatine staircase.

"What do you think?" Bana asked teasingly.

"I expect diamonds to cascade down from the ceiling any minute!" I gushed as he laughed.

Just inside the front door, I was already blown away. One did not know what to look at first.

The entire front hall had been created out of veined white Italian marble. A matching fountain in the center of the room was surrounded by green plants. A subdued gurgling of water eased its way through the fountain. The light fixtures were painstakingly detailed in Islamic style, and on either side of the room solid 24-karat gold lamps from floor to ceiling were fashioned as palm trees. The entrance area alone could have swallowed up the modest three-bedroom bungalow where I reside in LA. I could not even begin to estimate the total square footage of the palace.

The hallway floors featured designs of checkered black and white marble. The walls were festooned with mirrors framed either in Venetian glass or 24-karat solid gold. An elongated table in the dining room could accommodate 40 people at a sit-down dinner. When the palace finally opened, Nigerian National TV ran a live broadcast showing Bana's father entertaining his wealthy friends, including Chief Kabo, all decked out in their finest *babarigas*. As they were feted with endless silver trays of imported delicacies, the festivities were beamed around the nation.

We entered the upstairs salon in our bare feet, and I noticed that stepping on certain patches of the custom-made carpet hurt my soles. In certain spots, something was poking out from the detailed Persian carpet, which covered the entire room, wall to wall. Examining the design at close range, I discovered the "culprit." Infused in the carpet to enhance the beauty of the design was 24-karat gold wire. Oh, *now* I understood.

Most of the furniture was embellished with mother of pearl. Other pieces, created out of unusual wood from the Far East, were decorated with intricate designs of inlaid brass. Gold-embossed camel-hide ottomans rested your feet and had been carefully placed around the room. In the middle of the grand receiving parlor, the hide of a lioness sprawled out on top of the carpet. At the other end was a large zebra skin.

The master bedroom had a gold and white king-sized bed with matching furniture imported from an upscale store on Bond Street in

London. This same company had made various types of custom furniture for Queen Elizabeth at Buckingham Palace. A royal seal at the top of the canopy denoted the royal patronage. Most of the furniture that did not have a Mideastern theme had been imported from London.

Saved for last was *la pièce de résistance*, called "the gold room." Yes, the walls were not simply covered in gold leaf or gold over silver but made of solid gold bullion from floor to ceiling. The entire room gleamed so brightly that when I took the first photo, the flash bounced back into my eyes as if I had taken a picture directly into a golden-colored mirror. Looking around in disbelief, I had a hard time trusting what my eyes were telling me, and they revealed my thoughts. "This was President Bush's (41) favorite room, as well," Bana said, observing the look on my face. In more ways than one, I could see why.

When the palace was completed, Bana's father had also built a well-appointed mosque in the center of Maiduguri so that the towns-people would have an inspiring place close by to pray. The mosque attracted many worshippers who came from miles around to admire its beauty while practicing their religion.

Bana's father had meticulously assembled an elite group of Italian artisans, bringing them to Nigeria where they worked feverishly for a full seven years on this elaborate palace. I asked Bana if his father was pleased and if it had turned out the way he had envisioned. "My father was ecstatic with the work they did," he replied. "He knew that he had hired exactly the right team to create what he had in mind."

I could see that they had listened very carefully to his instructions as he described his ideal dream home, miraculously bringing it all to life in this stunning edifice.

"So, what do you think?" Bana asked me in a tempting way. "You are welcome to come back and stay in the palace, just like President Bush did a few years ago."

After all the carefully laid plans, the palace proved even too elaborate for Bana's father. He had an additional flat constructed on the compound nearby where he moved in with his four wives and all their children.

Bana drove us back to the airport amid the crowded streets of Maiduguri. The pilot was scheduled to operate the next flight back to Lagos and we were running late; about three hours behind schedule, in fact. That would also have an impact on other outbound flights, delaying them in a domino effect for the rest of the day. Whereas a western pilot would be chomping at the bit to be on time, the Kabo Air pilot was completely unconcerned.

Arriving at the airport, I saw a few passengers patiently waiting under a tree for the flight to leave. The flight seemed to be only half full, so at least we had not inconvenienced too many people. But as we approached the aircraft, I got the real picture. Dozens of passengers were jammed in together, sitting on the tarmac under the wings of the aircraft to keep the blazing sun off, as shaded areas were nonexistent.

On both sides, the patient tribespeople were seated under the wing's shade in the exact pattern of the wing above their heads. Now I could see that it was a sold-out flight.

Thanking Bana profusely for his wonderful hospitality, and feeling guilty for keeping the passengers waiting, I barreled towards the aircraft. The pilot just strolled along behind me with no sense of urgency whatsoever. In the States, they would have eaten us alive with complaints, but here nobody uttered a peep. The Hausas consider it Kismet. Yes, it was Fate. We were simply going to be hours late that day getting back into Lagos.

꙰

15

The Dichotomy of Kano —
Opulence and a Leper Sanctuary

Back in Kano, MD Hassan had arranged for me to visit the local leper shelter. I have always wondered why a disease that existed in the time of Jesus is still in the world today, often overlooked for funding and treatment. Leprosy causes loss of sensation in the extremities, along with destruction of tissue and possible blindness.

Our car had semi-official logos on the doors. We pulled up unannounced and immediately drew attention. Unlike the shelter in Sokoto, missionaries or other white people were a rare sight here. About seven patients and the gentleman in charge approached the car with acute curiosity. Peering in at me, they all smiled warmly, as if I was an old friend.

I greeted them with *"Sahnun-kahdah-zuah,"* (peace be upon you) to establish a connection. They returned the greeting, readily inviting me inside the compound. The man in charge, Hajji Abdul, was not a full-fledged doctor but had some medical knowledge. He was open, answered all my questions, and was pleased that someone from another nation wanted to know how this retreat was run. It was rough. The patients could not have been sweeter, but the conditions were dreadful compared to Sokoto.

The first room they showed me set the tone for the entire compound. On two double-sized beds, the bare mattresses were ripped open in several places. Flies buzzed everywhere. Five children slept on each double-sized mattress. Paint was peeling off the walls in the small, outdated dorms. Outside they had a giant metal pot where a lady was stirring some kind of stew for lunch, most likely goat meat and rice along with some vegetables.

This place was so much hotter than the sanctuary in Sokoto because there were no trees. Without vegetation, dust kicked up with each step. Everywhere you walked it felt as if the sun was trying its best to beat you down with its penetrating rays. To me, the desolation of this place was compounded by the fact that these people were also suffering from a disease that hearkens all the way back to Biblical times.

As I absorbed the atmosphere, one thing was obvious: these lepers all looked out for one another, like a commune. Children could go to any adult to ask for something, or to settle a small dispute. This was a remarkable mini-society within a society. I sensed the harmony of the people just flowing among them. You did not have to speak the language, just feel the energy.

Abdul took me to his office, which had unwashed walls of pastel colors and broken window panels. A large photo of Gogo's husband, the Emir of Kano, all dressed up in traditional finery, stared down at us from above Abdul's desk. Even though Nigerian officials had completely forgotten this place, the patients were not bitter. They consider it their destiny. I did not hear them speak ill of any government officials, although they may have seen the nebulous insignia on our car.

Pulling out file after file, Abdul was eager to show me a sampling of patients' records to illustrate improvements to their health. Positive things were being accomplished, and some progress was being made despite the acute shortage of supplies and amenities. His office was about twelve by sixteen feet with windows on each side. As we had been discussing the shelter, I looked around and was startled to see that at least 25 older patients, all men, had crowded in and were sitting on the floor. They were uninvited, but it was fine with Abdul and me. Neither of us discouraged them. We both engaged them in dialogue concerning their condition. They also wanted to be part of the discussion, to know what was transpiring. Disciplined and quiet, their body language indicated to me that they were respectful of each other. Kids were hanging in through all the windows. It reminded me of programs showing village life in Africa, but this was far different, having an impromptu forum in the manager's office of a leper colony. It was the only time in my life that I had a meeting with all lepers.

Abdul had to translate what they were saying because they had never been to school to learn English. I wondered how long these souls had been here. Some had lived here for decades, with no end in sight. When they began to lose feeling in their extremities, most likely they had leprosy. Despite their optimistic spirit, many of them looked tattered, drawn, and exhausted. However, in one sense they were fortunate to be here. Rather than suffering a homeless, lonely, and shunned life, as is the case in many developing nations, at least here they had a friendly community respite where they all faced and shared similar challenges.

While Yasser was still in Kano, the chief's attorney, Mohamed, lent us his car to explore the town. One day, when driving up to a roundabout, we noticed a young lady sitting with a baby in her lap and a toddler close to her as the traffic whizzed past. Part of her upper lip had been eaten away with leprosy, exposing her upper teeth. Unbelievably, she was smiling while holding out her hand for money.

We wanted to give her something but had to be careful. Someone might be watching, then zip by and rip her off once we were out of sight. We left and returned with a large plastic bag full of fruit, with cash hidden in between the oranges, mangoes, and bananas. Yasser stopped the car, and I went over to hand it to her. Given her situation, I was absolutely amazed at her demeanor. I squatted down, showing her the bag, surreptitiously pointing out the money. I wondered if her life would have been better living on a compound like the one in Kano.

I engaged some of the men in conversation to gain a better idea of how their lives were spent. I could sense the "seniority" of certain men sitting on the floor. Addressing one in the front row, I asked, "Can you please tell me what the patients here need most in your opinion? What would really help everyone?"

"Madame," he began, "There are two things that we would really like to have. The water well here dried up about five years ago, so we must fetch water from a well far up the road, about three miles away."

As he spoke, all I could think was that six miles is very far to walk, the heat is so intense, and water is so incredibly heavy. Many patients were missing fingers. How did they carry water under those circumstances? Once they dragged the water back home, they had to boil it so that they would not contract typhoid or another debilitating disease in addition to leprosy.

His voice did not contain any hint of resentment whatsoever. Some translated for others. Many of them had kind faces, full of light. It was not difficult for me to see beyond the illness that plagued them. "What is the second thing you need?" I asked.

"Some years ago, they began to build a mosque here so that we could have a place to pray," he answered. "After a few weeks of working on it, the construction team abruptly left and never came back." I began to wonder if that was all that the patients wanted for their isolated existence. "We would be so pleased if we had these things. A mosque is so important to us," he added.

The patients nodded in agreement. I also strongly agree that worship is an integral part of healing. That is why I envisioned a mosque to be part of the shelter I wanted to build in Sokoto, and had it included in the blueprints.

After discussing more about treatments and taking notes, I stood up to leave. All the patients rose to their feet, and we walked out into the bright sun. Outside, the energetic children were playing hide-and-seek just like they do everywhere else on the planet. Others had located sticks and tied used plastic bags to them to create rudimentary kites. As I walked with Abdul, the atmosphere was filled with the melodic sounds of children's laughter.

I headed toward the car, then heard a man's clear voice I will never forget. "Madame!" he said enthusiastically, "thank you so much for coming."

I whirled around to see a wiry man in a simple faded 'riga giving me the Hausa greeting of the thumb through the fist. I smiled broadly. Then I realized that he could not see me. He had been blinded by leprosy, but he had all the dignity in the world. His spirit had not been dampened. He had understood my intentions based on my voice vibration alone. His bright smile instantly won my heart. Stoicism presents itself in a million different ways.

"Thank you so much for your hospitality," I replied. Then I added, "*Al-Ham Duh lee-Lah!*" Praise be to Allah. The man emphatically repeated the words back to me.

Sliding into the car, I looked up at the entrance. There was Abdul, standing tall, with about 18 lepers of all sizes and ages. They were all vigorously waving the traditional Hausa wave, even though some did not have all their fingers. That image would be in both my mind and heart for many years to come.

That night, the chief invited me to join him for dinner at the guest villa, along with six prominent Nigerians, including the commander of the Nigerian Air Force. When the chief introduced me, one of the men in discord refused to shake my hand. He had never attended a dinner of this kind where a woman was present, and most certainly not one who was white, foreign, and Christian—that was way over the top. The chief shifted slightly in his chair, as if embarrassed by the gesture. I acted as if I was not offended. In every country, people become set in their ways and follow their customs closely. This time was no different.

Being surrounded by eminent Nigerian men made me flashback to a train ride in the late '60s from Paddington Station in London to my school in Somerset. My close friend Lotanna Ojukwu was the brother of Lt. Col. Emeka Ojukwu, who had attempted to break off Eastern Nigeria to create an independent state called Biafra. A horrific civil war had ensued, pitting the tribes of the East against the rest of Nigeria. The teenage son of Ojukwu's nemesis, the general he was at war with, also attended Millfield.

Lotanna once gave me his class photo where he had etched "VIP" above his head in ink. We shared mutual friends from African and European countries, spending many hours together attending sports games, dances, or Saturday night films. We always carried on in between classes kidding and laughing with each other. That day was no different, as we compared notes on how our holidays had been in our respective countries. As the train rattled through the Salisbury Plain near the monoliths of Stonehenge, the cabin door slid open. In stepped the son of the opposition's leader. For just a second or two, there was an awkward silence. Then we heartily greeted each other as schoolmates do, just as if everything was entirely normal. Naturally, I was anticipating that in no time we would be embroiled in a major political discourse of the Nigerian civil war, but no such thing happened as we glided through the verdant emerald-green English countryside that afternoon.

⊙

Now, being entertained by the chief and his elitist guests, I felt in some respects that events had come full circle. It was 27 years later, and here I was once again in the company of Nigerian men who had a strong hand in Nigeria's future.

Just to test the waters, the chief threw me a couple of curveballs that night, but I was up to the challenge. Politics was no doubt on his mind. He was close friends with "President" Sani Abacha, who had come to power by a coup d'état a few years earlier. The chief never called me Tania, but always addressed me as "Madame."

"Madame, how do you like President Abacha, what do you think of him?" he asked.

Each man at the table turned directly to face me to observe my reaction. Abacha was a big-time conspirator and nearly everyone in Nigeria detested him. He ruled with an iron fist and could be easily bribed by the usual suspects in Nigeria's political world.

"Jarma, I know that President Abacha has been a great friend of yours for years. Garba said you have known him since childhood."

The chief sat back, looking somewhat satisfied. His diamond-encrusted Rolex watch shone brightly in the chandelier's light.

"I sincerely hope that he can lead Nigeria into an age of prosperity," I added.

Nearly choking on my own words, it was difficult for me to utter such a sentence knowing how this loathsome figure was plundering Nigeria. I think the chief knew it, too.

After a while, he asked, "Madame, what did you do in Kano today?"

His question instantly reminded me of my childhood, "Darling, what did you learn in school today?" my mother had often asked.

Jarma had absolutely no idea where I had been. My exploration of the leper colony took him and his colleagues by complete surprise.

My favorite houseboy Isaac was serving us that night, which was fortuitous. He listened intently to every word and told me the next day exactly what they had discussed in Hausa while I was at the table. I explained to the chief in great detail my impression of the leper shelter, including my conversation with Abdul. Most importantly, I wanted to convey to him the dignity and the needs of the courageous lepers.

I explained to him that they had requested only two things: for a well to be dug and for the mosque to be completed. Everyone knew that the chief had the power to honor such requests, or at least talk to a government official about improving the compound's condition. He spoke Hausa to his colleagues. They all knew English, so I viewed it as a "private" conversation. They listened intently, nodding while he spoke.

As we finished the appetizer, the chief said in a loud voice to Isaac, "I feel like eating some meat tonight. Bring the monkey!"

The chief had wanted to tease me, but sometimes, I am sorry to say, they eat roast monkey in Nigeria. Even as busy as he was, he knew that I adored Kai. I thought about her often and hoped that she was happily settled in her new home with fellow chimps and the compound pooches. The chief laughed with zest as I protested his request for a simian entrée.

We all stood to say goodbye. The official who had earlier refused to shake my hand moved towards me with a smile, extending his right hand. "It was a pleasure to meet you, Madame," he said.

The next afternoon, Isaac and I went to an outside café that displayed three or four bottles of cheap whiskey. As we strolled past villas with huge satellite dishes, it was obvious that sports was not the only programming they watched. Isaac liked to walk hand-in-hand with me. Reaching over to take my hand, we leisurely made our way down the unpaved road. I could not wait to ask Isaac what the chief had said the previous night. His translation of what the heavy hitters were discussing and planning was always significant to me.

"Once you began describing the place where the lepers live, the chief could not believe his ears. I don't think he has ever had a guest from *anywhere* who has sought out a leper shelter," Isaac began. "He was quite impressed by your visit. Then he asked his guests, 'How is it that *baturia* (white woman) has come six thousand miles to show me something in my own backyard that I didn't know about? I have been unaware that such a place existed in Kano, not so far from my own home," the chief had added. "I will do what I can to see that they get access to water and that construction of the mosque is completed."

Sitting down for drinks and snacks, we spoke about many things. Isaac's original name had been Bana, as he was born a Muslim. In his late teens, he decided to become a Christian, changing his name to Isaac, much to the dismay of his father, who was a Muslim chief in a small village.

He got along well with everyone, and I never saw him be snarky. It was fun to spend time with him, as he gave me more insight into Hausa culture. As we rose to leave the cafe, about eight hookers sitting on a stone wall close by called out to us. They found our friendship amusing and wanted to get in on the act somehow. They reminded me of feline cartoon characters, aka "alley cats," all gussied up, posing along the wall. One could not resist the temptation. She called out "*Baturia!* Why don't you join us? Business is slow tonight, but if you work with us, we will certainly get more customers as there will be an even *bigger* variety to choose from!"

The girls roared and I chuckled, but Isaac was mortified beyond belief that they would be so bold. Muttering under his breath, "They are *not* decent women," he quickly ushered me away to the fading giggles of the local tarts.

Spending the rest of the evening visiting friends, we prepared to leave at about 1:30 a.m. Isaac could not get a taxi, so he hailed two scooters, negotiated a price, and we hopped on back. This is common practice in the North. Most Nigerians cannot afford cars or even bikes, so they step out to the curb, hail a scooter, ask how much, and ride along. It is relatively safe and has no bad connotations, hence the expression "scooter girl." I have been called that more than once. Well, how else are you to get around town?

Within minutes of leaving our friends, we arrived at a makeshift roadblock. The scrawny sergeant, wearing far too many stripes and medals, did not look friendly at all. Jumping off the scooter, Isaac explained in his soft voice that we were just on our way home. It appeared that Isaac could not persuade this skinny joker that we were just passing through. Abruptly ordering me off the back of my driver's scooter, I, too, courteously approached the sarge, using a quiet voice, explaining that I was a guest of Chief Kabo. He blew up. I do not think he liked white people.

"You are a LIAR!" he yelled at me, as I tried to keep my cool. "If you were *really* a guest of the chief, he would have provided you with a car and driver. You wouldn't be a 'scooter girl' here, using *that* for transport! Do you know the time? It's well past curfew."

Standing there as we were being berated, I began to wonder just how much this was going to cost me. I had about $40 worth of naira in my purse and about $20 in change. I certainly did not want to see us go to jail. Just the thought of it was extremely ugly, indeed. Who knows what we would find there? And how long would it be until my hosts discovered that we were really missing? The chief was always out of town, and Garba, who would certainly have realized that something was amiss, was down in Lagos, busy running the airline.

I felt around the inside of my purse as the sergeant continued upbraiding us for our bad judgment. Pulling out a couple of bucks, I handed them to him. He pushed them aside as a definite signal that the amount was not enough. I then handed him a ten-dollar bill, which he studied a bit. He made a little movement as to signal those twelve bucks, the equivalent of a half-month's salary, would probably do it. We were on our way.

Two days later, the chief asked me to go to the airport with him to greet the ambassador from Saudi Arabia, who was flying in from Lagos. We joined the caravan of four "Jarma" cars, riding in the chief's silver Mercedes SUV. At some point along the road, we came upon the sergeant, sitting outside his tiny, dilapidated post. He jumped to his feet to vigorously salute the chief as if he was the head of state. Then, peering through the window into the back seat, the hapless fellow spotted me. His face changed color, as it screwed up with recognition. "Madame!"

he exclaimed, saluting, and arching his back so violently that I thought I was going to hear it snap.

He knew well that the chief would not be pleased to hear a tale like the one from a few nights before. He could easily lose his job and not be able to find another one, ever.

To call overseas from Nigeria, you go to a special post where they have a bunch of loud ticking clocks, each situated in front of a phone. After your call, the clerk reads the clock and calculates your charges. I wanted to check up on Yasser to see how the laser operation on his eyes had been. The cash he had taken to Cairo had arrived safely and had been sent to my account in the States, so I was incredibly relieved about that. Now I wanted to know about his health.

Mohammed, the tall, distinguished man who always wore a beret over his salt-and-pepper hair, had been our driver when Yasser was in Kano. He took me to make the call to Cairo. He was dependable and always on time, and a rarity in Nigeria. Mohammed and Yasser had prayed together every Friday, so they understood each other well. He always drove us to the airport or the flight attendants' classroom.

"Yasser?" I began, "How are you, doll face? How did the operation go? How do you feel?"

I missed him terribly. I think it is even worse when someone has enjoyed a place with you and then left, rather than if they had never been there at all. There is not much to do in Kano, so it had been wonderful spending time with him.

He was not well. The connection was dreadful, wavering in and out. That did not help, either. "I am in pain, Tania. My vision is very blurry, and my eyes feel like someone threw sand in them," he complained.

Tears trickled down both cheeks, but I stayed quiet. What if he went blind? I would be devastated. He could tell by my voice that I was becoming more upset by the minute. "I keep them closed and resting every day," he added. "I thought that this doctor was good, but what if he didn't do the procedure correctly? I should have been out of pain by now."

There was a trace of fear in his voice. I was so upset by this news that I didn't know what to say. Since he had made so many friends in his short time in Kano, I assured him that everyone would be praying for him.

Feeling very low, I bid him goodbye, saying that I would call him in a few days. I settled into the back seat of the car and promptly burst out crying. Mohammed asked, "Madame! Are you alright? What happened? How's Yasser? What did he say to you?"

Bless his heart, the kind but reticent Mohammed knew that things were seriously bad.

Unable to stop sobbing, I felt dread right down to the pit of my stomach. Even so, I had purchases to make, and had laid the plans out to Mohammed before we left. In Nigeria, you must go all around the city to different areas to purchase goods. He knew all the stops, but I was so terribly upset, unable to relate our conversation without wailing, that he kept driving me in all the wrong directions for the balance of the day. He took on my distraught energy as if it were his own. That alone was enough to show me how much Mohammed truly cared for us.

16

Wedding Celebration at the Sultan's Palace in Sokoto

Flying down to Lagos while check-riding the crew, I wanted to catch up on any news from Garba. It was a good thing I stopped by. "Hajjia Tania!" Garba exclaimed. He enjoyed addressing me this way, which was a big compliment, meaning that I had embraced and understood their culture and religion. "There will be a big celebration at the palace in Sokoto this weekend. The Sultan's daughter is getting married, and you're invited. I have arranged for two 727s to fly the guests up from Lagos this Saturday."

My head began to whirl with the old familiar, "What on Earth will I wear?" thought as I considered this exotic invitation. I had brought several long-flowing silk skirts from the States, along with some imaginative accessories, knowing that these occasions would crop up.

As I contemplated the upcoming nuptials at the sultan's palace, I recalled the first time I was invited to a palace, also located in Africa. In the late '60s at school in England, my dear friend, Ethiopian Princess Sihin Asfa Wossen, had invited me to join her at her grandfather's palace in Addis Ababa for the Christmas holidays. No ordinary grandad, he was Emperor Haile Selassie; her father was Crown Prince Asfa Wossen, heir to the throne. A stunning young lady with classic features, aristocratic poise, and a great sense of chic fashion, she would have been a jewel in *any* family. Her popular sister Mary was also my friend.

My mother was thrilled at the invitation as she had always deeply admired the Ethiopian royal family. She vividly remembered when Emperor Selassie was *TIME* magazine's "Man of the Year" in 1936. The emperor had made a compelling speech before the League of Nations in 1933, strongly protesting the Italian invasion of Abyssinia, as it was then called.

I fantasized about the experience I would have being feted in the emperor's palace by his immediate family at my tender age of sixteen. The royal family was Coptic Orthodox, so the Christmas celebration would be an elaborate experience I would never forget. Sihin told me stories of how the emperor loved all kinds of animals. Boxers and chihuahuas kept company with trained peacocks, who slowly unveiled their feathers for foreign dignitaries at the snap of his fingers. Zebras, young lions, and "tame" cheetahs also lived at the palace. Once, Senator Robert Kennedy leaned over to pet one of the cheetahs. The large spotted cat snarled and swatted at him, sending him reeling, to the delight of the young royal children. A journey of that kind would be my heart's desire; a dream come true.

Suddenly, one day out of the blue, my mother began saying, "I'm not going to let my *virginal* daughter travel unescorted all the way to East Africa!"

Incredibly disappointed, I had no idea whatsoever why she had so abruptly changed her mind. The truth of the matter was that she was nearly broke at the time, and being such a proud woman, was loathe to admit it. She was ashamed that she did not have the funds to send me, or even escort me herself. Rapidly losing his life-long battle with alcoholism, my stepfather Bevo had been fired from a succession of jobs and had gone through his inheritance with a blow torch. We reluctantly declined the invitation, hoping for some last-minute unexpected stateside financial reprieve. Years later I told Sihin this over lunch. We had a great laugh about it. "We would have gladly arranged for you and your mother to join us in Addis, Tania," she told me, smiling broadly. "I had no idea until just this minute that is why you didn't accept the invitation."

Now I was going to have another shot at attending a special occasion in a grand African palace. This time, finances would not be an issue.

Saturday arrived. The excitement among the guests was infectious as we all gathered on the tarmac in Lagos, chatting. Ladies' brightly colored *boo-boos* and men's *babarigas* flapped in the wind. The setting would have made a great watercolor painting. I had decided on a mid-calf bright red skirt with a long-sleeved white blouse. Both were silk, and the outfit was punctuated by my favorite white leather belt, which had golden African animals running around it. I wore gold leather sandals which picked up the gold in the belt, along with my ever-present gold ankle bracelet. My skirt billowed as I walked across the tarmac with Garba and his closest confidants. Even though it was Western, my fashion worked well with this culture. It was stylish and appropriate for the occasion.

During the flight up to Sokoto, formal invitations were handed out. With a chuckle, I realized that this was the first time in my life that I had been referred to as a "distinguished guest." The plane was chock-full with an assembly of the Hausa elite.

Garba was busy with all his closest friends traveling together at the same time, so he arranged for Bello, whose hometown was Sokoto, to escort me throughout the day in case we became separated—a distinct possibility as the palace had mega square footage.

As the plane taxied to a stop in Sokoto, I could see Bello waving nonstop at us, wearing one of his many elaborate *babarigas*. This was one of those times when I really wanted to hug him hello but restrained myself in deference to their custom. Soon we were off to the Sultan's palace discussing events since Cicero's wedding.

Upon our arrival, I had a condensed lesson in what it feels like to be famous and easily recognizable, having people in your face every inch of the way. It was amusing in one way, but overwhelming in another. Once again, I would be the only Caucasian, foreign, non-Muslim woman at the palace. Everyone knew that in advance except me. That generated a tornado of interest, as people wondered why an exception had been made.

Tribesmen surrounded the car and began pressing in as Bello tried to help me out. I could not get the door open. He barked at them in Hausa, but I asked him to not become too impatient with them.

They had all come for a gander and were speculating about who I was, what my title was, and where I hailed from. They were scrutinizing why I was the only single woman invited. The wedding was going to be one of the major events of the year, if not the decade, so all the locals were inquisitive.

Finally, we slipped out of the human jam and up to the gates, where two of the Sultan's guards, both wearing bright red turbans, escorted us inside the white marble structure. The ceilings, walls, and floors were all made of white Italian marble. Large colorful carpets covered much of the flooring. Over the years, the sultan had been feted with many gifts of all kinds, particularly imported furniture and landscape paintings. Elaborate silver vases held dead flowers. Portraits of prominent Nigerians hung in the endless hallways. Running out of space, many had been casually stacked against the walls. The furniture had been arranged haphazardly. The sultan had some beautiful pieces, but not placed according to feng shui. This palace was not organized and decorated like the exquisite one in Maiduguri.

As we walked along, I saw gobs of men, but where were the ladies? I inquired about the bridal party. "The bride and her attendants are in seclusion in another section of the grounds," the poker-faced palace guard told me, "You will not see her today."

Disappointed, it was hard for me to imagine not seeing a bride on the happiest day of her life! What kind of gig was this? I had been looking forward to meeting her, viewing her elaborate bridal dress, and observing how the nuptials would be performed. I also wanted to see how the *Owambay* ceremony compared to Cicero and Amina's wedding celebration in Kaduna.

Finally arriving at the grand receiving salon, the bride's father, the sultan, was seated on an elevated throne enshrined with thick dark red curtains. Protocol dictated that each guest entered one at a time, removed their shoes, and bowed down while traditionally greeting the sultan. Patiently waiting my turn to be signaled, I paced my steps as I walked into the largest salon in the palace. Wearing a good-sized turban, the sultan was a tiny little man, nearly devoured by the oversized deep red pillows on his large gold-encrusted throne. If we had stood side by side, I bet he would have clocked in at about 5'2", nearly a head shorter than me. If I had run into him on the street in regular clothes, I would have been hard-pressed to recognize him.

Studying the sultan, I watched his body language closely. He had a bit of a regal attitude, somewhat stand-offish, perhaps "putting on a little dog" as my mother used to say. He did not resemble the affable Maazu, his younger brother, to whom I had presented the shelter blueprints to a few weeks earlier. How opportune it would have been to run into Maazu, but unfortunately, I did not see him. I am sure that he would have known where the wine cellar was, if one existed.

As I stepped in, I made the motion to remove my shoes and then bow, as I had observed the other guests doing. I could guarantee that both of my parents were watching from the great upstairs as their daughter bowed way down before this tiny potentate perched on a gold throne in the desert of Africa, certainly worlds away from McLean.

Waving his hand, the guard indicated that removal of my shoes would not be necessary. Throngs of male guests lined the walls all around the immense salon. Then, raising his voice so that all could hear, the guard proceeded to tell the sultan a big exaggeration: "Your Excellency, Madame Tania has flown all the way from the United States for the occasion of your daughter's wedding. She is here to pay her respects to your Highness this special day."

A big grin crossed my face. The whole world knew that I was in Nigeria to work for Chief Kabo, who was elsewhere in the palace partying with his buddies. He never missed any of those events that sported a lot of "hoopla" and celebration, regardless of these reason. As I remained half-kneeling, head slightly bowed, the sultan barely nodded in a casual way, as if to say "big deal." Escorted out into the great hallway, the guard then led Bello and me to other significant areas of the palace.

Outside, he showed us the stables for polo ponies and the stands where they sat to watch various sports. The loud and lively but friendly crowd outside, much larger than before, called to us as we climbed the bleachers. The minute I waved and greeted them in Hausa, the native cheers readily went up in return.

Then they took us into the wing of the palace where a large buffet from wall to wall was presented, laden with tasty treats. What made this section of the palace so unusual was that the guests here were the unfortunate of Sokoto. As tradition dictates, they had been invited to share the feast. This was the palace version of the same custom that had taken place at Amina's ladies' luncheon in Kaduna. I have never witnessed anything like this ritual in the West.

The needy guests, all men, shuffled down the buffet line. I am certain that it must have been overwhelming for them, as they naturally wondered just how much they could load up on for their families and loved ones. An artistic vast array of all the best foods available in Sokoto was displayed. If they stopped to pile on too much food, someone gently pushed them on as if to say, "Keep moving, fellas."

Thanking the palace guards, Bello relayed a traditional nuptial offering.

Once outside the palace gates, we were faced with the crush of onlookers again. They were asking all kinds of questions in Hausa and English about what it was like inside, how the sultan was, and which VIPs had attended.

Back home in Kano, the chief's house boys were all excited, particularly Isaac. "Tania, how was the wedding? We saw you on *TV!*" he exclaimed.

Unbeknownst to me, the ceremony at the palace had been broadcast live on Nigerian national television.

Soon, Garba invited me to join him in Lagos. The furious rainy season had begun; it was woefully sticky and humid. What I did not know was that heavy rain pisses off the mosquitoes big time. While they are breeding and having a good 'ol time in swamps and squalid waters after a downpour, they react like bees when a rock hits their hive.

Moses, one of Garba's houseboys in Lagos, joined us on the back patio. I had brought him a rare treat—some rum and T-shirts from Cairo. He was proudly sporting his King Tut T-shirt. We sipped rum and Cokes under the lush tropical trees and were having an upbeat conversation about recent events when Moses noticed that I kept slapping both my legs. "Madame," he said," I'm sorry that the mosquitoes are biting you."

I laughed, "It's no big deal, Moses. Please don't apologize. Let's just have a good time."

At that moment, having no real idea of the danger, it was going to turn out to be a very big deal, indeed.

17

Narrow Escape from Nigeria

In anticipation of working the Christmas holiday flight to Nairobi on his new private BAC-111 jet, I wore a lovely suit with a matching indigo-colored blouse. Upon boarding, I greeted Frank, one of the chief's bodyguards, and his colleague. I showed them all the emergency equipment, starting in the cockpit. Pointing out each piece, I described its function. I handed them both a pad and pen to take notes. It was unrealistic of the chief to think that anyone could learn all that a flight attendant has to know about one plane in an afternoon, but that was the norm. This especially applied to Frank, who was more caught up with having ready access to Jarma instead of running a viable operation.

This was typical of the impractical way the chief often thought. He already had knowledgeable flight attendants who would have relished working the trip to East Africa. Instead, he decided to have Frank perform duties that would be totally alien to him. Perhaps, in due course, Frank would turn out to be my "traitor."

What happened next will be seared in my mind forever. The chief was charging towards the plane, and before he even got to the steps, I greeted him heartily in Hausa. At first, I could not see his face but could tell he was obviously irate. Entering, with his face all puffed out, he looked enraged and was certainly furious about something, or someone . . . me?

"What are you doing on my aircraft?" he screamed at me, his eyes watering with fury. "You are *not* supposed to be on my plane!"

So taken aback I could hardly answer. I could not even begin to guess what he could be so angry about. As I tried to sort out different possibilities in my mind, he kept yelling in both Hausa and English, reminding me of a blowfish, which appears more than twice his size when threatened. He ranted for some minutes under the door frame leading into the cabin, laden with mother-of-pearl inlaid wood furniture. Standing inside, I was utterly stunned. He was waving his hands about as he often did, but this time in rage. This was serious business. His *babariga* had yards and yards of material and he appeared so large that I could not see my good friend and his right-hand man, Hassan, also a rather large man, standing right behind him.

Entering the cabin, the chief continued berating me as I shot occasional glances to Hassan with my pleading eyes as if to ask, "What in the hell is going on here?"

He had a sympathetic look on his face but we both knew that he was powerless to do anything. If he spoke up in my defense, the chief's wrath would then be unleashed towards him.

I explained that I had been asked to train Frank on the plane for the trip to Kenya. The chief would have none of it, interrupting me at every turn. His jugular veins popped out, his eyes were red and bulging. I remembered one of my late father's many expressions, "He was so mad he couldn't see straight."

I think I was witnessing that with the chief's emotional tirade. He may have seen two Tanias simultaneously.

"Why are you here? Who was that man, Yasser, you brought from Egypt? I don't think that he was a flight attendant! Precisely, what were both of you doing here? Who are you, *exactly*?"

I could not believe my ears. Hassan's eyes were tearing up in empathy. He knew me well, and how close I was to all Kabo Air's crews, hotel staff, and houseboys. Now it was all going to be flushed down the drain in one fell swoop.

As much as I tried, I could not win. As I began to speak in my defense, the chief interrupted me, shouting "Do I have to call immigration to get you off my airplane?"

Those very words struck a thunderbolt of fear straight into my heart. The trap door in my solar plexus's warning system slammed shut as acid surged into my stomach. My main benefactor could send me to the dogs in a heartbeat. We both knew it. I could always depend on Garba, but he was in Miami.

Promptly standing up, I looked the chief dead in the eye and said, "Have a good flight to Sokoto, Jarma."

As I raced across the tarmac to the terminal building, I burst out crying from fear, disbelief, and humiliation. All my cylinders were catapulted to full speed as my nerves went into overdrive. Two of the Kabo Air ground baggage men came running towards me. I used to love those two guys. One was about 6'6" and ebony-skinned, with the sincerest smile every day. I used to tease him, telling him that once Hollywood production cast him as a "character type" in a James Bond film, his life would never be the same again. He loved it, and always laughed as if he was hearing it for the first time.

His coworker, whose spine was not erect but twisted, was about 4'5" tall. He used to do something that I have never seen at any airline, and I have worked for nine. Once the aircraft was all "buttoned up" and completely ready to begin moving, he would pull the blocks out from underneath it. Then, as the engines began to scream, he would "pronk;" that is, he continually jumped straight up and down in one spot to give them an animated send off. It must have given his knees hell, but it was so much fun to watch, and he enjoyed doing it, knowing that the passengers were also enthralled by his display. We all have our ways of auditioning, I guess.

Now that both men were being so kind to me, I became even more upset. Taking me inside, the Kabo Air ground people gathered around, listening to what had happened. Everyone knew that the chief was a moody enigma, but they also knew me well as a real straight shooter. All of us were perplexed by the chief's behavior.

Time was running out as the afternoon wore on. Now I had to get out of the country *pronto;* not an easy proposition. It was December 21, four days before Christmas. Nearly all the flights went north to Europe and then onto the States. My head was spinning as I had a million things to do before I left. Having lived there for nearly five months, I had accumulated aircraft manuals, clothes, and all the usual things. First, I had to make the rounds to say goodbye. The hardest part was bidding farewell to the flight attendants. I interrupted their class and had decided to just tell them that something unusual had happened back home, and I would have to return that very night. I certainly did not want even more trouble from the chief.

"Hello, everyone. Sorry for interrupting your class. Something unexpected has come up in the States and I must fly back in a few hours."

My voice began to crack. Some of them asked when I would return, but others knew it would be some time. The Nigerian "telephone tree" was at work again, and some had already heard from the airport personnel that something lousy had occurred between Tania and the chief.

They all rose and came up to me, surrounding me. Most were crying. Each one showed, in their own way, what we meant to each other. I had also been the liaison between the crews and the chief, trying to improve their working conditions, so now that I was leaving, their situation would most certainly deteriorate. One was so upset that she could not even hug me. Weeping, she waved me away. Another said she always admired my camaraderie with all of them, and how I tried hard to help them. One of the gals had rushed off to get a going-away card, and they were hastily passing it around, knowing that I had to make my flight plans to leave. Everyone signed it. To this day, it is nestled in my 1996 diary. With tears in her eyes, Amina Garba, whom I had been so close with, hugged me last. "We will miss you terribly here. May Allah keep you well and safe, Tania, until we see you again."

Getting back in the car in my rush-mush mode, I asked Mohammed to get to KLM as quickly as possible. Barreling off toward the ticket office, my thoughts were racing at the speed of sound. I had tons to do before taking the red-eye back to Europe, and I was not even sure I could get on the flight. It was not a favorable time to make last-minute travel plans. I had casually let my ticket expire six weeks earlier, foolishly thinking that I would revive it at my leisure whenever it looked as if it was time to return home. Mohammed could sense my nervousness and stepped on the gas. I was thankful to have such a great driver . . . and friend.

Thank God the KLM office was quiet. There was more good news, as I handed my old ticket to the attractive blond-haired Dutchman who was also the office manager. "Ms. Anderson, you greeted me recently when I boarded a Kabo Air flight in Abuja. It is good to see you again."

Another minuscule lesson on what benefits come from just being friendly. I giggled, so relieved that he remembered.

Looking for a flight, he kept banging away at the keyboard. I was trying hard not to act nervous, as I certainly did not want him to think that I was in a rush to get out of Nigeria due to nefarious activity. Then my inner voice said distinctly, "He will get you out tonight."

Ah, the voice! What a relief. As any "non-rev" (non-revenue airline employee) knows, the most welcome sound in the world is that of a ticket machine beginning to click as it spits out your boarding pass. Even though I was "full rev," it still sounded musical to me. I was *very* grateful to make a quick getaway.

The handsome, no-nonsense Dutchman had gotten me out on a flight that very night.

Back at the hotel, I was rushing around like a deranged woman. I had so many people to say goodbye to. Not only incredibly emotional but also exhausting. Suley, my favorite housekeeper, Abdul and the front desk guys, along with Natania the engineer all came by as I was frantically packing. Sorting my things out in double time, I gave them T-shirts, tapes, foreign magazines, clothes, and gifts for their girlfriends. I also had something nice to give to the Dutchman for his wife in sincere appreciation for getting me out of Kano on such short notice near Christmas.

Whenever I travel for an extended time, I take various gifts with me. Some could be given as house gifts, while others are more expensive and meaningful, just in case the occasion arises. It had. A pair of Claddagh 12-karat gold earrings in their original box, which I had purchased in Shannon, was tucked into my purse.

Confusion reigned in my room as an endless stream of friends came by to wish me farewell and perhaps pick up a trinket or two. I was also processing memories of Yasser and the great times I had enjoyed in Nigeria with him as I expeditiously plowed through my things. Three hours remained. The phone rang. It was Mohamed, the chief's attorney.

"Tania, what on Earth has happened between you and the chief? Are you alright? Are you going to stay in Nigeria? Don't worry, the chief will be fine in a few days, and it will all be forgotten."

Thanking Mohamed but still upset and realistically afraid, I told him I was planning a hasty retreat to America via Amsterdam that very evening. He immediately offered me a ride to the airport, the perfect case scenario. Mohamed was articulate and knew well how to navigate through the officials at the airport. I was still appreciative that he had accompanied Yasser six weeks before.

Hearing some shuffling noise, I whirled around to see Suley, who had always pleaded with me to help him get to America. Trying hard to hold back tears, Suley and I spoke for a few minutes, then hugged, and he left. It was a bit too much for both of us.

An hour later, when I had made a serious dent into packing, my intuitive voice told me to go downstairs and find Suley. I had never been to the housekeeper's quarters before, so I had to look around. I strongly felt that I needed to find him. It did not take long. He was face down on his bed, sobbing loudly. It was such an emotional sight. The "room" was miserable, perhaps four feet by six feet. The "bed" was one of those one-inch mattresses that you throw on an outdoor chaise-longue. What lousy conditions. Surprised, he stood up and we hugged for a long time. "I don't know if I will ever see you again, Tania," Suley said, "but I certainly hope I do. Please write and keep in touch, and call when you can. Tell us that you made it safely back to America. I also wish you a wonderful Christmas."

Again, it was difficult to say good-bye.

"I took Yasser to the airport, but I certainly wasn't expecting to take you so soon," Mohamed the attorney said as he wound along the streets of Kano. "Often we think about him, and now we're going to miss you as well."

Sighing, he jokingly repeated he had missed his chance to take me out before Yasser came. Moving on to a more serious note, he had no idea what had gotten into the chief, either. He was as perplexed as anyone. "Tell me, what happened?" and as I began to explain the chief's tirade for the hundredth time that day, he shook his head in disbelief.

As I bade goodbye to the loyal counselor, I wanted so much to give him a big hug. I had no idea when I would see him, or any of them, again. With his staunch devotion to our friendship, he had come through like a trooper for Yasser, and now for me.

Ascending the steps towards the KLM plane in my sundress and sandals, I was glad to see the Dutchman greeting passengers. "Welcome aboard, Tania."

I fidgeted in my purse for the gold Claddagh earrings, then thrust the velvet box into his palm. 'What's this?" he asked, smiling.

"Those are for your wife because I don't have any suitable gifts for men on me," I joked. Shifting my voice to a more serious tone, I added, "You have *no* idea how much it means to me that you got me on this flight."

Reaching the back of the plane, I saw a row of four empty seats. Wow, I thought. The Dutchman really buffed me out! I settled in, spreading my things across. Squatters' rights, you know. Just as I was beginning to play my music and enjoy the feeling of "living large," a whitish-faced young lady from Holland approached my row. I immediately recognized that her pale-white complexion was not her normal color. She was super ill. Often when you get sick in Africa, there are any number of culprits: most often food, bugs, or water. Perhaps you forgot to close your mouth when you were in the shower.

Straightening up, I offered her the other three seats so that she could stretch out and sleep, which she did for the entire six-hour flight. I was also quite ill but did not know it yet. The infection was in me, but it had not manifested itself at that point. It would still take another ten days.

As we roared down the runway in our pristine 747, now surrounded by Europeans, I had such mixed feelings. Tears welled up in my eyes. As the jet's nose lifted up from Nigerian soil, I viewed the sprinkling lights of Kano from above. My adopted African home reminded me of diamonds on black velvet. As it slipped away from my line of vision, I gazed up to see my favorite constellation, Orion, as exquisite as ever, reminding me of my first night on the balcony in Maiduguri. Thoughts on many levels ran through my mind as I revisited all the images of Nigeria I was leaving behind. Taking out my diary, I began to recollect those impressions. With overwhelming relief, as we flew north towards Amsterdam one thing was certain: I was safe.

Feeling somewhat guilty, I furtively swiped a blanket off my flight which landed in Washington. Sporting my African look in December weather, I had the usual colorful sundress and bare legs with sandals, so I not only looked out of place but was freezing my ass off in 23-degree weather. I used the unflattering blanket as a pashmina while I waited for the bus. What a sight. I just could not wait to get home to tell my friends about my abrupt departure from Kano.

Relieved when Cicero answered the phone, I was yakking at 90 miles per hour, describing every last detail. I was hoping to get some good insight from him as he knew the chief and was familiar with the customs in Nigeria. Poor guy, he could not get a word in edgewise, but I was frustrated, running on nervous energy, and looking for any clues to reveal the origin of the chief's tirade. He put his wife Amina on the phone.

"Tania, Garba is flying up tomorrow from Miami. Would you like to greet him at the airport with me?" That was super good news. Garba had a level head and would most certainly be able to make sense of the events that had transpired earlier that week. It would also be fabulous to see him on *my* side of the Atlantic.

So as to not to look "down and out," I wore a black suede mini skirt, a sexy black blouse, suede boots that came over the top of my knee, and my mother's black diamond mink coat. Strolling down the jetway, Garba was astonished. "Hajjia Tania, what are you doing here? I thought that you planned to stay in Nigeria until spring!"

"Oh, Garba, it's such a long story. Why don't you come back to my flat for some champagne and I'll tell you everything? We have so much to discuss, and I need to ask you some key things, as well."

Knowing he loved champagne, I bought a bottle of Veuve Clicquot, which we served at Pan Am. As we spoke in my condo, I held steady, telling him the entire story, trying to remember every detail as best I could. He was sympathetic, deeply concerned, and asked pointed questions. But just like everyone else, he found it a complete mystery that the chief had exploded like that.

After listening carefully to my recollection, Garba said, "Tania, let me make some phone calls. I will get to the bottom of this. I certainly don't understand why that happened, but I'll have a much better idea after I speak with certain people."

The next afternoon, we met at a café. "Tania, you will never believe this," he began. He was searching for the right words. "You know those sycophants who are always swirling around my brother? You also know how I can't stand them," he added. "They realized that you and the chief were becoming closer as you stayed on in Nigeria. They were trying to get rid of you, get you out of the way, so that they'd have a clear crack at my brother."

Garba wanted to say something else but hesitated. "Tania, I'll just tell you straight out. The jackals who surround the chief told him that you were a CIA agent and he had been duped by you. It made him absolutely furious to think you had tricked him." Smiling, Garba said, "Of course I know that you are not an agent . . ."

I interrupted, "Well, Garba, come *on*! First off, if I was an agent, I would speak fluent Hausa-Fulani. More importantly, I would have spent all my time outside the hotel constantly trying to gather information, not wandering the grounds with a chimp on my hip. Now that I think of it, what on Earth would be worth spying on, anyway?"

A slight smile broke over my face. Even though the experience had been harrowing, it did have its kooky side. I have been mistaken for an agent a few times in the D.C. area. Four years later, I was cast as an extra on TV's *The West Wing* as a secret service agent since I have the "Fed look." In reality, only my closest friends knew I had gone through a series of interviews to become a field agent for the CIA in Los Angeles in 1981. But the question remained: what was there to spy on in Kano?

What Garba told me made some sense of the absurd things the chief had asked me that day. Upset about what had happened, Garba wanted to help, but the chief was very bull-headed, and even his favorite brother could not persuade him otherwise. We decided to have some fun and visit the National Air and Space Museum, a place I never tire of. From an aviation background, Garba loved seeing the vast aeronautic displays.

Two days after Christmas, missing my friends in Nigeria, I decided to call Isaac, Titus, and the other house boys at the chief's villa to see how they were doing. I wanted to wish them a Merry Christmas. I heard someone pick up the line. The chief never answered the phone, as someone always grabbed it first to screen all calls. For some inexplicable reason, this time he picked up the receiver.

"Good evening, this is Tania calling from America. Is either Titus or Isaac there? May I speak to either one?"

I was astonished to hear the chief's voice, but even more surprised to hear how he carried on, as if everything was completely normal. "Madame, how are you? How was your flight? Are you happy to be home? How was Christmas?" On and on.

Flabbergasted, I replied, "Everything is fine, yes, chief," as he impatiently yelled non-stop for a boy to fetch either Isaac or Titus.

It was probably the first time in his life that someone called him asking for the *houseboys*. It was perpetually the other way around—somebody was always desperately trying to get past the servants to take advantage of the chief somehow.

I would never hear the chief's voice again.

⌒☙

One of two things must have transpired after I left Nigeria. Either someone "in the know," like Garba or the attorney Mohamed, had convinced the chief that he was way off base about my status. Or, perhaps he became spooked, thinking that if I *was* the real thing, there could be trouble down the road. Agents who have been wronged have a way of exacting revenge, you know.

Isaac came to the phone. It was good to hear his voice and listen to what had happened in the six days since I had left. I felt as if I had been gone forever.

"Merry Christmas, Isaac. Thank you for always showing me around Kano, I really appreciate it. I fondly remember all the fun times we had together." I told him.

"Merry Christmas, Tania." Isaac replied, "You know we miss you so much here. Everyone sends greetings to you."

Soon Garba left Washington and flew back to Lagos, as I got ready to fly down to Cape Canaveral for the launching of the space shuttle.

⌒☙

Welcoming Garba to DC

An official at NASA had given me two VIP invites to see the launch. The timing could not have been more perfect. I was anxious to ingratiate myself back into my own culture, and what better way than to witness the launch of a space shuttle? The ticket was golden: that is to say I would be seated in the bleachers three miles from the launch site among the NASA employees. None of that "touristy" talk, like, "Where are you from? How is your vacation going?" We knew exactly where this intelligentsia was from: NASA Headquarters.

My friend Kay flew in from the West Coast for the launch. We were surrounded by astronauts, engineering professors, and the scientists who were conducting an experiment with lab rats on board. We were the only people sitting there who did not work for NASA. It was engrossing just to hear their intriguing conversations. The countdown began as I readied my camera. The loudspeaker advised us that "the shuttle gathers significant speed right after launch, so you better pay attention, or you'll miss it. It will reach orbit a mere eight minutes after takeoff, so you must move at lightning speed to get a good photo."

The countdown began. The air was supercharged with excitement and anticipation. People were chattering animatedly, but stopped, almost in unison, and crooned "OOOOHHH" every time the computer halted the countdown for a few minutes. When it resumed, everyone spontaneously clapped and shouted "Yeah!"

The shuttle blasted off the launch pad with a thunderous clap, spewing out bulbous clouds of exhaust. Big and small birds alike, terrified by the violent gust of wind, flew erratically to safety every which way. I continually snapped the launch, watching it through my lens. You must keep your eye on it, or it will be out of your line of vision in no time. Everyone excitedly cheered the shuttle on as they might do at the Kentucky Derby when a favorite horse tears down the track.

The conversation between the astronauts and mission control was heard over the loudspeakers long after takeoff, drawing the spectators into another aspect of this sensational voyage. The space crew was spirited far beyond the stratosphere traveling at 17,580 miles per hour.

The employees clapped loudly at their project, which had come to fruition in a most dramatic way. I was thrilled for all of them who had contributed to this space flight. What a feeling for the NASA employees, surrounded by their colleagues, knowing the significant contribution that each had made to this magnificent journey into the heavens. As I continually took pictures of the launch, I was overcome by emotion. Beneath my sunglasses, tears streamed down my cheeks, this time with joy rather than despair. In stark contrast with my ugly exit from Nigeria, the launch made me feel so glad to be an American, back in America. The sharp clack from the sky signaled the rocket breaking the sound barrier. Kay and I strained our eyes to watch the shuttle until it became a miniscule gleaming dot in the bright blue sky.

A few days later, back home in Virginia, I woke up one morning with a headache so violent it felt as if someone had taken a sledgehammer and whacked me in the middle of my cerebral cortex. I had not partied the night before, or even the two previous days for that matter. I could not think of what may have caused the horrendous headache. I had never felt one like this before, parties or not. I rolled out of bed, took two Anacin, and tried to go about my day. No luck. I was completely down, just for an old headache. I drank hot mint tea as my roomie rubbed my head, but it continued.

Cicero and Amina called to ask how the space launch had been. That was great timing, as Amina solved the mystery about the headache. "I'm certain you have malaria," she said, "because of the way you describe your pain. It is the first symptom you feel, and the last thing to go."

"What else can I expect?" I asked.

"You will have cold and hot sweats, too."

They were not far behind. My sheets were soaking wet. I just could not get comfortable. The thermostat in our house was set at a perfect 70 degrees, but I made everyone nuts while I constantly adjusted it up and down. The headache was nonstop, pounding through every part of my brain. No region was left alone. Previously, I had not known there were so many areas located inside my skull.

I had already scheduled a medium reading with my dear friend Steve, so I decided to put off making a doctor's appointment until I heard from him. I am not certain how much American doctors knew about malaria, anyway, unless they have spent time in the tropics. Being cautious, I had taken anti-malarial medication religiously throughout my stay in Nigeria, but to no avail.

I called Garba in Lagos. A growly voice answered, "Hello?"

"This is Tania calling from the US, is Garba there?"

"Tania, this *is* Garba."

I had not recognized his voice at all. It was the voice of a man who smokes three packs a day. "Garba, I have malaria," I said.

"I have it too," he groaned.

He had the exact same symptoms that were making me sick. We had been foolish to stay outside on his patio after the rains because that is when we had been bitten. Had I known, I would have urged our group to move inside.

During my reading, Steve advised me, "Jonathan (my healer in spirit) is here. He wants you to do the following things: drink as much fresh orange juice as you can, as it is so helpful to you for fighting the malaria. Take Motrin instead of Anacin for your headaches. Take Vitamins B1, B6, and B12. In addition to drinking orange juice, drink lots of chamomile tea."

I was lucky. In eight days, while following the advised regimen, my malaria was nearly gone, except for the nagging headache. Just as Amina had advised me, it was the last symptom to leave my body.

After my five-month stay in Nigeria, I would never see the chief again. Several years later, while I was half a world away working on Steven Spielberg's *Catch Me If You Can* in Los Angeles, the chief was in the ancient city of Kano, trying to pull all his companies together so they would benefit from a strong and united cohesiveness.

One night in early April, he called an unexpected special meeting with his three brothers and trusted aides from the various Kabo companies. Gathered around the large oval dining table where I had broken bread with him many times before, they made a true effort to iron out their differences. The discussion was spirited and somewhat contentious at first considering the astronomical assets involved, but then smoothed out.

Garba later told me that after some hours of an intensely powerful tete-a-tete between the prominent men, a denouement was reached.

The meeting was adjourned shortly after 3 a.m. Bidding his colleagues and brothers goodbye, the chief climbed the stairs to his marble bathroom for the very last time to draw a bath.

As the sun peeked over Kano's horizon, Jarma's wife was suddenly awakened to the disturbing sound of rushing water. Jarred awake, she promptly sat up in bed to witness a rising flood. Realizing it had originated from the bathroom, she slogged her way down the hall through the swirling water to find the chief's soaked body sprawled on the floor.

At the age of 62, he had been felled by a massive heart attack. The towering figure who had been so authoritative in "the China of Africa" was gone without a moment's notice.

18

President Clinton Honors President Mandela with Solid Gold

"President Nelson Mandela is currently in New York, scheduled to speak before the United Nations later today. Tonight, he will fly to Washington, D.C., to be honored this week by President Bill Clinton, who will present him with the Congressional Gold Medal," the television anchor announced.

The Congressional Gold Medal is the highest honor that the United States can bestow upon an individual from another country, although some have been awarded to Americans. Congress was going to present the award to President Mandela for his "life-long dedication to the abolition of apartheid and the promotion of reconciliation among the people of the Republic of South Africa."

The first recipient was George Washington, in 1776. In modern times, Prime Minister Winston Churchill, Mother Teresa, and His Holiness the Dalai Lama have also been honored.

How was I going to find a way to meet Mandela? I considered him to be one of my "major gurus,"—that is to say, he resided in an exclusive, tiny group of public figures whom I held in the highest esteem on this planet. A humble, but larger-than-life human being, Mandela had spent his entire life making a *real* difference in this world. A partial list of my other "gurus" also includes the Dalai Lama, Mahatma Gandhi, Martin Luther King Jr., Oprah, Bono, Mother Teresa, and my personal friend, the Rev. Steve Woods. All these enlightened people "walk the walk" when making their contribution to humanity, and are not dissuaded by the nay-sayers. No question the world is a better place because they lived in it. Along with millions of others, I also deeply loved and admired Princess Diana, and was heartbroken when she died.

Most major religions teach that if you can forgive a person, or group of people, for betraying or mistreating you, you will set yourself free of that binding handicap. Then you can move forward without hindrance. Mandela exemplified that adage. I am endlessly amazed that he was able to forgive his jailers on Robben Island, well known for its institutional brutality, after a staggering 27 years of being incarcerated and abused. He even invited the prison guards to his presidential inauguration. Talk about redemption. Life can present some remarkable surprises.

Just two weeks after being released from almost 10,000 days in prison, instead of relaxing from his ordeal, or "going to Disneyland" as we like to say, Mandela was already actively engaged in fostering peace between the South African tribes. During an emotional speech in Natal, Mandela urged his followers and their opponents to abandon their weapons, bringing to a halt their ruthless slaughter. Historical records show that, despite gloomy predictions the world over, the transformation of South African apartheid to a democracy, however fragile, was achieved with almost no bloodshed. No doubt we can thank Mandela for the peaceful transition.

Who was the chump who said that you never meet quality people in bars? When I moved to Alexandria, Virginia, in the late '80s, the bar I patronized attracted a real cross-section of engaging people whom I befriended. Among these new pals was an FBI agent who is a lifelong friend, Bill, who became my tenant and confidant, and Jerry, a fun-loving Congressman on the Ways and Means Committee. That's *right*, I would call Jerry and see if I could wrangle an invitation to the ceremony. He had invited me to President Clinton's swearing-in six years before; perhaps he could work a little magic again. I could not get to the phone fast enough. While I waited for the Congressman to come on the line, I was already planning what to wear: a bright green silk suit with the emerald and diamond ring that my Godmother Elva gave me to match. To carry the energy of my mother and father, I planned to wear the gold necklace and matching bracelet that my father gave to my mother in Venezuela before I was born. I chose the green suit because of its significance. Green is not only the color of springtime and money, but, more importantly to me, healing. Black Italian wing-tipped shoes rounded out my ensemble. Now, who on Earth was I going to invite? What a hot, *hot,* ticket.

Jerry came on the line, interrupting my rapid thoughts. "Tania, what's up? How have you been?"

"I'm fine, Jerry. Hey, listen, I have a favor to ask, if you can possibly do it . . ."

Laughing at my boldness, Jerry said, "Actually, you are in luck. Bonnie and I will be out of town, so two invites are yours."

"Wow, Jerry, thanks a million! I'm so jazzed!" I replied excitedly.

"Just swing by my office early so you can pass through security in time to get a good seat. You want to have a good view. I hear there will be a few Hollywood types attending as well. Have fun," he added.

Thanking him profusely, I hung up. Immediately picking up the receiver, I sought to invite someone who would really appreciate the occasion. I decided to call three Nigerian friends, one at a time. I knew they would relish the rare opportunity to witness a fellow African being the first one honored with this eminent award. I called Kofo Akinmade, then Ali, then Dauda. Regrettably, none of them could make it. I would go alone.

Entering the spacious Capitol Rotunda where the ceremony was to take place, I found a good seat. High-profile senators, congressmen, actors, ambassadors, and the South African delegation all paraded into the grand circular room. Elegant marble statues of previous presidents were stationed around the perimeter. Eight large portraits depicting key events from our history hung from the walls. This is the hallowed room where the assassinated President Kennedy's body lay in state in 1963. I gazed straight up at the spectacular mural, reminiscent of the Sistine Chapel, on the ceiling high above. Absorbing the ever-increasing, highly charged atmosphere, I began to spin a little, like swirling in a vortex. We were sitting in the precise center of the Capitol Building, the seat of our American government.

President Mandela arriving at the US Capitol

Utterly awestruck observing this scene, I felt miniscule in stature, and a bit in thought, as well. This is where decisions are made that, for better or for worse, impact us globally. In the building where I sat at that moment, the nerve center of our world, discussions take place every minute of every day that can have a profound effect on my future, and for millions of my fellow citizens.

The spirit of my father Glenn appeared close by. I could "see" him sitting next to me, smiling with approval that I was about to witness a historical event as he often did. *Hello, Daddy, I just knew that you would be here.* Had he lived, there was no doubt that he would have encouraged me to be engaged in some aspect of the political process. An integral part of his life, he was frequently up on Capitol Hill.

I glanced at the program. Oh, no. At the bottom, it read, "Absolutely no flash photography allowed." I was *ruined!* Taking photos was not only enormous fun for me, but they helped me immeasurably to describe an impression of something meaningful. They also kept fond memories alive.

I kept an acute meerkat lookout, watching and waiting for someone to break this rule. That would be my signal.

Pin-striped suited officials sat across the aisle, most carrying the *Washington Post,* screaming tales of President Clinton's misadventures and impending impeachment. It felt odd for me to read that banner headline, when momentarily I would see the main subject of that day's scandalous news in person. Our president was about to walk out any minute to honor his close friend, whom he admired greatly.

Danny Glover strolled in, taking a seat near Senator Edward Kennedy and his nephew, Congressman Patrick Kennedy. Close by, the South African delegation, complete with translators, were resplendent in their brilliantly-colored traditional African costumes, in stark contrast to the dark conservative suits worn in Washington. After Labor Day, but still hot, nearly everyone was already in their "winter uniform." I like to joke and say that I moved to Southern California so that I would be able to wear white with no shame in between Labor Day and Easter. I favor imaginative sandals, bright colors, and never any pantyhose if I can get away with it. In this crowd, you could readily tell the Hollywood peeps from the diplomats, legislators, and their aides.

Activist Dick Gregory arrived, sitting not far from Bono, wearing his signature sunglasses. The Rev. Jesse Jackson leaned over to speak with the parents of Fulbright scholar Amy Biehl, who had been brutally murdered in South Africa while on an extended trip to assist in South Africa's first democratic election. After details of the tragedy had been featured in the world press for months, her parents made an extraordinary gesture to forgive the murderers of their gorgeous, vivacious daughter.

Representatives Maxine Waters, Ron Dellums, and Newt Gingrich, along with Senators Carolyn Moseley-Braun, Alfonse D'Amato, and Strom Thurmond all stood to join President Clinton in welcoming President Mandela to the dais. Gingrich, in his opening remarks, had likened Mandela to George Washington, referring to him as "the father of a multi-racial democracy."

Mandela, humbled in his posture, approached the podium. A look of gratitude and vast excitement shone on his face. He was absolutely glowing. Men can sometimes be radiant, too, I have discovered. Just like a bride on her wedding day, men brighten up considerably when it

President Mandela after receiving the Gold Medal

has something to do with power, honor, love, or a combination thereof.

This was the second significant occasion Mandela was celebrating in quick succession. He was not only going to receive the solid gold medal, but he was also a newlywed, recently married to Dr. Graca Machel, the widow of the president of Mozambique. She was concerned with resolving the plight of children around the world who were drafted or kidnapped and forced to fight in conflicts or civil wars. Standing in the front row, she took a quick bow to the hearty applause of the audience when introduced by Clinton. She was sparkling. It was obvious that they were still on their honeymoon.

This was one of those rare occasions when partisan politics were temporarily put aside, as politicians came together for a common purpose. For a while after such events, it appears as if all is well in paradise, and contentious issues have been forgiven between the parties, but do not be fooled. Once they return to the gallery, the caustic barbs fire away again almost immediately. Some of the legislators in the room were hell-bent to impeach Clinton, but for a couple of hours, the adversarial undercurrents went on a short hiatus as everyone took a temporary break. I was always tickled by one legislator's observation: "After 6 p.m., we are all friends on the Hill."

Sure, as they merrily head off to any one of the numerous Irish pubs dotted around the Capitol, all is forgiven, at least during the time you can consume a few happy hour cocktails.

Another of my favorite D.C. expressions is, "If your dog thinks you are the greatest person in the world, don't get a second opinion." Yup, you see a lot of canines in the capital city.

Clinton had developed rosacea (redness on the face) from all the stress and political fallout, but he was still wearing his wedding band. Just before the ceremony began, he leaned over, whispering something witty into Newt's ear. That summer they had frequently clashed as bitter political rivals, but this day they heartily laughed, covering their mouths like school kids. I would have loved to have known what two men, from opposite ends of the political spectrum, found so mutually funny.

President Clinton welcomed the room full of dignitaries gathered for this grand occasion. Glancing at Mandela, he began:

> *To my friend, President Mandela: Americans as one today, across the lines that divide us, pay tribute to your struggle, to your achievement, and to the inspiration you have given us to do better. Others have said with profound conviction and eloquence what it is that we love and admire. Today we offer the man who has received the Nobel Prize, the highest honor within the gift of this country. The thing that always humbles me when I am with Nelson Mandela is the sense of serenity and peace and engagement in the moment. And so I say to all of you, we should not waste our days; we should make more of our days.*

Looking over at Mandela sitting close by, he added:

> *And, finally, in forgiving those who imprisoned him here, reminds us of the most fundamental lesson of all: that in the end, apartheid was a defeat of the heart, the mind, the spirit. It was not just a structure outside and jailhouses within which people were kept; it was a division of the mind*

and soul against itself. We owe it to Nelson Mandela not simply to give him this award, but to live by the lesson he taught us and to tear down every last vestige of apartheid in our hearts—everything that divides us, one from another. For those of us who have been privileged to know this remarkable man, no medal, no award, no fortune, nothing we could give him could possibly compare to the gift he has given to us and the world. The only gift that is true recompense is to continue his mission, and to live by the power of his profound and wonderful example. Now, as prescribed by law, it is my privilege to present the Congressional Gold Medal to President Nelson Mandela.

The applause in the room was so loud it almost shook the ceiling light fixtures loose. Everyone jumped to their feet.

President Mandela admired the precious medal, showing it to the audience. He then handed it to Rep. Waters for "safekeeping" and stepped up to the dais. After thanking Clinton and Congress, he began:

There is one regret I've had throughout my life: that I never became the heavyweight boxing champion of the world. I'd like my friend, Evander Holyfield, to know that today I feel like the heavyweight champion of the world. It has been my great privilege to serve a people whose bondage to an inhuman system evoked the solidarity of all those who love freedom and justice; a people whose triumph over the divisions of racist doctrine has given new life to humanity's hope for a world without hatred and discrimination. I am conscious that in bestowing the Congressional Gold Medal upon me you are evoking these bonds between our nations . . . . it is in that spirit that I humbly accept the award. As one who has dedicated his life to the pursuit of unity, I am moved by the consensus in your nation's regard for the achievements of my people. And I feel a great pride in the fact that with a few citizens of other countries who have received this high honor, the name of an African has been added.

President Mandela spoke of how "countless ordinary American citizens responded to the call to join the worldwide anti-apartheid campaign." Acknowledging Amy Biehl's parents in the front row, he noted, "Among those we remember today is young Amy Biehl," adding, "She lost her life in the turmoil of our transition."

In the final few moments, after thanking Congress again, the stoic and dignified Mandela closed by saying, "There is still in all of us the capacity to touch one another's hearts across oceans and continents. The award with which you honor me today is an expression of the common humanity that binds us, one person to another, nation to nation, and people of the North to people of the South. I receive it with pride as a symbol of partnership for peace, prosperity, and equity as we enter the new millennium. I thank you." he concluded, to thunderous applause. Most had tears in their eyes.

As Mandela concluded, caught up in this exuberant historical moment, I leaned over, whispering to Dottie, a congressional aide, "I just *love* that man!"

Clapping, she smiled and nodded. On stage, Senator Strom Thurmond, in his mid-nineties, then the longest-serving senator in US history, had taken an unauthorized snooze earlier while everyone listened to Clinton. As Mandela's speech ended, awakened by Earth-shaking applause, he rallied and stood up, vigorously patting the African president's arm, then, in a touching moment, hoisted it up high. In the 1980s, he had led the charge of voting for a provision declaring Mandela's African National Congress a terrorist group. How times had changed.

Rising to their feet, the audience reacted with uproarious applause and cheers as his acceptance speech ended. "Ladies and gentlemen, please stay in your seats while the presidents are escorted off the stage."

Rapidly moving into key positions, the Secret Service surrounded Clinton and Mandela. However, it was obvious that Mandela was not ready yet to give up his few precious moments in the sun, as he stretched down to greet well-wishers, enjoying every single second. Plenty of hugs were exchanged on the stage; not a common sight in our nation's capital. Mandela's wife hugged Amy Biehl's mother.

Then something happened that made me oh-so-happy. Many of the "stiff suits" in the Rotunda whipped out pocket cameras and snapped away in defiance of the warning. Flashes went off all over. Grinning like a Cheshire cat, I abruptly stood up. Sucking in my gut, I did the "crab dance," meaning I moved sideways with the adept speed of a well-practiced square dancer. In seconds, I was up front, right under the podium.

"God Bless you, President Mandela, I love you!" I crooned, more than once, from directly below him.

Coming closer, he leaned down, giving me a cordial handshake. "Congratulations, Mr. President!" I exclaimed, smiling broadly.

"Thank you," the jubilant Mandela answered in a gentle voice before an official caught his attention.

The air was mega-charged with high energy. The Secret Service team scanned the audience nervously in every direction. Clinton looked over affectionately at his dear friend, smiling warmly. Swarms of admirers pressed in to shake hands with Mandela and to greet him personally. Well-coiffed ladies in smart designer suits positioned themselves close to him. Fellow South Africans, overcome by emotion, called out, "Madiba!" As the recipient of so much loving energy coming from all directions, Mandela did not know which way to look first.

A series of clicking sounds boomed from behind me. The sounds' intonations immediately commanded Mandela's attention. I recognized that the man was addressing Mandela in Xhosa, Mandela's tribal language. Whatever his fellow tribesman was saying, Mandela was certainly elated to hear it so far from home. Their conversation in Xhosa sounded harmonious to me. I was standing in between the cherished South African president and one of his citizens, exchanging constant clicking noises back and forth. For the second time that day, I would have given anything to have known what was being said.

Right behind Mandela and Clinton was Robert Kennedy, Jr., smiling at the dignitaries. Quickly snapping one last photo of them, I felt that it would be a good one. The presidents were escorted out.

While the subway clacked towards home, I sang Mandela's name repeatedly like a jubilant child. It has a melody to it, anyway. I was in a blissful, dream-like state. So grateful that Fate had granted my wish, I had met two of my "major gurus"—Mother Teresa, and now Mandela. More opportunities were on the way.

The timeless photo of Clinton and Mandela dazzled me. I had it enlarged and called the South African Embassy for Mandela's address. The receptionist was quite snooty. "You can send it to President Nelson Mandela, Pretoria, South Africa," she sniffed.

Taking a cue from the Brits, I huffed, "That simply won't do. I attended the Congressional Gold Medal Ceremony and would like to send him a particular photo which I'm sure he will like."

She snapped out of it and gave me a good address.

I had this strong, intuitive feeling that he would not only receive the photo but would write me a thank you note. After several weeks with no word, I said to my friend Kofo, "That's funny, I had this powerful feeling I would hear from Mandela."

Weeks passed and nothing came. Then, one day I reached into my mailbox and one particular envelope tingled in my hand when I touched it. As I separated it from the others, I noticed the detailed presidential seal, designed with a silver multi-colored hologram on the envelope. Ahh, crooks beware; you will have a tough time duplicating this seal. Opening it gingerly, I drew in my breath.

My intuition had been right on the mark. In fact, my favorite African leader had replied promptly to receiving my photo, but his answer had been addressed to Falls Church, VA, not including "USA." His letter had traveled all the way up to Vancouver, Canada, where it was sent back to Pretoria. The envelope then crossed the Atlantic once again, this time headed towards my home in Virginia.

I love you, President Mandela. I do, I do.

NELSON MANDELA

Ref: Sb 20000112 anderson R (KN)

12 January 2000

Ms Tania Anderson

Falls Church
VA 22041
USA

Dear Tania Anderson

RE: PHOTOGRAPH SENT

I acknowledge with thanks receipt of your letter addressed to Mr Mandela.

Thank you for the time and trouble you took to send the photo it is greatly appreciated.

Mr Mandela has asked me to convey his best wishes to you.

Yours sincerely

KATHERINE NDEBELE
SECRETARY

PRIVATE BAG X70 000, HOUGHTON, 2041, SOUTH AFRICA
TEL: 27 (0)11 728 1000/1100, FAX: 27 (0)11 728 1111

President Mandela's thank you letter to me

19

The Aura of the Dalai Lama

"There's a blonde cobra slithering around the flower beds, and tons of bats are screaming throughout the lobby!" Our colleague Anne exclaimed to us as we entered the New Delhi Hotel on our return from Nepal.

"Per and I saw a beige-colored cobra, about three feet long, prowling through the flower bed just outside the coffee shop a while ago," she continued, "and a large Hindu wedding with hundreds of guests will take place out there this afternoon!"

Danish Per readily nodded in agreement. Apparently, things had gone south during our short absence. Animated, articulate, and always fun, Per and Anne were ever-so-ready to deal with any unexpected crises that might crop up on or off the plane. Workers hammered away outside, building a wedding platform. On the grass, piles of fresh flowers waited to be placed for the nuptial decorations. "Is the hotel doing anything about the unwanted beasties?" my friend Donna asked.

"They have a couple of 'serpent wranglers' out there, but I doubt if they are making any headway. For everyone's sake, I hope that they flush the snake out soon. Everybody here wears sandals. They were most casual when I asked them to do something about it," Anne added, with tension in her voice. She sighed in resignation.

"Hey, how was Nepal?" Per asked.

"We had a great time," Donna replied, "the elephant safari was fantastic, and the landscape was gorgeous."

My thoughts were elsewhere. "By the way, has anyone checked, or do they know if the bats are rabid? That's no joke. I spoke to a Filipino doctor once who treated people with rabies, and it's brutal. I have also seen bats flying all around the atrium. Not to mention the dried-up fountain where the mosquitos are enjoying an ongoing festival."

Some type of animal-related caper was always happening in India. Once, when Donna and I were riding in a tuk-tuk (a three-wheeled taxi with a lawn mower engine), a man with a large platter on his head walking along caught my eye as Donna was speaking. I have trained my eyes to give certain difficult things a quick once-over to determine whether I should give them a second glance. If the scene is too rough, I will not look again. This scrawny man had a platter loaded down with freshly-skinned bloody lamb skulls, and as Donna was talking, I averted my eyes, consciously thinking, *I do not need to look at that sight again.*

"Perhaps the hotel staff should place a few mongooses in the garden to do what they do best and ferret the cobras out," Donna said to Anne, adding, "we saw one of those shows by the road where the mongoose beats the stuffing out of the cobra."

I chimed in, "What a macho little animal! The minute they took the lid off the basket, the mongoose made a beeline for the cobra, which was swaying back and forth to the keeper's flute music. Confusion reigned with all the onlookers and the other snakes at the scene, but the mongoose was totally focused. He waited for precisely the right moment, then bolted upward, propelling himself up behind the cobra. He latched onto the back of his head right at the neck and hung on for some minutes while the snake writhed wildly, fighting for his life. The razor-sharp teeth of the mongoose were imbedded into the cobra's neck, close to where the heart is located. He hung on for dear life. If he let go, the tables could immediately turn, and he could be killed in an instant. The cobra looked as if he could not believe what was happening. It was all over in a few tense minutes. The keeper casually put the mongoose back in the basket and came around to collect tips. When he inadvertently kicked the top of the basket off, the mongoose, still licking blood from his face and paws, sat up at attention, ready to jump out again for another round with a new competitor."

The little critters are relentless and fearless. Carefully watching the snake's rhythm, they know exactly when to strike. An F-16 pilot in Japan once told me that he witnessed a mongoose in a match with a rattlesnake. Before long, the mongoose lost big time because the rattler made continual violent strikes. Not having the slow, methodical swaying of the cobra ruined the mongoose's strategy, taking him by lethal surprise.

Seated in the atrium's center, we noticed some unusual activity across the lobby. "I wonder what is going on over there," Per said.

Six lean Indian soldiers marched in, each with a long-bayoneted rifle chained to their waist. Their black Labradors sniffed at anything within range, as if to prove their worth. Bomb sniffers in our modest hotel were not the norm unless the wedding party had invited some real heavy hitters.

The soldiers got into the elevator and stopped on my floor. I followed them to investigate. The guards were setting up a post in the large suite at the end of the hall, two doors down from my room. Then I noticed three men dressed in smart suits. I introduced myself. They were Tibetan, and my heart began to beat a bit faster. Even as a teenager, I admired the Tibetans, their beliefs, their spiritual gifts, and their luminous leader, His Holiness the Dalai Lama. The more I learn about the Tibetans, the more I love them. I used to join them for their traditional annual New Year's celebration, called Losar, whether in D.C. or LA.

I could have never foreseen that the Dalai Lama would be staying at our dirt-simple hotel near the airport, but the Tibetan advance team told me that the Indian government treated his Holiness to the suite whenever he returned to India from abroad. He was scheduled to arrive from Sweden in the wee hours. Even though I was whipped from our trip to Kathmandu, I was determined to stay up and see one of the worlds most beloved and revered human beings.

While looking outside my window to see how the wedding was progressing, I changed into a turquoise and gold silk Punjabi outfit that my friend Mary Lou Karch, another Pan Amiga, had given me. The festivities were now in full swing. It was a feast for the eyes if you enjoy a panorama of color. The wedding chamber was decorated in a fresh flower mosaic of brilliant hues. Many delicate flowers dangled down over the two "thrones" for the betrothed. Dozens of guests mingled on the lawn, some wearing Parisian silk suits while others wore saris or Punjabi outfits of every shade imaginable. The late afternoon golden light of the setting sun added the perfect tint to an already vibrant scene. I was itching just to get a closer look. I asked the Tibetan corps (their version of our Secret Service) if they were certain their leader would arrive after midnight. I certainly did not want to miss the arrival of His Holiness if I happened to be snooping around a Hindu wedding in our cobra-infested garden at the exact same moment he was walking down the hallway just outside my room.

Earrings and rings featuring my birthstone, aquamarine, enhanced my blue outfit. I slipped on gold sandals. Wearing this national costume, I would blend in quite well, at least until they heard my American accent. I did not even want to shark some buffet treats, I just wanted to see the wedding couple up close. After introducing myself quietly and inquiring about them, I got my wish. I was not disappointed. They were not only physically stunning, but coming from wealthy families, were dressed up in a way that is right out of a mythical tale of fantasy. I had never seen such a pair in my waking life.

The bride wore a full-length golden dress, elaborately embroidered with even more gold. A matching headdress was held together with a solid 24-karat tiara. A large, detailed, solid-gold necklace dazzled at her neckline. Heavy solid-gold bracelets like layered chandeliers cascaded down from the bride's arms a full ten inches. Garlands of fat pink and white flowers flowed from the newlyweds' necks. Both had red dots in between their eyebrows. The groom's ornate headdress, created in gold and silver, was reminiscent of a maharaja's crown. He wore a modest full-length white and orange robe with simple white socks. The wedding couple was just as gracious to me as if I had been a fully-fledged invited guest, even though they knew I had weaseled my way into the party.

Back upstairs, I resumed my conversation with the Tibetans while waiting for His Holiness to arrive. They related some extraordinary stories, and we enjoyed passing the time. I told them about one of my big dreams: to make a spiritual journey to Tibet one day when the time is right. I described how I have occasional visions of people who I do not currently know but will recognize when I finally do travel to Tibet. Over the years, I have had glimpses of my future trip there through a series of dreams, astral travel, and visions, which I record in my dream diary for reference later.

A fruit basket had been delivered to my room upon our return from Nepal, so I offered it to the Tibetans and Indian soldiers. One Indian took an apple, then cut it into bite-sized pieces with his bayonet. Yuck! The rifle, still chained to his waist, looked so ancient to me. What if I was a soldier in close fighting and my opponent grabbed the rifle and bayonet? I could be skewered like a shish kabob with my own weapon.

The Tibetans particularly admired Richard Gere, who was devoted to their spiritual leader. They told of the time Gere met the Dalai Lama up in Dharamsala, and how he modestly approached His Holiness. They smiled as they recalled how Gere appeared to be in awe of the leader, entering the room in a quiet, low-key, respectful manner where the Dalai Lama was perched on his hand-carved wooden throne. Suddenly, the Dalai Lama cracked a joke, laughing heartily. Bellows of laughter filled the cavernous room as he had some fun with the reticent devotee. Gere, now at total ease, formed an immediate, well-known close friendship with His Holiness.

The elevator doors opened and His Holiness emerged, closely followed by a group of officials. Standing in the doorway of my room, I was astonished. Even though he had been traveling for hours, he looked totally refreshed and relaxed. I had met Mother Teresa only two weeks prior, and now in the same country I was going to see another inhabitant of this Earth whom I hold in the highest esteem. Delighted and grateful for all these experiences, it seemed as if India was working some type of magic for me.

The omniscient Dalai Lama is another individual who is in an exclusive group of people who are closely connected with spiritual powers described in Buddhist teachings. He has a timeless look. If I did not know his age, I could have never guessed it. His face is luminous, and there is light all around him that reaches far out beyond his physical body. He walks like an ordinary man, but he is anything but ordinary. If you simply placed him in an environment where he was not known, he would immediately draw people in with his unique auric charisma. They would feel his love for his fellow man, and the attendant vibrations he sent out in every direction. It is also this constant flow of light that reaches beyond, touching all kinds of others, inviting their vibration into this special wheel of life. Feeling that energy, people are strongly attracted to the enlightened person who is sending the signal out.

Hardly able to say a word, I just wanted to take it all in as he strolled down the narrow hallway toward us. Wearing his familiar saffron/maroon robes, he walked slowly, smiling while acknowledging each person as he passed them on the way to his suite. I stood there in my Punjabi outfit with my hands folded in supplication. As he reached me, I welcomed him, saying *Tashek Deley*, the Tibetan salutation, loosely translated as "All of Buddha's blessings for you." He smiled broadly, and returned the greeting, *Tashek Deley*. He looked pleased that I greeted him in his native Tibetan. He always looks happy, even in trying times. Despite the tragic occurrences in Tibet, his love of humor, and his Buddhist faith that shows no bitterness, has sustained him and carried him along all these difficult years since 1949. He is simply a remarkable human being.

Less than an hour later, I was "in the arms of Morpheus" (the God of sleep in Greek mythology) as my Godmother Elva used to say. I entered a place of deep peace that was in the astral, combining both real and imagined visions. My months in India made me feel as if I was living partially in a fairy tale, with all the vibrant customs and never-ending adventures, both animal and human. India is indeed filled with endless visual effects of every kind.

Incidentally, we never heard about another blonde cobra sighting. With all the loud wedding activity and live Hindu music taking place in the garden, I am sure that the serpent was not looking for a nerve-jangling fracas, either.

Later that month, Donna and I stumbled upon traditional Indian nuptials of a different kind. Returning from an elephant safari north of New Delhi, we asked the driver to stop for a break. Our crew was straining their eyes to see what dozens of buzzards had just found when a Honda playing festive Hindi music, decorated with hundreds of fat canary-yellow marigolds from the hood to the trunk, pulled in. A young man in a beige suit wearing a gold and pink turban got out. In perfectly accented English, he greeted us, asking where we were from. He wondered what we were staring at. I was even *more* curious as to why his car had marigolds all over it. "We just got married," he replied, smiling broadly, pointing to one of two ladies in the back seat.

He appeared to be such a nice young man, but he was only sixteen, not even out of school. After we offered congratulations, I asked if I could take a photo of him with his new bride. She was elaborately dressed in bright red and gold silk from head to toe with matching gold jewelry. I love taking photos of people who are so different from Westerners and felt that the newlyweds would take a beautiful photo. Her face was completely covered. For some minutes, he tried to cajole the bride into getting out. She refused. It was not because she was tired from the ceremony, or did not want her photo taken, but she was extremely upset, and would not stop crying.

The young man seemed kind enough, and well educated for his age. With a sympathetic smile, he said, "She didn't want to get married."

As we began to wonder if it was to *him*, he went on to explain, just as if he was reading our thoughts. "I love her very much. She didn't want to leave her parents and come with me, but I will show her a good life," he sighed.

His new bride had just turned ten years old.

20

The Way You Look Tonight—A Visit to Mother Teresa's Orphanage

Calcutta is a rough place with its blistering heat, not to mention the humidity, punctuated by frequent whiffs of a "low tide" stink. You do not even want to know where the smell is coming from because that will certainly cut the adventure short. The poverty is so all-encompassing that the casual visitor is overwhelmed. Once I saw a lady rushing alongside the fence of the Victoria Museum, stark raving mad, shouting at the sky nonstop in Hindi, totally naked. Poor lady did not have one single possession. Nothing at all. Even though she appeared to be in her mid-sixties, she was probably in her early forties. Hardship does cruel things to people, and their faces show it. The locals admit that "New Delhi is much cleaner." I began to wonder what their frame of reference was. How does one define clean? New Delhi was scheduled as our next destination. But first we had to deal with swampy Calcutta, which the British originally chose as the capital city when they colonized India.

Have you ever noticed how particular things associated with your new destination run through your mind as you try to link up different impressions and comparisons? As our crew of 21 stuffed themselves into nine taxis, I tried to recall anything historical about the Brits in occupied India. What happened when the "Black Hole of Calcutta" incident occurred? Having come from Great Britain with its chilly temperatures, the English must have been absolutely miserable in this steamy climate a century before the advent of air conditioning. One consolation was to wash down their fears with copious amounts of gin and tonics, on the assumption that the quinine-based tonic would keep the disease-filled mosquitoes away.

After an 18-hour day, our crew was bushed and looking forward to our layover. Our nine cabs were positioned like a convoy when suddenly there was a commotion involving one of the taxis up front. The taxi driver got out, raised his arms in alarm, then returning to the cab, sped off with our colleagues. At the hotel, the rest of us were itching to know what had happened. That same driver nervously grabbed his fare and roared out of the hotel compound, not looking back. "What was that all about?" asked our captain incredulously.

Cows are sacred in India, and it seems like those bovines know it, too. Lounging in the medians under the trees, they drink water from wells meant for humans, and raid people's flower gardens, leaving cow pies behind with abandon. Without a care in the world, they meander around the big city highways, often to the sound of screeching brakes.

A young calf, perhaps a teenager, had jaywalked, stepping out haphazardly into the road. The taxi driver, busy speaking with the crew about things to do in Calcutta, did not catch the movement fast enough and *kaboom*! He hit the youngster. The driver was not exactly sure what to do. Should he try and rescue the calf, or hope that nobody had seen the incident and act as though nothing had happened? If you try to help, an unruly crowd of religious zealots might appear out of nowhere, and then you *really* have problems.

Happily, as the calf staggered to his young feet, seemingly none worse for wear, the taxi driver zoomed away, desperately hoping that there had been no witnesses other than the Americans.

Once unpacked, I decided to visit Kalighat, where Mother Teresa created her original Home for the Destitute and Dying in 1952. It was founded after she came upon a dying man in the gutter, all alone, suffering terribly. Saddened and greatly disturbed, Mother Teresa held him in her arms until he died.

She always looked for the goodness in poverty, and the home has graciously treated countless patients over the last 71 years. As we entered the hospice, we saw a long dormitory for men, with one down the hall for women. The place was clean and relatively free of offensive smells. The welcome fragrance of exotic incense wafted through. I was immediately aware that some of these patients suffered from more than one disease. Some had unbelievably pulled through and had been restored to health, prompting the Missions of Charity in later years to develop an educational program to teach them skills for re-entering society.

In short order, Kalighat taught me a quick and powerful lesson about human dignity. As we walked along the men's dorm, each of them greeted us by putting their hands together and saying *namaste*. I love what it means: "The God in me recognizes the God in you."

Some patients were so desperately ill that they could only raise one hand to their face, but they were determined, nonetheless. Others struggled to sit up in bed to politely greet us. Some secured the buttons on their simple cotton shirts. One man gestured to me, pointing toward my camera. Even though I love taking photos to capture any intriguing moment, I respect people's feelings anywhere in the world, so I was quick to indicate that I would not take *any* photos. He requested exactly the opposite. Sister Anne Therese, whom I had met at Mother Teresa's home, said he was so thrilled at his recovery from his debilitating illness that he *wanted* me to take his photo to illustrate his joy at being well enough to sit up again. When I returned to the States, I sent the pictures to Sister to pass on to the patient. I admired him greatly; he had all the grace in the world, and it showed.

I noticed a young man on a simple cotton stretcher close to the entrance. He looked to be about eighteen. Even beyond the scruffiness he was handsome, with a gentle face and big eyes. But just like any of us, he was having a tough time with life. Who knows what disease he had, or how many? I took the mala (garland) of heavenly jasmine from around my neck to place it around his. So weak, he could not lift his head much, but then I slipped it around his neck. Even in his dire straits, he had the most beautiful heartfelt expression, making me feel I had known him before. It was not difficult at all to peel away the layers and see beyond his serious, oppressive illness to recognize the true beauty of his soul.

Sister Anne Therese took us to see the morgue. A hand-written sign on the wall said, "I am on my way to Jesus." The simple morgue had slots for six corpses. Thankfully, only one body shrouded in white cloth was "resting." It would not be there for long. Without air conditioning, bodies must be hustled out in short order.

Even though the sign mentioned Jesus, the sisters kindly took in people of all religions, including Hindus who cremate the dead, and Muslims, who must be buried within 24 hours of death.

At night, most whippet-thin homeless in Calcutta sleep "spoon style" on tiny mats alongside the roads, dozens sleeping together. Who is going to steal anything? Everyone is in the same boat—destitute. In the wee hours, the old wooden cart comes around as in medieval times. Attendants go along, checking each person's pulse. If one is not breathing, they simply load the body onto the cart—raw stuff, but a basic fact of everyday life. Once full, it rolls off towards the town's center to add more bodies to the pile for the next day's pyre, fueled by wood and cow dung cakes.

In India, you must have a strong stomach if you are going to navigate the experience successfully. Behind Kalighat, on a broken-down patio, was a cement block about three feet square. At 4 p.m. every day, officials bring in a goat. Slitting its throat in front of everyone, it then gets skinned and roasted. All the severely deprived locals, including the Untouchables, know this and come daily to wait for the feeding. I did not stay for the ceremony, as the smell was already overwhelming. Blood from previous slaughters was never hosed off, and baking in the Indian sun, the stench got progressively worse in the heat. Flies swarmed about everywhere, with more on the way.

I asked Sister Anne Therese about an orphanage close by. She offered to take me along with two colleagues, Deborah and Kathy. We piled into a taxi. At the orphanage, the Missions of Charity sisters were greatly understaffed, scurrying about to take care of their charges, but they welcomed us warmly and offered to show us around. They were clearly devoted to the Almighty's work.

We wondered why the girls far outnumbered the boys. We learned that most of the girls, even though healthy, were simply dumped in trash cans or abandoned on street corners; a result of the ancient dowry custom in India that made girls a liability. Parents of a female must come up with a substantial dowry, even when poverty-stricken. This is prohibitive for the great majority of families. Sometimes, as a necessity for survival, they try to get rid of the girl, often with tragic results.

Other young girls were seriously ill or had deformities that appeared to be birth defects common in India. Those young innocent souls already had at least two strikes against them. As we entered one room, it was just chock-full of kids wandering around in different directions. The sisters were doing their best under the circumstances, but it was a real challenge. This is a story without end. Every day, from the first light of dawn until long after dark, they devote their lives to helping any way they can.

One tiny girl in a pale blue dress, sitting on the floor in the middle of all the activity, spotted me from across the room. At first, I did not see it, but then I noticed her arms and legs were twisted in different directions that practically rendered them useless. She began to drag herself across the floor towards me as I moved towards her. I reached her side, squatted down, and brought her into my arms for a hug. I instantly realized that it would not have even mattered if I had spoken fluent Hindi, she just craved the reassurance of the human touch. And what would I have said? We held that embrace for a long time, as if neither of us wanted to let go. I stroked her long dark hair gently. All the noise and chatter in the room seemed to fade away as we exchanged energy.

As I held her, I wondered what I should do next. It was such a personal moment, one that surpassed time for me. When that moment ended, it was gone forever, but the image of it occupies a distinctive place in my memory. I did not even know this girl's name, where she was from, or what her life had been like so far. What would her future reveal?

While I was absorbing the entire atmosphere of the room, a soft singing voice became audible close by. It was Kathy. She had reached down, scooped up a baby girl, and was pretending to dance with her. The child loved it, giggling like kids do when they hope the fun will never end. The sound of her laughter was melodious, immediately brightening the room. Kathy began to move around the floor in a waltz as we all stopped to watch. She looked so lovingly towards the baby as she sang the song Frank Sinatra made famous, "The Way You Look Tonight."

Even the sisters took a little break from their hectic activities to watch Kathy serenade the entranced Hindu child. It was heartwarming to see those Indian children interact beautifully with us Americans who had traveled halfway around the globe. It clearly illustrated to me once more that all of us just want love and acceptance, no matter who we are or where we hail from.

Occasionally in life, certain interactions make time stand still for a moment or two. I truly felt in that instant that time had stopped for a brief period as they danced around the imaginary ballroom.

To this day, back in the opulent environment which is America, every time I hear "The Way You Look Tonight" I revisit that touching scene again, where two souls from opposite ends of the Earth stopped time, coming together in gentle harmony for a few unforgettable moments.

21

Building Houses in the Land of the Lemurs

As we flew over Antananarivo, I felt "plum wore out" as they say in the Deep South. My eyes felt like hot coals and my body was gritty all over. I had flown all the way from Los Angeles but had missed the connection from Paris to Madagascar. I then flew the twelve-hour-red eye to the lovely French resort island of Reunion and on to "Tana," as they call it for short. As we made our final approach, I wondered if the Malagasies at the airport would be buzzing pests and aggressive like the Nigerians. If so, I did not have the energy to fight them off. Sometimes in exotic places, I felt somewhat like a gazelle on the Serengeti—open season, if you will. It is essential to utilize all my senses, especially when traveling alone, although, I must admit, I have witnessed some goofy things when visitors are traveling in packs.

Madagascar is the fourth largest island in the world, located east of the South African coast. It hosts a unique menagerie of wildlife including lemurs, civet cats, aye-ayes, fossas, large chameleons, and tropical butterflies. Even boa constrictors have their dull brown colors highlighted by patches of shiny cobalt blue. The people are descendants of explorers who set sail from places as far-flung as the Philippines and Sri Lanka. Their embassy in Washington sent me some cultural info, which included a reference to their "turning of the bones" ceremonies which kind of spooked me, but I will get to that later.

I love Africa, and was really looking forward to joining my group, whom I had never met before, assembled by Habitat for Humanity in Atlanta. We were scheduled to build three houses in two weeks. Looking over the advance trip info from our leader Lynn, there was much to be considered. Each of us was told to bring flip flops, so when we showered, parasites would not be able to burrow into our feet. Camping showers were a must. The sun warmed the water all day for a hot shower at night after work. We were advised to "practice squatting" before we left home for using pit latrines. Not to mention bringing toilet paper and handy wipes. I must admit I carefully studied the liability clause and had to pause for a moment when signing the part confirming I understood if I was kidnapped, Habitat would not negotiate for my release.

What was I getting myself into? If that was not enough, there was plenty to be considered in the health arena. I had paid over $600 for shots. When picking up my prescription to ward off malaria, even the pharmacist teased, "Why don't you save yourself some trouble and rent the cartoon *Madagascar* instead?"

Plus, the itinerary had changed. The group was all excited about visiting a gorgeous beach, but then word came that the side trip had been canceled because of a "flu" that made people's bones sore. I had not even left the States yet, but I was pretty sure that I knew what that meant. "Whoa, they are talking about dengue fever which causes severe pain in the bones," I commented to my friend Sudd. "That's no joke!"

I understand that Africans will downplay something serious because it could have an adverse effect on tourism, but they also naturally have a much higher resistance to infections than we do.

After going through passport control, I scanned the crowd in the arrival area. I was dragging a ton of construction tools, spare clothing to leave behind, a sleeping bag and pillow, trowels for brick laying, work gloves, towels, flashlights, a bottle of vodka, and medicine for any kind of trouble. A fist full of syringes in their original wrappers had been kindly donated by my friend Warren Brown in case of a medical emergency. Just when I paused to drag my things further, I spotted a friendly young man in a Habitat for Humanity T-shirt, with a bright smile and a hand-written sign with my name misspelled, "Tanya."

"Edwin?" I asked, relieved. "You are my new best friend!"

He laughed, and from that moment on, for the next three weeks, we were almost inseparable.

Required to give a presentation for my class at UCLA before I left for Madagascar, I was three days behind the team when Edwin picked me up at Tana airport. The hotel Edwin had selected was modest—so modest, in fact, that his room had no running water. Still in my skunky clothes which I had been wearing for more than 36 hours, I heard a plaintive knock at the door. "Tania, I must change rooms. Mine doesn't have any water."

Ahhh, welcome to Africa! Inviting him into my room, I pulled out photos of lemurs. These amusing primates with foxlike faces and wide eyes are unique to M'car, as they call it for short. They come in over 100 varieties and different colors. Naturally curious, they are not afraid of humans. In earlier times, many Malagasies kept the gentle creatures as pets, and I bet they made great babysitters, keeping the kids amused for hours on end.

After all, these little guys are the real celebs of M'car. Sensing my love of the handsome little animals, Edwin invited me, "Tania, if you aren't too tired, there's a private, natural habitat 45 minutes away where you can observe them in close proximity."

"Really?" I asked excitedly, gaining a strong second wind just at the thought.

What a cool thing to offer me. After all, the team had already been there three days and had not seen one lemur yet. Fresh off the flight, I was about to meet an entire troupe.

Without even bothering to unravel my luggage and change, Edwin and I were off to visit these cunning and agile arboreal animals. Enthralled from the minute we arrived, I asked the taxi driver to join us. These are critters who obviously like to have fun. I swear they have a sense of humor, too. The one who stole my heart was black and white. He liked to gently tease the others. He swung along the branches of the trees, constantly trying to engage the ring-tailed lemurs and sifakas to party with him by gently prodding them in a tickle-like way with his monkey-like paws. What a doll; so photogenic. I was a goner. I quietly and carefully brushed against his long, bushy black and white tail with my hand, just to test the waters. He did not complain. Even though I was dying to touch him, being jet-lagged and a bit delirious, another time would be better when my senses would be more acute. In addition, if he did bite me for some reason, that certainly would not be an intelligent way to begin my journey.

Edwin and Malala were our Malagasy hosts, cheerleaders, cultural ambassadors, and translators for three languages. Tops at what they do, everyone loved them with their boundless energy. The group of 14 volunteers, 12 Americans and two Canadians, were in another city, Fianarantsoa. We would join them the next day after a bumpy eight-hour bus ride. Edwin and I had plenty of time to bond on the way, while viewing the lush green rice paddies framed by imposing mountains. I picked his brain about life in M'car, so by the time we joined the others, I was pretty much up to speed.

Arriving at the bus station at midnight, our group leader, Lynn Twitchell, wearing a flowing sundress, greeted us with hugs. I had spoken to Lynn on the phone and knew by her voice vibration and devotion to Africa that we would get along great. A veteran of an impressive nine Habitat builds in Africa by 2008, she was ready for more. Certain individuals with particular personality traits truly love Africa, and Lynn had the understanding and adaptability that is needed big-time. In Africa, I have found you go with the flow. Things happen on their time, not ours. A natural diplomat and liaison with empathy, Lynn adored people and their various cultures. She would have made a fantastic Pan Am purser and I told her so. That is a giant compliment from a Pan Amer because we can be clannish *and* opinionated. She possessed all those flexible qualities it took to navigate the globe successfully. She kept things in order while simultaneously joking about it all with aplomb.

The previous day, she had fallen straight into the rice paddy's mucky water but took some ribbing about it in a real sporty way. Foul! I am not very coordinated, so when it was my turn to go to the paddy to fetch water to mix the mortar with, I made up my own little mantra for protection. As I walked along the narrow, slippery, and crooked path in between the paddies, I repeated "I am as sure-footed as a mountain goat."

The Gods must have been on my side, for I was spared that nasty experience. The Malagasies observed that "the white people are like us when we take the cows down to the watering hole. They leave clean but come back muddy and dirty."

Africans instinctively know that Westerners are somewhat prissy. After a day of construction, there were also logistics involved. Ten people in our house divvyed up three outside camping showers every day after working on the site. However, there was one advantage—no set rules. On a Habitat build in the States, they will not even let you on the site without proper clothes, sturdy shoes, and a hard hat. In M'car, I wore a Tahitian sarong, skinny top, cheap flip flops, and a 50-cent straw hat. My construction gloves hung from my waist, perhaps a couture fashion statement. Just trying to maintain a little decorum in the bush.

A place like Madagascar will force anyone to change all their habits. For the entire three-week stay, except for the last two days, none of us had access to e-mails, cell phones, air conditioning, or TV news. I am a news hound, as my parents were, and it was the first time in my life I had gone for three solid weeks anywhere in the world with no info concerning current events.

Habitat had the operation down to a perfect science. The house we slept in had just been completed by previous volunteers, then the owners helped work on the new homes with us. When those homes were ready, we would leave, and the new occupants would move in.

As you entered our house, all ten pairs of shoes were lined up in neat rows as if it were a temple in Nepal. I slept on the floor in between four other gals—Natalie, Bridget, Sherri, and Sarah—in the sleeping bags we had brought from the States. Whew! There is nothing in the world like having a hot flash in a stinking polyester snooze-bag when there is not even any air conditioning to help offset the temperature of your sweaty body. The silver lining was when I got up to use the latrine outside of our house and breathed in clean, fresh air and was rewarded with the spectacular and brilliant sight of the Milky Way, highlighted by the constellations of the Southern Hemisphere. At least one large cluster of stars dazzled in every single section of the sky. Sadly, there are few places in America where one can see stars like that anymore. Maybe Alaska.

Once you arrived at the outhouse with your toilet paper in hand, you fumbled for the flashlight, and then squatted, which was not easy. It was tough on your creaking knees. There was also a broom for . . . well, you know. No shortage of mosquitoes buzzing around, either. I could not help but think in an environment full of unusual beasts, what if a scorpion bit you on the bum while you were simply doing the "bathtub squat?"

The Habitat crew from Ireland had preceded us, leaving behind fun souvenirs, clothes, and practical items. Jacques, a charming man who looked after the main house, wore an emerald-green "Security" T-shirt every day, a gift from the Irish vols. Perhaps it had been used for a rousing Saint Patty's Day party back home. Rail-thin and spry with a drawn face, I adored Jacques from the moment I laid eyes on him. He appeared to have had a tough life, but he displayed great equanimity in his devotion to the group and was as reliable as the sun. He cheerfully helped the ladies, Habitat homeowners, prepare the food every day after they came back from the marketplace with fresh produce. They also laundered our clothes in the rushing river.

If all of us could get along under these conditions, we could get along anywhere. Tremendous harmony flowed through our entire group. Everyone felt it, including our gracious hosts. They fixed delicious meals for us, which were a vegetarian's dream. Grown in rich soil, the various organic vegetables were bursting with flavor. Fresh-baked French bread was served along with roast chicken or zebu, water buffalo meat.

Grace was said before every meal, and even though extremely cozy, about 27 of us squeezed in to break bread together three times a day. We discussed the progress of the build and any improvements we could implement. We also related any blessings or events that had occurred which were meaningful to us. After dinner, our Malagasy hosts played the guitar, leading us in traditional songs. We were truly an eloquent ensemble, joined together from two separate ends of the planet.

After each meal, we separated edible scraps for the dogs, often something bland like rice or fish bones, but they ate it anyway. If they do not compare notes with their American canine counterparts, I think we will be okay. More than once, I witnessed turkeys fighting over banana peels, while squawking, pulling, and gobbling—quite an unusual and hilarious sight. Yes, this was *Africa*.

To pump some finances back into the local economy, tools that we had not brought were rented. To keep things on track, two masons were hired for each house. We formed a "fireman's line" and tossed the roof tiles from one to another and then up to Scott, a fellow volunteer. He diligently and lovingly placed them on the roof slats, one by one, just as if he was building his own beloved home. A high-energy devoted worker, Scott was a true team player. He also displayed good creative talents as an artist as he arranged those tiles.

Believe it or not, the scaffolding was made by lashing strong branches together. None of them broke. The future homeowners of these three houses were also encouraged to help with the construction, referred to as "sweat equity." Everyone pitches in, and each person "brings something to the table."

A black parrot watched us from a small tree every day. Nobody had taught him any words in either French or Malagasy, and it did not seem that he aspired to be a linguist, anyway. I began to tease him that he must work for the National Security Agency (NSA) since he was watching us so closely without offering any info about himself. Nicknamed James Bond, he did liven up considerably one day when Scott offered him a banana, sliding down the branch of the tree using his feet like a skateboard to get the fruit. It appeared that James was somewhat skilled after all.

The daily salutations from the children were a welcome sight. The entire village knew that the *vazaha* (foreigners) were in town. Lining the dirt road every day as we walked towards the construction site, they called out *vazaha!* It means "person with a wide view of the horizon or world," which I consider a great compliment. The children were gorgeous and genuinely friendly. They laughed and giggled, acting as if they were afraid of white people, but the next day they were back for more. I noted in my diary, "being exotic here can be quite tiring in this heat," as the kids called out "vazaha!" repeatedly, waiting for us to respond in kind. This ritual of sorts took place every time we walked back to the house for meals.

The villagers were endlessly fascinated at how well we worked under their conditions. And I was continually amazed as the neighbor's children, some as young as five, picked up as many bricks as they could handle and helped move them for us. We rented two carts from the locals, and our team gave the children rides back and forth to the dirt pile while others also "transported" dirt in simple but strong straw baskets.

Nobody ever asked the kids for help, but they gladly and voluntarily became part of our multi-national team. I wanted so much to engage these energetic children in some fun. One day, I tried in vain to recall the words to *"Freres Jacques."* I did not get too far with the ancient French song, but the children danced and squealed with delight just the same. They were charming for days and endeared themselves to all of us when they sang "Happy Birthday" to our colleague Chris for his birthday, in both French and Malagasy. Another time, we visited the local school, and the Westerners led the Malagasies in a rendition of "If You're Happy and You Know it, Clap Your Hands." The children danced and clapped, looking at us for clues to the foreign jig. Their bright and lively eyes readily showed their eagerness to be part of the gathering.

After lunch on an exceptionally hot day, a volunteer from our group went upstairs for a little snooze. With absolutely no air conditioning and only a rickety little fan for comfort, he peeled off his clothes and fell asleep. Just outside the bedroom window was a staircase running up to the neighbor's flat. Before long, the word got out that a white man, sleeping naked, was sprawled out on the floor with his pale jewels there for all to see. A group of teenage girls gathered. They had never, *ever* seen anything even close to that, I'm sure. What an eyeful! And, because our crew ate at that house every day, they knew that our group was friendly. They were trying hard to be quiet, for if they were discovered, the fun would surely end in a heartbeat.

You know how, even when you are in deep sleep, you have the impression that some living thing, maybe even a pet, is eyeballing you? A few suppressed giggles escaped. Then the startled and lethargic guy was awakened to a rather large, young female audience outside. Laughing wildly, they all quickly scattered in different directions as if he might come out growling like a grizzly bear. Later, I just had to joke, "Do you realize that 20 years from now, those gals will still be saying, 'Do you remember the time we saw the naked white man?'" And I bet they will not forget one single detail.

We soon set off for a trip to the rainforest of Ranomafana to visit the wildlife in the jungle, including the nocturnal inhabitants. Our simple motel rooms were located along the banks of the main river. The dramatic roaring water kept the air smelling fresh. Cold water came gushing down from the mountains through a series of large waterfalls. Many children swam and frolicked in the wide river, but for some unfortunate souls going to work, the only way to reach their destination was to either walk or swim across to the other side to reach their jobs. Many hiked up their clothes to help balance themselves against the strong current. Supplies were transported on their heads. As the sun set after a long working day, I watched these same laborers return to the muddy banks to ford the river again on their way home.

Ranomafana gave us an opportunity to get close to numerous kinds of lemurs. It was delightful to watch them at play. It was almost as if they knew it, too, like kids who show off because they know their parents are watching. They are not afraid of humans and their only real enemy is the fossa, a rarely seen, mid-sized, cat-like carnivore. The frisky lemurs romp and have fun with other lemur species, and then come closer to humans, as if posing for pictures. They are physically beautiful, always photogenic, and come in many different colors, from striped to auburn.

The rainforests are teeming with all kinds of wildlife, including leeches. The little bastards are tiny, but when you pull them off, the "incision" mark they sliced into you was the same size as the circumference of their head. Remaining vigilant, we rechecked that our socks and pants covered our legs entirely. Like the Amazon, the forest is also loaded with medicinal plants. Edwin pointed them out to us, identifying each one.

A regional guide took us on an incredible hike, an exploration that revealed the diversity of the island's beauty. It reminded us of Arizona, Colorado, New Mexico, or even the area near Ayers Rock in Australia, but one thing was for sure, it was stunning. Around every corner, we witnessed another heavenly view of nature's splendor. Enormous rocks could be seen for miles around, revealing lush green valleys in between. Pristine waterfalls beckoned swimmers. Sections of the landscape were mountainous, then the land suddenly flattened out to reveal endless skies like those in Montana.

Earlier in the trip, I had mentioned the Embassy information I had concerning the "turning of the bones." My fellow volunteers reacted as though I was telling a tall tale from a fable. Africa is diverse, and sometimes foreigners want to take it a big step further, exaggerating the customs they practice. But the truth came to light when Lynn, the group leader, asked the new guide why the rocks were displayed in such an unusual way at the mouth of a cave. "Oh, that's *famadihana*," replied the guide, adding casually, "or the turning of the bones."

He explained more details while I was entertained by watching the perplexed, and somewhat horrified, expressions of my thirteen fellow volunteers. They practice a custom of digging up buried relatives and then wrapping them anew in colorful and expensive clothes. The corpses are then paraded through the streets while locals celebrate before reburying the bodies. In addition, if your family moves from one village to another, most likely there will be a trip to the cemetery to dig up grandma's and grandpa's bones to accompany the family to the next destination. Like the West, when we transport sentimental and treasured possessions from one city to another, the Malagasies do as well, except that the move contains bones, and lots of them. An unusual ritual to say the least. Eyebrows flew up as jaws dropped.

We traveled to a traditional African lodge with thatched roofs. As tons of our bags were being unloaded from the top of Claude's bus, I noticed a colorful rainbow arc signaling the end of a perfect day. That night, word reached a local choir called *Firenga Bevata* that the Habitat people were in town. They arrived to sing *gratis* for us, with voices like angels. The dance troupe, choir, and actors explained each cultural vignette before singing. All were dressed to the nines in their tribal clothes saved for special occasions. Three ladies wore orange, green, and red sarongs with inscriptions. I asked Edwin to translate for me. Tigers raced around the edges of the first one, with the words "Blessing is powerful."

The green one depicted villagers laboriously tilling the soil with help from a zebu (water buffalo) saying, "There are no bad jobs on Earth." I might be hard-pressed to push that philosophy in America.

The one with red hearts dancing all over it advised, "Do not fight someone else's destiny—you will be extra tired." Not bad advice for those who envy the good fortune of others.

The troupe added amusing props to portray a particular type of animal, individual character, or chief in their storyline. It was their honor to entertain us, thanking us kindly for building homes in their country. They never asked for donations.

As the departure date neared, we felt sad that soon we would be going our separate ways. The team became quieter, not as lively and rambunctious as before. I had scheduled myself to stay three days beyond their departure date because my inner voice had advised me to stay a while longer. I also figured that by then I would know the ropes and feel comfortable, even by myself, after the team left.

Armed with a big umbrella to keep the strong sun at bay, Lynn gathered all of us together to celebrate the dedication of the new houses at the site. Present were the three families who would be the homeowners, the neighbors, the masons, and the children who had helped us along the way. The local chief thanked our team. The sun was blazing hot as we all stood around Lynn. She had secured three Bibles, one for each of the families. Lynn conducted services and the dedication in English, followed by Edwin and Malala, adding to her words in both French and Malagasy. Each attendee was teary-eyed at our ceremony. It had been uplifting and encouraging to see how the construction had progressed each day since we had arrived. Now it was nearly time to depart for good.

The Malagasies also had plenty of kind things to say. Gerard commented that he had never seen two cultures work more closely together in such a unified way. Pierre, a Malagasy with a French name, added, "The Americans and Canadians are certainly much friendlier than the French!" The entire group laughed.

Claude, our driver with his big red bus who transported us the entire time while we were in their extraordinary country, could hardly control his tears. "I have been a bus driver for more than 15 years," he began, "and I have driven people to every part of this land, as I know much of this country without maps. My customers have come from all over the world, but I have never been treated as kindly as all of you have been towards me. You have made me part of your incredible family, and I will never forget your generosity. I'll always remember how you included me in all your luncheons and dinners, and the parties, too." Turning to Lynn, still trying to keep the tears under control, he added, "Mama Lynn, I have never met anyone like you before and I will always remember you with love. You are truly the 'Mother of Africa.'"

Driving for umpteen hours back to Tana, the bus was nearly silent. We planned for some last-minute shopping, regrouping, and for an opportunity to meet Habitat's chief architect, Daniel Simpson, an American. I joked with him that we were fortunate to have gotten away before the latrine, a giant hole in the ground, was dug. That would have taken some real man or woman power in that heat. He explained to me how it cost a mere thousand dollars for each house to be built. That was it, from start to finish. Four to five family members could live comfortably in the two-story house. While on the road, we did have a couple of "homestay" opportunities, spending a night or two with a Malagasy family to see for ourselves firsthand how they live in a Habitat house. We observed up close the remarkable benefits of having one's own place to call home.

Weeks later back in the States, I ran into an interior decorator at a party. Her client had asked her to order a $9,000 bathtub with all the water jets and nonsense coming out of it, just for one lady and her hubby to enjoy. As the decorator proceeded to describe this foo-foo tub, I did not hear another word. I was listening to the words running through my head. All I could think of was, "Nine grand! That would be NINE houses to benefit about 54 Malagasy people." Those words went through my mind repeatedly as I mused over the polarity from the African perspective.

That night, we had our farewell dinner. Lynn presented thank you gifts to Edwin and Malala—briefcases to keep their travel plans in order. She presented Claude with a book, lovingly signed by the team. After a delicious dinner topped off by *mousse au chocolate noir de Madagascar*, we boarded Claude's bus for our last ride together. Heading out to the airport for our final *adieu*, the images of our experience played through my mind. It was difficult to say goodbye to this dedicated, closely united group as Edwin, Malala, and I went down the line hugging and kissing each one. I wondered if I had made the right decision by staying on a few more days without my dedicated co-volunteers. I had.

A pastel-colored French hotel sits near the center of Tana. It has a/c, lush tropical landscaping, a salad bar (*what?*), and TV broadcasts beamed in from every corner of the globe. Still teary-eyed from the goodbyes, Claude drove Edwin and me to the hotel on our final outing. He said how difficult it would be to acclimate himself to an entirely new group arriving from Europe early the next morning.

Bidding our final goodbye, we wished Claude all the best in his travels.

My hotel room cost the equivalent of perhaps three months' salary for the average Malagasy. As we entered, I told Edwin he could watch

TV all night if he wanted, that I would not mind. He confessed that he had never been inside a hotel that even slightly resembled this one, so lavishly and cheerfully decorated. Downstairs, Edwin, a vegetarian, was delighted when the restaurant made a special dish just for him. After all that he had done for us, I was happy to offer him a new experience.

Saturday morning, Edwin took me to his English class to meet his friends, including Andry, who hosted a weekly hour-long radio show that could be heard far outside the capital. Once Andry realized I did background work, thinking I was a fully-fledged actress, he quickly invited me to be interviewed on his *live* radio show that evening. "Andry, in all fairness, you don't understand. I'm not really an actress, it's not right for me to exaggerate. I have only had one speaking part, and that was a fluke. I was 'picture picked' to play someone's conservative and fussy mom."

I declined to tell him that it had been a porn flick, even though I had kept all my mom's clothes on and did not even have to smooch. "I do background work, which means what it sounds like. On the set, when the crew thinks we can't hear them, they refer to us as 'props with appetites,' hardly a compliment. We're at the bottom of the totem pole."

Not dissuaded at all, Andry excitedly asked, "Tell me what productions you have worked, and I'll research them on the internet, then interview you tonight on my show, okay?"

Andry eagerly welcomed me to the radio station. He could not wait to begin peppering me with tons of questions about Hollywood and every single movie I had ever worked on. Who was in it, how did they look? How was their acting up close? Were the film crews treated well? What was the pecking order of the actors? I had an advantage explaining many of these things because I worked on private jets for five years out of LA. Often, actors I had seen working their craft on the set later traveled on our jet, so I had the chance to observe them in an entirely different environment.

The radio show was a blast, and I ate up every minute of it. The passion clearly came out in both of our voices. Instead of commercials, they took breaks by playing melodious African music. I had so much fun that occasionally I interrupted myself, moving on to an anecdote or humorous story that I thought the audience would like better than the one I was just in the middle of telling, *sorry!*

Before the show, Andry suggested I visit a friend's private house in the countryside where the lemurs run wild, but they will also eat out of your hand. I was blown away. The man whistled and, recognizing the call, they swung from branch to branch, hitting the ground, running towards us like canines. Our host poured some peanuts into both of my palms. Instantly I had three sports fans at my side: Mom and Pop eating out of my left hand and Sonny Boy on the right. They were so gentle, taking my hands with their tactile paws and directing them in a position to make the feast easier to eat. Completely enthralled, I was in critter heaven. When the young son finished the peanuts, he licked my entire palm for the salt. The he did something we all did as kids. Sitting back on his haunches, he licked his own fingers one by one to savor every last taste of the treat. He then put one of his paws on his knee like a human does when they are contemplating something. The sifaka family won my heart in no time. With their white and rich auburn-colored fur I had some *real* "A-listers" seated around me.

On his radio show, Andry brought up our trip to the lemur garden, asking about my visit. He immediately realized that he had made a big mistake if the audience was ever going to hear about the musings of Hollywood, as there was plenty I wanted to discuss about these darling animals, totally unique to Madagascar. Aired live, we spoke for an hour. Later employees from the American Embassy told me how much they had enjoyed the live broadcast bantering between us.

Despite numerous mishaps that could be lurking around every corner on any construction site, something magical happens on each Habitat build. Madagascar was no exception. Virginian team leader Tom Gerdy, who has freely given tons of his energy and expertise to Habitat, has observed the same thing. The owner of a construction company and a veteran volunteer of numerous builds, Tom told me that he had precisely the same impression. Somehow the Almighty shifts the energy force in all of us, giving us stronger drive and endurance. In 2000, I met Tom on a "Blitz Build" in Los Angeles named "Hollywood for Habitat," with a thousand novice volunteers running around the site.

Mom, Dad and son sifakas

Some were A-list actors, others were "wannabes," but everyone was dedicated. Nobody was injured except for minor things. The progress of the build just flows, as people unite with the same desire to give the gift of a home while working cohesively together from every background imaginable.

The day before we left Fianarantsoa, the families, neighbors, and volunteers had gathered at the local school for some sweets, juice, and just a great heaping of positive energy. Our entire group had bonded in almost indescribable ways. We sang "We are the World" together in that dusty little room. All ages and sizes held hands, swaying to the sound of our voices wafting out over the houses. Thousands of miles away from North America, the fellowship shared would have been immediately palatable even to a stranger. Yes, we are the world, an infinitesimal part of it.

But . . . you just have not lived until you have built a house or two in Africa!

22

Utilizing My Experiences as a Volunteer on Capitol Hill

"Don't tell me what you believe," the speaker began, "tell me what you *do,* and I'll tell you what you believe."

In the two spheres where I reside—Washington, D.C., and Los Angeles—you hear far too much of "I am, I have, I want." The chic lady was speaking on behalf of the humanitarian aid provider CARE to an audience of more than 600. She was about to make short work of that doctrine by teaching us how important a first impression, and hopefully an impact, we could make on our legislators. We were training to lobby on behalf of the world's impoverished people. Less than a mile from Capitol Hill, nicknamed "The Hill" by Washingtonians, we were learning the value of lobbying our senators and congressmen concerning issues close to our hearts. "We never lobby for salary, but always for *passion,*" I like to say as we hike down the endless grand, cavernous white marble hallways of Congress.

Think about it for a minute: you possessed keen lobbying instincts even as a small, tender child. Remember asking your parents to purchase brownies, cookies, and Cokes? You had already figured out that you would get a sugar high from it, along with a caffeine buzz, to boot. You wanted more. As you tugged on Mom's sleeve, you persistently built your case, perhaps even presenting evidence, "It's on sale," or witnesses, "Helen's mom buys it for her family." By nature, I have this theory we all possess the inherent gift to "lobby," or persuade someone else to see things as we see them, at least to a certain extent.

I was first introduced to "volunteer lobbying" through our Pan Am flight attendant union, the Independent Union of Flight Attendants (IUFA) in 1990. The US Capitol Handbook, the 'Bible of the Hill,' was presented to each of us along with an expedited briefing. This handbook lists all the legislators with their biographies, committees, and contact info. We were then escorted into a large room inside the Cannon Building just in time to hear testimony regarding airline regulations before a panel of congressmen led by Rep. James Oberstar. As we entered, I sucked in my breath. The sense and feeling of power permeate the air in Washington. It is not only the architecture, but what it represents and how our democracy is run. Millions of Americans will never have the opportunity to witness any of these proceedings in action. In another sense, often it is difficult to digest the entire legislative process, and the thick, multi-faceted ambiance which accompanies it. Power has a definite, forceful aura that can be intimidating.

Struggling with an oversized metal door, holding it to gain access to one of the House-side buildings, a little girl said to her mother, "I think I know why the doors and halls are so large. They are trying to make you feel small."

I smiled at the observation and continued to grin at my thought right behind it: *Yeah, but we aren't going away anytime soon.* Thanks to laptops, millions of us who would have been in the dark about any given issue in the '90s are now well-apprised, and much better equipped to plead, or even demand, what we feel our legislators should do concerning a particular issue. If you want to track the status of any legislation listing all the co-sponsors and last-minute updates, there is a website with the current info. I felt grateful to our union for having introduced me to this process of learning about the workings of the Hill. As I walked the halls of Congress, my father's energy was right alongside me.

We took our seats at the hearing as Rep. Oberstar listened to testimony from flight attendants from various airlines, both commercial and charter. The employees were not in uniform, so their airlines remained anonymous. In the last story, a flight attendant told the panel that he had worked a five-hour flight from LA to New York. As he prepared to leave the plane to go home, his supervisor boarded to advise him that he had been re-routed. Another short flight would have been agreeable. However, this charter airline was going to send him with a jumbo jet full of soldiers, as part of Operation Desert Shield, all the way to Saudi Arabia. Even if they had left New York that very minute, a non-stop flight all the way to Dhahran would have been fourteen hours. Then he would have to wait for several hours while they unloaded the military equipment. On top of that, crews did not spend the night in Saudi Arabia, so they turned around and flew to safety in Rome, another five-hour flight. To be that tired, after 30-plus exhausting hours, is worse than being wild-ass drunk. If there was an emergency evacuation, the flight attendant might have a difficult time trying to save *himself.*

The point had been made. Not long afterward, Rep. Oberstar supported legislation that strengthened our union's call for "duty day limitations" of fifteen hours. I had sampled a taste of what can happen when concerned citizens come together to make their voices heard, thus instituting change. On the agenda that day was the campaign for smoke-free skies. We lobbied for a prohibition on smoking, not an entirely popular quest. Once a burly pilot, an avid smoker, barked at me, "What do a bunch of f….g Pan Am flight attendants think, that they'll prevent smoking on planes?"

A few years later, after some hurdles, it became a reality. Imagine how many non-smokers over all these years have been spared the ill effects of second-hand smoke due to this legislation.

One of the benefits of becoming involved was it brought me into contact with others who share similar ideologies to my own. Lobbying is a fertile ground for new friends. It is the voyage we take together. If the struggle was easy, it would not be half as much fun. Do not just complain about the state of affairs, *do* something about it. Lend your talents.

World Wings International, the philanthropic organization of the Pan Am flight attendants, with a membership of thousands, selected the Cooperative for American Remittances to Europe (CARE) as its designated charity. It was a great fit, as Pan Am people share the same global mindset. Founded in 1946, CARE dedicates itself to improving the quality of living for the disadvantaged in 73 developing nations. That year, they flew their nutritious food packages to destitute civilians in Europe, ravaged by World War II, which had ended only months earlier.

CARE addresses the underlying causes of poverty by working closely with the impoverished in the areas of health, nutrition, economic development, water purification, education, agriculture, and eradication of disease. In 2004, when the Indian Ocean tsunami hit, about 200,000 were killed in more than 12 countries. Tens of thousands were devastated, but CARE hit the ground running. Established offices complete with supplies were able to operate immediately and effectively in some of the hard-hit areas.

They also extend micro-credit. My favorite concept is the one developed by Muhammed Yunus, founder of Grameen Bank in Bangladesh. His bank lent amounts of $100 each to more than six million indigent, fledgling entrepreneurs to get them started in the business of their choice. Women in particular use the funds to benefit their families. The repayment rate of these loans is an astonishing 98 percent. Grateful for the opportunity to be given a viable chance to improve the quality of their lives and those of their families, the new businesspeople work diligently to return the funds to lenders.

CARE also has a similar pay-back rate. One example was a young lady, Violetta, from Ecuador. A petite native Indian, she was dressed in traditional bright clothes to attend CARE's 2006 annual conference. Her face was marked with red-colored crosses on both cheeks. She had borrowed $80 for a sewing machine. She busily sewed all kinds of clothes to sell in her village. She hired her sister. They purchased a second machine and brought their cousin on board. By the time she paid back the loan, her business was well on its way. When I approached her to congratulate her, she spoke little Spanish, as her native tongue was a dialect from the mountainous region of Ecuador. She was thrilled to be honored for her success. She was surrounded by Meg Ryan, who had introduced her, Senator Barack Obama, and Dr. Helene Gayle, CARE's CEO. Violetta obviously knew who Dr. Gayle was, but I am not certain that she knew who the other two were.

Our tables were divided into states. Once seated, we became acquainted with other constituents from our congressional district. We had scheduled meetings in 200 congressional offices. We were given talking points for the three main issues to discuss with our legislators. Group leaders from each district introduced fellow lobbyists to facilitate the meeting. We were provided with packets containing CARE's background information with congressional delegation biographies. We familiarized ourselves with our legislators' profiles and how they had voted on key issues related to our concerns.

If they represented a political party other than our own, we were advised to acknowledge their positive achievements. We tried hard to "stay on message," although I know well that when people feel passionate about particular issues, sometimes that is not so easy. The best part was discovering that often the constituent is educating the legislator. They cannot know everything; it's beneficial for them to hear different points of view. We mentioned that we would follow their voting record after returning home, thus holding them accountable for their decisions.

"It is good to read *The End of Poverty*," began Rep. Lois Capps, a California congresswoman, who was also a registered nurse. "Bono from U2 is doing so much for the millennium goals. People cannot work on an empty stomach. Wherever we are, our goal is saving lives, not preaching."

After a productive meeting, our group walked out into the reception area. I could not help but notice a good-sized surfboard bolted to the wall, along with other surfing-related artifacts. Photos of the sweeping California coastline brightened the room. Gidget, the celebrated Malibu surfer girl, would have been right at home. Laughing with my fellow volunteers, I observed, "You would have to be from outer space not to realize that you were in the office of a legislator from California."

We headed over to the Senate buildings, passing the US Supreme Court, another landmark. The steamy June heat reminded me of "Sumatran summer." Our briefcases got fatter by the hour; most of us had blisters underneath our pointy-toed heels. In LA, I wear Bohemian dresses and sandals. "Inside the Beltway" or on the "Hill," I go through a metamorphosis, emerging in a proper silk blouse, pencil skirt, and Italian wingtips.

Next, we visited Senator Barbara Boxer's office. Over 50 of us were jammed into the meeting room. Before even a word was spoken, our presence sent a strong signal to her aides how passionate the advocates were, and that CARE had strong support.

Then-Senator Barack Obama

"If you work to empower women, you work to empower a nation," Senator Barack Obama told the rapt CARE supporters later that day in the ballroom. It was the first of many times I would hear him speak in person. "We have an obligation to see these women as our mothers, sisters, and daughters. That is why we must speak out for them when they can't," he added to strong applause. "Enhance the economic power of ladies, tapping into the potential of those who are *already* doing the work. Without educated women, developing nations can't compete in a global economy. I wrote *Dreams from My Father,* but it was my *mother* who shaped my passions. It's important for us to be agents for organizations like CARE. We all need a sense of purpose and hope in our lives. We can't always see the progress being made, but things happen if people imagine."

Concluding, he added, "Ask your legislators how they are supporting people in developing nations, so they know you're following what they're doing. Legislators will respond to the squeaky wheel back home." I grinned, recalling the 'squeaky wheel' comment also suggested to us by Rep. John Conyers.

Something empowering did happen the final day. Late afternoon, near quitting time, CARE learned that Rep. Ted Poe of Texas was submitting an amendment to cut foreign assistance programs by $600 million. A group of CARE advocates rushed over to his office, fervently explaining why he should not support this amendment. A Black minister from Texas told Poe, "If you offer this amendment, you're going to have to come and tell my congregation why you wanted to cut funding for poor people all across Africa."

Later that afternoon, Rep. Poe withdrew his request.

Another cause close to my heart was the creation of a cabinet-level Department of Peace (DOP). It is hard to believe, but the idea actually stretches way back to 1792. It was first conceived by Benjamin Rush, a co-signer of the Declaration of Independence, who was also a physician and humanitarian. Benjamin Banneker, a noted Black scientist and editor, shared the vision with Rush. Over the years, more than 90 pieces of legislation have been introduced calling for a formal structure in our government that focuses on peace. To date, none exists.

The DOP would research and utilize proven methods of peaceful solutions to international hostilities, using the best practical knowledge available. The department would continually advise the president and Congress of viable techniques in peace-building processes between nations. It would also examine US foreign policy, making expedient recommendations of ways to approach the root causes of war. In times of crisis abroad, the Secretary of Peace would also be present in the Situation Room of the White House to provide the president with alternatives to war; solutions that could bring a less contentious outcome. Domestically, the Peace Academy would complement the Military Academy, working closely with them to help resolve conflict between nations by closely examining effective peace-building skills. In the US, it would address violence of all types—domestic, gang warfare, child abuse, elder abuse, even abuse to animals. Before the gangs get to them,

Dr. Helene Gayle, Senator Obama, and Meg Ryan

children at an early age would be taught essential tools of non-violent conflict resolution, utilizing proven ways to "wage peace." They would learn alternative ways to resolve differences that are not acrimonious. As Nobel Peace Prize winner Archbishop Desmond Tutu has noted, if people can co-exist peacefully *after* a war, why have war in the first place?

Best-selling author Marianne Williamson co-founded the Peace Alliance, a nonprofit organization that leads a grassroots campaign that supports this legislation. "The primary function of a United States Department of Peace will be to research, articulate, and facilitate nonviolent solutions to domestic and international conflict," she tells supporters. "Today it is time for our own generation to respond to a great historical challenge: to interrupt the patterns of violence which threaten to destroy not only our own way of life, but all human civilization." The mother of a beautiful daughter, she adds, "This will be our generation's gift, should we choose to give it: to our nation, to our children, and to the progress of the human mind."

Fellow volunteers whom I have met on this journey have all brought incredible energy to the process. We share similar goals, so we bond well. I also strongly believe that it has much to do with mindset. How different would our culture be if it we made it a priority to utilize peaceful values as our *leading* ones? Only a handful of universities award bachelor's degrees in peace. Imagine modern technology focusing its goals on supporting this kind of gentle culture. In the future, what would it sound like to hear a child ask, "Mother, what is war?"

I ask myself how this world might be different if all the greatest minds, coming from a myriad of occupations, tossed all their brightest ideas into the ring to come up with the most beneficial solutions for all concerned? What if my boomer generation, so outspoken in the '60s, "rose to the top of the tank" again, demanding a paradigm shift of peace? How would that affect a shift in consciousness? I love it when Marianne Williamson speaks about these ideas. Traveling all over our vast nation, she has seen and felt this yearning by watching the enthusiasm on supporters' faces. "I see it in the eyes of my generation" she has often said.

Attendees had what I call "the bright eyes look." They were old souls with much light in their eyes, here to usher in a new age of thinking. I easily felt the energy of determination swirling around the conference ballroom like a benevolent *dervish* on a spin.

A vast array of citizens from all walks of life supports this legislation. The late Senator Vance Hartke introduced this bill back in the '60s. These days, his son Jan speaks on behalf of creating a DOP before large audiences, emphasizing to them how we are all interconnected. Then Congressman Dennis Kucinich picked up the torch, re-introducing the bill in 2005.

Singer Judy Collins, Steven Tyler of Aerosmith, Dr. Patch Adams (who was portrayed by Robin Williams in the film), Deepak Chopra, Walter Cronkite, and actors Frances Fisher, Amy Smart, and Joaquin Phoenix all traveled to Washington to attend the conference, many lending their talents. Archbishop Desmond Tutu, Darryl Hannah, Paula Abdul, and Willie Nelson were also active patrons.

Supporters flew in from over 35 nations to attend the national conference. It is enlightening to hear how we can work together to make this vision a reality in our lifetimes. Attendees take significant time off from work, spending their money to fly thousands of miles to our country to see what they can learn and contribute. They come from Africa, Asia, and Europe. It is heartwarming to listen to what they say, which is essentially that we must live in a peaceful world. These dedicated volunteers are lobbying their own governments for the equivalent of a Peace Department.

Noted author Barbara Marx Hubbard told the attendees, "We need to develop social synergy in our society and scan the globe for innovative programs concerning peace. Then we should utilize them."

The late Walter Cronkite, CBS News anchorman for nearly twenty years (and my mother's absolute *favorite)*, added, "We should build an infrastructure of people who spend their lives in service to others."

Dr. Patch Adams, dressed head-to-toe in comical, mismatched clothes, asked, "What is your love strategy? I mean the philosophy of love and how you utilize it? Certainly, the DOP is a love strategy. How about tripling teachers' salaries and have them teach love?" he added to thunderous applause.

The stunning Judy Collins led our group of over 500 in an uplifting and inspiring version of "Amazing Grace." Reminiscent of the '60s, people swayed gently to the music holding hands. Before leaving, Collins concluded, "In order to create energy and power, you have to break down the secrets and discover what they are."

Marianne Williamson stepped up to the podium. She has an almost magical way of speaking, often with thousands in attendance, whom she holds spellbound. "There is a historical context to what we are doing. Big decisions are not coming from depth of wisdom or instinct. When people are metaphysical, or come from a spiritual background, when they speak about taking a stand, they mean from within. All miracles begin as we consider there might be another way. Deep wisdom is always counter to the status quo. Self-awareness is the key. Turn love into a *political force*. Politics is like your health. If you are seriously ill, you want to check out many different ways to get well. With violence, we wait until it occurs, and then try to suppress it," she told us.

At the end of the speech, she added, "I envision our presidential candidates addressing a Department of Peace idea and putting it high on their agenda." Then, with a knowing smile and a wink, she added,

"We are all harnessing a strong energy field here, although, you might not want to say that to your members of Congress," she concluded, to gales of laughter.

By February 2010, 71 members of Congress had signed onto the legislation for a Department of Peace. Two senators were co-sponsors, but both have since retired. While trying to obtain more signatures, volunteers all over the US have approached their city councils to formally endorse a DOP. We then had 34 city council resolutions, including Atlanta, Chicago, Cleveland, Detroit, Minneapolis, Newark, and San Francisco.

On Pearl Harbor Day, December 7, 2007, we were thrilled when the Los Angeles City Council formally endorsed a cabinet-level Department of Peace, joining the other cities. Volunteers Jerilyn Stapleton, Terry Mason, Tory Haslinger, and Mel Taylor had worked diligently and tirelessly with a devoted group of volunteers for two years, lobbying our city council members one by one. We were in City Hall as they voted. It was unanimous. Tears welled up in our eyes as we hugged each other. We heartily thanked council member Bernard Parks for introducing the resolution. I felt satisfied as I remembered how this group of unpaid volunteers achieved this milestone. In America's second largest city of twelve million people, we were given an early Christmas gift.

In February 2007, we descended upon Washington to lobby the new Congress, which had only been sworn in two weeks earlier. One of the highlights of the conference would be watching Rep. Dennis Kucinich re-introduce the bill, HR 808, from the floor in front of Congress. In the same room where the annual State of the Union address is given by the president, we would be seated way up high in the gallery, with a sweeping view of all the proceedings.

We climbed to the top of the marble stairs to enter the gallery. Just before we walked in, they took every last item from us, even our purses. I felt a bit naked, but naturally I knew it was necessary. Our group watched intently as Kucinich approached the dais. Stating the name and number of the legislation, he gave a description of the bill. He spoke to a hushed gallery. For Washington regulars, all of this is no big deal. But always swirling around in my head is the respect I feel that this is where laws are introduced, debated, argued over, and passed every day, no matter how large or how inconsequential they may seem. Witnesses to a tiny slice of history, I wondered if this was close to what our forefathers had envisioned so long ago. After some minutes, he stepped away.

Our group filed downstairs to the ground level, chatting excitedly about what we had just seen: a small sampling of the legislative process that would positively affect generations to come, if passed. Our fellow volunteers, some from countries where it can cost you dearly to either protest the government or have the temerity to think that you can advise leaders, had just witnessed our legislative process in action. In most countries, you would not even be able to get *inside* a government building.

In the United States, by expressing our desires to Congress on any given issue, we are exercising our right guaranteed by the Constitution. This is one of the pillars of our democracy that sets us apart, making the distinction between our form of government and most other nations on Earth.

As we exited the Capitol building, I noticed a bridge of light in the sky; a not-so-pale rainbow arcing over the Mall, the patch of green grass that runs from the Capitol Building to the Washington Monument. Considering it a positive sign, I pointed it out to the others, who also took it as an encouraging symbol that we were on the right path.

A few minutes later, next to the exit, a cluster of people had gathered. At first, I could not see the object of their attention. Moving in closer, I saw Rep. Kucinich. Wearing a crisp suit, I spotted a small copy of the US Constitution inside his breast pocket. One at a time, he shook hands with each individual, genuinely thanking them for taking the time and effort to travel to Washington in support of this legislation. Powerful decisions that create laws and affect infinite lives are made every day in this large white, historic building called the US Capitol. But sometimes, and just as essential, Washington can be gracious, too.

In 2023, Congresswoman Barbara Lee is now the sponsor of HR 1111, The Department of Peacebuilding.

Princess of Sikkim (left) 1967.

Photo- Makoto Asai

23

Boomer Reunion on the Island of Crete

And did those feet in ancient time, Walk upon England's mountains green: And was the holy Lamb of God, On England's pleasant pastures seen! And did the Countenance Divine, Shine forth upon our clouded hills? And was Jerusalem builded here, among these dark Satanic Mills…I will not cease from Mental Fight, nor shall my sword sleep in my hand: 'Till we have built Jerusalem, in England's Green and Pleasant Land.

William Blake

Softly I hummed the sound of Blake's melodious tune as I gazed down from my airplane window at the vibrant green hills of Somerset, where I had attended Millfield School for four memorable years. This bright sunny day in England encouraged my thoughts to relive all my memories, which seemed like another lifetime. Returning to England on such a sentimental occasion felt as though I was coming home again. The recollection of those years and all that had happened—the international friends I made, the new experiences, the cultural differences, the unfamiliar lifestyle—played clearly through my mind as I remembered the words to *Jerusalem*, our school hymn. Blake had written England's popular song believing that Joseph of Arimathea had traveled to Somerset with Jesus in their early years. At Easter and Christmastime, services were held at Wells Cathedral, where the song was sung by the students and teachers from Millfield.

As our plane descended into London, I was looking forward to once again seeing my close friends, Maamoun and Mona, who were flying in from Saudi Arabia. Pleased that it was sunny, always a special treat in the UK, I wore my sunglasses and proceeded into the city. I had two days to "muck about," as we used to say, before I was to meet up with them at a hotel on Kensington High Street. Just saying the destination to the taxi driver conjured up memories of running around London like renegades between the time the school train from Somerset reached Paddington Station and when our flights were scheduled to whisk us back home to our countries, dotted all over the globe.

When I first arrived in London in 1966, Carnaby Street was *the* hottest, most stylish place to visit. The shops on this tiny street were colorfully charming and inviting, heavily stocked with the latest fashions. As time progressed and the hippie age set in, our activities turned more towards hanging out on King's Road, the artsy Portobello Road, or Abbey Road, made famous by the Beatles on their album cover, the area where my guardians lived. We also loved the giant park of Hampstead Heath where couples often got married, dressed like gypsies, surrounded by wispy trees and carefully tended gardens. I frequently visited Biba's Boutique, where nearly all the clothes were black and the lipsticks were reddish black. I do not know which came first, the popular Rolling Stones song "Paint it Black," or Biba's Boutique. In 1968, at age 16, I had returned to the States dressed in black, from leather hat down to my boots, topped off with an old, worn-out English Civil Defense coat. Even my hose was black. Setting eyes upon me at Dulles Airport for the first time in six months, my mother took one look and gasped, "My God, darling, you look like Rasputin!"

I inquired, "Who is Rasputin?"

Now, 37 years after leaving England, I entered the grounds of Kensington Palace where the gorgeous Princess Diana had resided. I had always loved her from day one. Inside the palace, I lingered at the enormous windows directly overlooking the imposing gates where countless bereaved admirers left an ocean of flowers and cards for their beloved princess. I tried to envision how remarkable that sight must have been to behold, however tragic but also pregnant with massive love and devotion.

Downstairs, I was about to find out that commoners could have tea in the extensive gardens surrounded by carefully manicured bushes and roses of all colors. Queen Victoria's room overlooked this area. It did not take long to fall right back into old habits. I sipped some Earl Grey tea with raw cane sugar, along with a variety of scones while reading (not *The Sun*!) the respectable *Times*. On that midsummer, sunny afternoon, I entered deep thought, pondering how my life would have been vastly different had I remained in London all these years.

Waiting in the hotel lobby, my heart picked up speed in anticipation of being reunited with my treasured friends again. The minute Maamoun emerged from the revolving glass door, I was on him like "a cat on a mouse hole," as my mother used to say. I gave him five hugs, one from each of our mutual friends who had been based with me in Jeddah. Mona was right behind him, laughing. I cherish spending time with them anywhere. There are certain undeniable traits that cosmopolitan people possess. They inherently know how to communicate well with others anywhere on Earth, just as if everyone grew up in the same neighborhood.

Upstairs, I toasted with a celebratory glass of champagne while they finished packing. We were returning to Millfield to visit their sons, Ahmed and Ameen, for the annual Parent's Day ceremonies.

As Maamoun drove us through the countryside down to Somerset, *Jerusalem* was playing through my mind as if I was listening to a CD, particularly when we reached the area where Stonehenge is located on the Salisbury Plain. We were approaching a mystical place that is one of the planet's most popular archeological sites. People come from all over the world to see it, awed by its formation and significance. In a straight line across the green fields, Millfield is about 35 miles away from the ancient mysterious circle. A light summer rain cleared the air, and the old, familiar smells of the countryside began to reach my nose, summoning even more images from my past.

We stayed in a quaint but well-equipped country estate, complete with all the English traditions. The next day, we navigated the narrow roads over to Glastonbury to visit Ameen, their youngest son. The program listed a wide scope of activities for visiting parents, ranging from art and technology to international sports displays. We listened as gifted students played classical music, filling the hall with angelic sound, as the child prodigies diligently played the challenging symphonies. I was pleased to see that after nearly four decades, the traditions of this international school were still honored.

Outside, relatives in saris and Punjabi outfits mingled with robed parents from Africa and the Middle East as they had for decades. I flashed back to when my mother attended in 1967. The guest of honor was Her Highness, the Princess of Sikkim. I distinctly remember her arrival. Her attendants bowed slightly as she emerged from the large sedan wearing a stunning turquoise bakhu with metallic gold trim that shone in the sunlight. Outside the gates, foreign guests were held up in their Rolls Royces and Bentleys while a herd of meandering cattle made their way from one pasture to another. Cow pies obliterated the narrow road, a clear reminder that we were still in the country. Locals gathered to watch, and as my mother arrived, all dressed up for the school ceremonies, wearing beau-martin minks over her shoulders, a local Cockney fella called out to her, "Cor, look at 'em *cats!*"

We joined Ahmed, their eldest son, for a delicious salmon salad served with champagne. Now fourteen, the same age Maamoun was when we met, the resemblance between father and son was striking. On the wall, old black and white photos from the late '60s showing the boarders of the house called out to me. I pored over the pictures, finding a couple of my former good friends. Where on the globe they were now? What had their destiny become? Were they living full, happy lives? Would I recognize them if I saw them today? Even more frightening, would they be able to recognize *me?*

Strolling up the main driveway, we approached Millfield House, where our headmaster and founder of the school, Jack Meyer, nick-named "Boss," had lived and worked. The first boarders resided in this original house. Memories flooded back as I studied it. Rob Van der Hart, Maamoun's mentor and professor of philosophy from Oxford University, had joined us. He listened as I pointed out where we used to grab freshly baked pastries and tea every day at 4 p.m. It was also the spot where we all milled about during breaks, endlessly flirting with each other, acting like fools to impress the opposite sex. Like a ghost, I could almost see Boss emerging with the ever-present pipe in his hand, observing the students. The aroma of the tasty cakes and crumpets permeated the air. I easily remembered the unique cars from the '60s parked along the driveway. Looking across the field, I recalled the helicopter that landed on Parent's Day in 1967, carrying one student's VIP parents from abroad. Private transport by 'copter was a novel thing in the '60s, to say the least. I easily envisioned my closest school friends—from Ethiopia, South Africa, Nigeria, Thailand, Ghana, Saudi Arabia, Kuwait, Iran, Hong Kong, Singapore, Brunei, the Emirates, and Greece, just as if they had suddenly reappeared from my past. Ringing in my ears was their vibrant laughter, but I also clearly recalled their lament at missing their cultures and homelands, far, far away from England's verdant countryside.

I gingerly stepped into Boss's old office, almost as if trespassing, but I did not want to disturb his ghost. I do not know why I felt a bit reticent; perhaps because I had admired him so much. His illustrious career as an educator began by instructing the turbaned sons of Maharajas in India during the 1930s. His teaching career had taken him all over the world. Even though he was long gone, he was still alive in my memory. As headmaster, he had almost barricaded himself in that musty room with tons of files, newspaper clippings, and old books. Even in the '60s, Boss was regularly sent newspaper articles from around the world of anything printed about Millfield. He constantly smoked, just as my father had. I was always concerned that one night he would peacefully fall asleep with his pipe in his hand and set all of Millfield House ablaze. I had the serious hots for a handsome guy from Tehran who lived upstairs, so that worried me, as well.

Eight hundred boys and 230 girls were enrolled. The girls were always invited to visit Boss for their birthdays. He asked all about how life was at the school—how our professors were, what was happening in our home country, and our dreams of the future. He had an extraordinary memory, recalling minute details of my life back home, including exactly where I lived near the Potomac River. Boss remembered that my father had designed and built our Tudor home. At the end of the meeting, he would present me with a nice box of chocolates, a real treat. For all the wealthy kids in that school, our weekly pocket money was one pound, the equivalent of $2.40 a week. A candy bar cost six cents, and movies charged four shillings, or 48 American cents. A developed roll of film wiped out half.

When I commented on how clean Boss's office was, the two professors inside burst out laughing, as they knew well what a packrat he had been. Just standing in that room with its musty smell felt as if I had stepped into a time machine. In one sense, it seemed as if it was yesterday, in another, it felt like a scene from ages ago.

Professor Van der Hart and I went to see the stables. Even though I was not a good rider, I loved being around horses and meeting other equestrians. All riders comprised a small society within Millfield and knew each other well. I easily befriended the Middle Eastern students, all excellent horsemen. As I drew my breath in, taking a sniff of the old familiar equine scent, I remembered the many different horses we rode, their colors, and how their personalities were as individual as humans. I could hear the long-ago voice of our crusty, ailing instructor, Captain Hern, ordering us to ride properly in formation, as if we were preparing for a regal visit. I could see the friendly man from Dublin with curly ginger hair, speaking with a strong Irish accent while helping around the stables. Just like a pirate, he had a hook instead of a hand extended from his right arm. The horses really liked him. He worked hard keeping the stables clean while carrying tied bundles of hay on his hook. I often wondered if the weight of the bundle would one day yank out the poor chap's hook attachment off his arm, but it never did.

That night, I enjoyed a somewhat peaceful sleep. I felt at home in one way, but my mind was still restless. I was processing the many memories of then and now, infusing them into my present, pondering what it all meant to me after these many years.

Stuffed into the car with Mona and her sons, we rode along as Maamoun drove us back up to London. Mona and I had some fab quality chatting time while her husband navigated the motorway's thick traffic. After goodbyes and bear hugs, they left me off at a hotel close to Heathrow Airport. I decided to call Yasser's cell. I had not heard his voice in years. The last time I had seen him was in Jeddah, nearly ten years before. Our split had broken my heart and remained fresh in my memory.

"Who is this?" Yasser asked, in a very curious-sounding way.

I bet he nearly did a back flip when I said it was Tania. Thinking I was in the States, he asked where I was calling from, and was astonished to hear what I told him. "You are *where?*" he exclaimed, sounding dumbfounded.

Based in Cairo and flying for British Airways, he was at a hotel a mere ten minutes' walk away. "I'll be right over!" he exclaimed, ringing off as the Brits say.

I rushed to the ladies' room off the lobby. I had been in the car all day and was probably a bit 'ripe' as my mother used to say. Not only that, but who wants to look like a rag for her former lover? I frantically dug through my purse for all the flattering make-up—lipstick, eye shadow, foundation—I could grab. In ten minutes, I was back in the lobby. Wearing his sharp uniform, Yasser arrived shortly. He immediately spotted me from across the crowd.

We embraced for the first time in a decade. During the entire operation, we flew out of Jeddah, and later when we stayed in Cairo and Nigeria together, this was someone who I had been very much in love with. It felt uplifting to see him again, and he looked exactly the same. We laughingly and spontaneously said that to each other, almost in unison. "Tania, you still have that sparkle in your eyes, just like I remember from ten years ago," he said, his eyes glistening.

"You look the same, too, Doll face!" I enthused.

Studying his face, visions of our time together played through my mind. I had been so crazy about him that I asked my gifted medium, Steve, about it. "You and Yasser vibrate on the same frequency," he told me without hesitation.

It took me many months to get over our break-up, but now it felt wonderful, even refreshing, that our relationship and care for each other had come full circle in a way.

I had felt so alone when he left Kano to return home to Cairo; I had missed him terribly when he did not fly the Hajj with me during our last year out of Jeddah. I was deeply upset when we parted, living thousands of miles away from each other.

Yasser and I have mutual friends in Nigeria, Egypt, and the States, so there was tons to discuss. Time was short, as he was scheduled to fly to Muscat that night. After bidding each other a heartfelt goodbye and promising to stay in touch, I walked across the street to dine in a pink-colored pub.

As I slowly ate dinner, my mind was running overtime with thoughts of my visit to England, absorbing Millfield and then being reunited with Yasser, two distinct and powerful parts of my past. Watching the sunset through the pub's windows, I began to unearth the impact of my emotions after having taken a big step into my distant corridors of time.

⁓

"There she is, wearing a bright sundress as usual! Hey, mate, welcome to Crete!" Emlyn's boyfriend shouted as I emerged from Customs to hug them both.

Em was an Englishman whom I had worked with on a private B-727 out of LA for over five years. Intelligent and fun-loving with a great sense of humor, Em and I had flown all kinds of VIPs to four continents. My "airborne hubby" and I had our share of skirmishes, but we loved each other dearly and worked well together. "Tania, I love you to the bone," he once said.

When we unexpectedly lost our jobs in 2005, he searched for an island home in the Mediterranean. He found a bright, two-story house overlooking the sparkling Aegean Sea. In the distance, purple mountains capped with snow served as a backdrop to the sweeping vista. His house faced west, and the sunsets with their array of colors were spectacular over the water as lights twinkled from the yachts below.

Em navigated the old goat trail, now a paved road, towards their new house, set high on a hill overlooking several villages below. Along the coastline, beaches were as individual as flowers. Stopping at one of many tavernas on the waterfront, we ordered breakfast—some toast and grappa, a drink made from the fermented skins of grapes that will kick your ass. The water appeared chromatic—it was a clear, pale green at the shore, becoming darker green, and then blue as it became deeper.

"Tore has been asking about you, Tania. I've told him many of our airline stories, the places we've been together, and how you crave adventure," Em said.

Tore, their Norwegian neighbor, lived in a charming yellow house with cobalt blue trim. He relished the same stunning view from his large veranda. Often, they partied with the close-knit ex-pat British community. Em was busy getting ready for a Fourth of July pool party for me. There is nothing like Brits throwing an Independence Day party for a Yank. I would return the favor by making some killer mai tais for the beer-guzzling gang.

The car wound its way up towards the top of the hill. We stopped at Tore's house. Em shouted out his name. Emerging from the basement, Tore's friendly face had angular features. Tanned all over and dressed in shorts, his chest was covered in bits of white paint. "Hah-low, Tan-yah!" he said, when we were introduced.

The Swedish gals at Pan Am were always making fun of the Norwegians' accent, which I had never heard. Now I had an idea. It was quite sing-songy, with up-and-down inflections.

Tore joined us for lunch at Octopus Taverna, an out-of-the-way bistro patronized by the locals. It overlooked an inviting turquoise-blue colored lagoon. One small boat entertained a few swimmers with soft music. Sunbathers relaxed on the rocks. We ordered grilled octopus and calamari, but I have never seen it like that in America. It was lightly fried and had fat fingers, like a child's hand. We devoured the tasty island food and admired the view as I related stories about Somerset. Right away, I belonged in Crete. We toasted the good fortune of being reunited once again. Leaning in closely, Tore asked me to take my sunglasses off. They were quite dark, and he wanted to see my eyes. "Is that all you want me to remove?" I jokingly asked as I pretended that I was going to peel off my sarong.

I had not realized how handsome he was. At 6'5" tall, perfectly proportioned, with sandy-colored hair and blazing blue eyes, his appearance was true to his Nordic roots.

The Fourth of July party was to start at 6 p.m., but Em's neighbors were so anxious to romp, most arrived two hours early. It was home away from home for the expats. The weather is gentle, the air fresh, the views overlooking the sea are striking. The sunlight always dances on the water; gold flecks on azure blue. Numerous types of beautiful plants are easily grown, something even the local goats know. Instead of sifting through discarded goods like in Nigeria, the goats purposely invade people's gardens, selecting only the best succulent flowers. Worlds away from stinking, neurotic, and loud urban living, nature in this island has a sense of complete harmony. The inhabitants reflect the ambiance well.

Reggae music played throughout the night as Em's guests chugged the mai tais I had lovingly concocted. Some wiggled to the music while the more adventurous skinny-dipped in the pool, splashing around. Others caught up on the latest news in the expat Brit community. The sounds of our party traveled far throughout the tranquil island air, floating down to the villages and beaches below.

Even though I was now in Greece, another Millfield reunion was on the horizon. I had decided to Google my old boyfriend, a gifted and well-known musician named Ross Daly. We dated for a year at Millfield when we were both seventeen. I had fallen madly in teenage love with Ross, a tall Irishman with deep green eyes and reddish-brown hair. On the PC, his name was the first, second, and third one that popped up—bingo! I sent him an e-mail and dreamt that night that he had responded. The next morning, I received a welcome reply, which was beautifully illustrated with Arabic calligraphy. I was amazed at how we still shared so many of the same interests and philosophies after all these years. We have both always loved animals, so it was no surprise to hear that he had adopted at least a half-dozen Cretan and Minoan dogs. One photo on his website shows Ross on a motorcycle with two contented-looking pooches, a hound and an Alsatian, sitting patiently on a small Persian rug lining the sidecar. Ross and I were always curious about world events and cultures. We share similar political views, and the same affinity and respect for foreign lands with their diverse cultures. He has visited many countries to study music, further enhancing his remarkable gift. I have discovered that the uniquely gifted people I have met over the years are most modest. Long ago, I think Ross lost count of how many instruments he can play, some found only in Crete.

In 1975, Ross settled in Crete and spoke Greek with a Cretan accent. He was well known on the island for playing their native strings. He founded the Musical Workshop Labyrinth, featuring an extensive exhibition of rare musical instruments. Music students from all over the world attend seminars in his village. Classes are held where Ross teaches them how to play. The home he shares with his talented wife, Kelly, who also plays in his ensemble, is not far from the ancient Bronze Age Minoan Palace of Knossos, the most magnificent of four Minoan palaces.

"Ross, what a beautiful home you two have," Em gushed as he was greeted by the latest canine adoptee. It was decorated exactly the way I would decorate mine if I had a nice budget, with relics from their world travels. Persian rugs accentuated the décor, along with intriguing mementos and antiques from the Middle East. Handmade delicate instruments of varying kinds decorated the wall. White prayer beads hung over a four-paneled, hand-carved wooden screen. Suspended from the ceiling were filigreed bronze light fixtures. Incense that reminded me of the souk in Jeddah wafted through the air. The only item in this timeless collection of decorative artifacts that would have given away the date was one lonely, snoozing TV set. Everyone settled in for an animated conversation while Em scratched the pooch's ears.

Something remarkable occurs when looking into an old friend's eyes, whether they are gals or guys. When I have been separated for many years from someone, once reunited again, I find it fascinating to look right into their visual orbs. For me, it is like connecting in an absolute way with your friend again. Their eyes represent their soul and their light, instantly transporting me back to the conversations we had years ago. The spark is so strong that even though we are having a modern-day conversation, it is as if I am listening to two parallel discussions at the same time. The eyes signal soul recognition and indicate that you have a powerful history with that individual.

A dear friend I have known since we were both twelve speaks with me about this often. Whatever "inner sonar" we possessed as kids intuitively led us to many of the best prospects to befriend for our lifetimes. It is fascinating to contemplate how friends from my deep past have turned out to be so like me, sharing many of the same philosophies in life. Many thoughts do not have to be spoken; they are automatically understood.

Ross, now with shoulder-length salt-and-pepper hair and a handlebar mustache with the same smile as always, beamed as Em related some of our zany tales. His green eyes were exactly as I had remembered. I flashed back to when we were both seventeen. I had looked into his eyes so many times as we walked around Millfield. Students were closely monitored all day long, so there were few opportunities to have any kind of privacy. Sports were also watched closely, and students got into as much trouble for skiving sports as if they had cut a class. We did learn, however, that golf was rather lax, so we signed up. Strolling about the extensive gardens behind Millfield House while in deep conversation, we pretended to improve our shots. At least we gained some rare quality time together. On Saturday nights, everyone went to the cinema, considered a real treat even if the film was lousy. We all piled into the stuffy, two-story cinema house, devouring fistfuls of delicious English chocolate. Some bravely smoked a quick fag surreptitiously. We constantly looked around to see who was paired up with whom, or who had broken up with their love.

As the spring afternoons lengthened, Ross and his best friend, "Chili" Wilkerson from Los Angeles, would spontaneously jam in an emerald green field on their two acoustic guitars joined by another close friend, Jeff Rock, also from LA. Everyone knew how gifted they were, and instantly a crowd gathered. Their sound was synchronized perfectly as dozens of cross-legged students sat quietly, completely drawn into, and enthralled by their extraordinary music.

On Saturdays, they sometimes held folk concerts for the esoteric group as a fun alternative to the hokey "hop" dances. Both were only teenagers, but you would have thought that they had played together for ages. Perhaps they had. Maybe this was not the first lifetime that these musicians had created original melodies together.

The summer of 1969 arrived, and the attorneys for my late father's estate arranged for me to join a small tour to visit seven countries on the continent. I should have been thrilled, but instead was distressed that I would be separated from Ross for ten weeks. In my teenage mind, I would have much rather spent the summer with him in the local village of Glastonbury than to travel all over Europe with women I had never seen before.

One day while lamenting the thought of not sharing the beautiful English days of summer with him, a smile crept across his face. The first stop was Paris, where I would join seven gals who had flown in from the States. Ross mentioned that he had heard it was eight pounds to take the ferry across the Channel. From there, he would hitchhike to Paris. *Voila!* I checked the itinerary. I was booked at the Normandy Hotel.

The Summer of 1969 was the height of the hippie era. Ross and I were right in the middle of it, usually dressed in a way that suggested we had escaped from a wagon train heading west. We were not dirty, but colorfully attired, using much imagination. Often our clothing did not match, but who gave a damn? Everyone dressed like that during "the summer of love." All eyes were on San Francisco, but we definitely had *our* version in London. My long skirt was usually paisley or a similar design, topped by a low-cut peasant blouse with a mirrored vest from India, accented with two scarves to battle the dampness. I had flowers in my hair. My shoes were suede squaw boots up to the knee or hand-carved, solid wood Dutch clogs which clacked loudly as I walked. Ditching his tweed coat or Shetland sweater, Ross usually wore a type of Pakistani shirt.

Once, while we were sitting at Piccadilly Circus, a tourist bus stuffed with boisterous Americans pulled up. A woman busting out of her polyester outfit immediately began snapping photos, while screeching to her husband in a rowdy Bronx accent, "Ralph, look! European hippies!" She was pointing directly at us, as if we were part of a freak exhibition who did not speak English. I walked over, looked her square in the eye, saying in a gentle voice, "Actually, I am from *McLean, Virginia!*"

Across the Channel in chic Paris, we encountered the same treatment, but for a different reason. Staring rudely as we entered the lobby, I think the fellas at the Normandy Hotel were perplexed as to how we could afford to stay there until they checked my bill, all pre-paid. They had yet to learn the lesson that even though people sometimes dressed like peasants, they might not necessarily be rag-tag bumpkins. When I wore my micro-mini skirts, the Parisians stared at that, too.

Upstairs, Ross and I got into some heavy smooching. Even though I was horny beyond belief, I was still afraid of "going all the way," as we used to put it, so when he began wrestling with his trousers, I exclaimed, "Ross, no! You know I can't do that!"

Who knows why I was hanging onto my virginity. maybe Mama had poisoned my head a bit too much.

My room had a balcony overlooking the boulevard, but Ross and I were itching to explore all the sights of Paris, especially the artsy areas. I distinctly remember our cruise down the Seine, captivated by all the sparkling lights, sounds, and sights. We savored a sampling of French cuisine including *la langouste froide, le chateaubriand béarnaise,* and *les fromages varies.* With disdain, we gladly skipped the *grenouilles provencales*—sauteed frog's legs. Ross kept his arm around me as we cruised below the brightly lit magnificent *Tour Eifel.*

To celebrate Bastille Day, we visited a gypsy-like café. A guitarist, singer, and magician entertained celebrants while we danced slowly, but more importantly undisturbed, to relaxing music. No conservative teacher was lurking around the corner ready to pounce and break us up from our slinky dancing to give us defaulters. At last, we were on our own. It felt absolutely divine to enjoy complete freedom.

On our last night, we went to the famous Lido de Paris Cabaret, a complete eyeful for *both* of us. Gorgeous ladies with giant tits and tiny waists tastefully dressed in endless feathers, jewels, and multi-colored costumes cascaded down the elaborate staircases. Superbly choreographed and richly titillating, we devoured yet another gourmet meal while being entranced and bedazzled by the retinue of beauties. At school, if we had even been in a room without a teacher, we would have been punished for a "private assignation." Now we were scot-free in Paris, drinking champagne all night while ogling boobs galore as world-class dancers cavorted about.

In D.C., we considered ourselves quite sophisticated, but we had absolutely *nothing* to compare with The Lido. As far as I know, we *still* don't. Ross and I danced until dawn, then strolled along the banks of the Seine. It was my wish to remember that magical, romantic scene forever.

We laughed at his ingenious plan of joining me in Paris. We were only 17 and had finally managed to run Scot-free and unescorted for a few blissful days in one of the world's most beautiful cities. We felt as if we had pulled off a pretty good one.

After those heady days in Paris, Ross returned to London and I flew to Spain, the land of my father's ancestors. Watching Apollo 11 live, I stayed up all night with the Barcelonians, joyfully enthralled by witnessing Neil Armstrong bounce around on the moon's surface. My small tour flew onto Nice, and then drove to the cosmopolitan resort Juan-les-Pins. I missed Ross already, and watching couples stroll along the romantic beaches of southern France did not help my moodiness. However, before long, I snapped out of it and thoroughly enjoyed every minute of the next seven weeks exploring Europe, from the canals of Venice to a trip behind the Iron Curtain in Hungary. I must say, I received a quick lesson on male anatomy below the belly button as I studied Michelangelo's David in Firenze for quite some time. I thought to myself, "So that is what a man's privates *look* like, but how do they *work*?"

Christmastime arrived, and Ross informed me of the grim news that his parents were abruptly pulling him out of Millfield to send him to another school. Pure exuberance flipped to complete anxiety. The concrete decision had been made, so it was hopeless to explore any avenue that might allow him to stay. Bidding him a tearful and prolonged goodbye, I left London and flew back to the States for five weeks of Christmas vacation with my mother and stepfather Bevo in worlds-away Hendersonville, N. C. Disheartened, I could hardly finish a train of thought, much less a sentence. Although thrilled to see my mother again, I retreated to my room for long hours, woefully playing the same Led Zeppelin songs repeatedly while scribbling in my diary.

I was going to be separated from my love Ross forever, and there wasn't a bloody thing I could do about it.

∽

My mother was overloaded herself that Christmas, but she tried hard not to let it show. My stepdad Bevo had undergone cataract surgery the month before, and it had not gone well. During the operation, the anesthesia had begun to wear off, and he felt the physician scraping along the top of his eyeball. In an urgent tone, he informed the doctor that it felt like his optic nerve was about ready to burst wide open. The surgeon stiffened up. With a glowering look, he barked back, "Would you like me to *quit?*"

Astonished and taken by complete surprise at the doctor's blatant and cruel insensitivity, Bevo meekly implored him to continue.

Now two months later, both of his eyes still looked like blood-red oranges, oozing every day. He constantly had to change the dressing. While my mind was obsessing about losing Ross, 3,800 miles away, the increasingly despondent Bevo was circling an emotional drain. One day when mom was out, I came home to find him suicidal. I will never forget his words. A patch was over one eye. With the other bulging eye glaring straight ahead, he kept saying in a voice rife with resignation and despair, "If I can't see, I can't work. If I can't work, I can't support your mother." A handgun was in his lap.

Immediately suspending all thoughts of myself, I tried to gently console him. I desperately hoped that my intuitive mother would sense something was wrong and come home sooner rather than later. I sat down right next to him on the sofa, stretching my arm around his broad shoulders. The gun stayed in his lap; it gave me the creeps to think that he might pick it up at any minute. I certainly did not want to touch it but was ready to intervene if it came to that. I was increasingly relieved that it remained where it was. Even in that agitated state, Bevo realized that he was too close to the edge of a cliff.

I chose my words carefully as I looked him straight in the one "good" eye. I was trying hard to instill a sense of optimism in him. Admitting that his eyes were taking far too long to heal, I told Bevo that if he would be patient, the good Lord would see him—and his eyesight—through this crisis. Even though Bevo and I fought often, and loudly, much to the dismay of my mother, I knew that he was a wounded soul and had been since childhood. He never forgave his parents for abandoning him at age six. Now, fearing that loss of vision would destroy his life, his fragile personality began to crack under the pressure, adding another difficult dimension to his alcoholism.

Fortunately for both of us, it was not long before my mother came through the front door. Our conversation had probably lasted 30 minutes, but had seemed like hours, as things do when they are incredibly stressful. Bevo's eyes eventually did heal, and the incident with the gun was rarely ever mentioned again.

One bright spot that season was that my mother, a true animal lover, had adopted a darling little squirrel monkey named Tikki. She let him out of the cage often, and he would run rip-snortin' through the house at Mario Andretti speed, getting into everything that was not nailed down. He brightened my spirits considerably.

Upstairs in my bedroom, my world was spinning out of control. My school was not up the street, it was an entire ocean away. Ross seemed to be even further. A moody teenager, I contemplated my situation day and night. However, my gloomy thoughts were frequently interrupted by the overly energetic Tikki, who would scream with delight every time Mama let him out of the cage. No room was off limits, and in Tikki's case, anything he found became his. My father used to joke, "Possession is nine-tenths of the law."

Tikki must have been listening, as he was a true believer in "finders keepers." Tossing my mother's makeup every which way, he would then scurry across the stovetop at Mach 3, knocking pots and pans clanging to the floor. It was a miracle he never got burned. Swiping any piece of fruit, he would hurriedly scarf it down, throw the peel on the floor, and then wipe his tiny hands on the brocade curtains in the living room. Later, he would stretch out on the side table to relax under the lamp's warm light, looking like a sunbather on Miami Beach, while I gently stroked his small fuzzy body.

Tikki was a welcome relief from my world of heartache. Knowing how amused I was by his antics, my mother began to let him out more frequently, braving the ensuing mayhem, to pull me out of my depression. She must have been thinking to herself, *oh, the things we do for our children.*

⌒⊘

Now it was 38 years later, summer of 2007. I was worlds away from sprawling Los Angeles, happily conversing with Ross and beautiful Kelly on the sunny patio of their home in Crete on the Eastern Mediterranean Sea. I could not have imagined this sparkling, bright moment of my life in my wildest imagination, but here it was.

⌒⊘

Em and I climbed the sun-bleached white steps toward a lookout point I had discovered on a previous trip to Santorini. The large patio sits atop an ancient volcano, revealing one of the most beautiful vistas I have seen in any country. The island is crescent-shaped, overlooking a few small islands that rise from the dazzling deep blue sea facing west. Along the black volcanic rock, quaint white stucco homes dot the hillside, punctuated by endless bright tropical flowers of every color imaginable. The town of Thira, built on top of an inactive volcano, is located hundreds of feet above sea level. From this height, we had a 180-degree view of the western edge of the island. The homes, bistros, and shops, almost all of them white stucco, run straight up the side of the cliff, adding to the allure of this captivating view. Every direction we gazed in was "picture-postcard beautiful." Adding to the intrigue of this mystical place is the belief held by many that it sits above the area where the civilization of Atlantis existed.

We settled in on white wicker chairs, surrounded by bougainvillea, oleander, and hibiscus plants. In the distance, we could see the village of Oia, with the white houses spilling over the solid black rock, looking like milk foam on top of an espresso. Below, black sand beaches were squeezed in between the sharp hillside bluffs. Dozens of donkeys brayed and groaned as they carried endless overweight tourists from the cruise ships on their tiny backs up the grueling, steep, stone pathways to the top.

Em and I sipped wine as people began to gather along the volcano-top to watch the sunset. We reflected on some of the bewitching times we had enjoyed, flying A-list passengers to the far ends of the Earth.

"Tania, Tore is pretty crazy about you. I told him all about you before you joined us in Crete. I bet that he'll come to LA this fall," Emlyn said.

"Em, this is the second time you have been involved in a good matchmaking scheme," as we chuckled, enjoying our wine.

A few minutes later, Louis Armstrong's "What a Wonderful World" was gently playing on the patio. The timing was perfect. I had always loved that song, Armstrong's unique voice, and the memories that came with it.

It was a heavenly scene. As the sun dipped lower toward the horizon, the white houses changed color from pale pink to bright orange. A single large sailing ship was heading toward the sun, in between two islands. "You know Em, we have had blessed lives. We have experienced so much, met such a variety of fascinating people, and visited so many countries. And here we are in another gorgeous setting, only a two-hour ferry ride from your new home in Crete."

He nodded, not taking his eyes off the sunset for one minute, as if the sun was going to escape, and he was going to miss the final act of nature's show.

"When I was flying the Hajj operation out of Calcutta," I continued, "I met a sincere and spiritual Indian man named Abdul. On the five-hour flight to Jeddah, we discussed a myriad of things—life, religion, India. As he disembarked, he told me that he would pray in Mecca that my crew would fly him back home. Six weeks later, when he boarded my plane again, we were delighted, greeting each other like old friends. Once more, we spoke of many things. I asked him all about his experience performing the Hajj for the first time. When we landed in Calcutta, I was sorry to see him go, but he said one of the most beautiful things to me I have ever been told by anyone."

"What was that?" Em asked, his face aglow with the final light of the setting sun.

"As we bade each other goodbye, he said, "I will pray for your golden life, Tania.""

Sitting back in my chair, in between the fat pillows, captivated by the sun's divine light on the sea, I reminisced at what a considerate gift that was, saying those remarkable and powerful words to me. I have never forgotten Abdul's gesture of kindness.

And I believe that Abdul got his wish.

Acknowledgements

I wish to express my heartfelt thanks and much appreciation to the six brave souls—Chris Beakey, Jim Burke, Al Topping, Renee Boyd, Shirine Gill, and News Tiki who so generously offered to read my memoir cover to cover. Your evaluation, assessment, and feedback are immensely valuable to me.

I would like to acknowledge the contribution of my old friend, Ron Davies, erstwhile curator at the National Air and Space Museum, who freely and painstakingly proofread and edited infant stages of this book, not once, but twice, making valuable red-pen annotations on every page! Ron, writer of airline history books, including one about Pan American, was a world expert in every aspect of airline history. He died in 2011, and I miss his raconteur tale-telling about the airlines, especially about his and my favorite airline, Pan American.

I am grateful to the late Warren Brown, gifted *Washington Post* columnist and book author, who consistently gave me sage advice and suggestions of how to improve my narration. Warren sadly passed before he could edit my memoir.

Deep thanks to the late Julian Myers, my professor of entertainment PR at UCLA, who introduced me to some valuable authors' clubs.

For my fellow Pan Amers—Gunilla Crawford, Vince Rossi, Cicero M. Fain III, PhD., Kevin McDonald, Jim Shaughnessey, and Donna Stromick Hazelton, who relished many of these journeys with me and helped make them golden.

To Al-Hajji Garba Shiitu Kabo for your marvelous support during my "Nigeria years," and Sam Gaude who taught me about Nigerian culture.

An enormous thanks must go to Rev. Steve Woods and Kofo Akinmade, my dear spiritual friends who consistently kept me on track and focused for eons, and to Per Clausen, who like me approaches life with an open heart.

I appreciate all the support I received from my "high school" life-long friends from Millfield School in Somerset, England—Shiekh Maamoun Zahid, his beautiful wife, Dr. Mona Kholief, Bill Wilkerson Jr., Dr. Katrina Wood, and Lotanna Ojukwu.

Thank you to Mrs. Helen Meyers of Charleston, S.C., who has believed in me since I was eight years old. I eternally appreciate you!

Over the years, I was always delighted when my dear friend Cat Sines asked how my book was coming along, and I know that Dr. Shelly Ovsak, D.B.A. had faith in my memoir.

I must also thank Steve Chelski, Esq., and wife Joyce Margolin for proofreading some chapters, and recognize Tom Gerdy, volunteer extraordinaire, who has built more houses for deserving families than even *he* can count.

Thanks to Russ Mannex, my "in-house" techie who was my captive audience, and Sudd Dongre, who built my website. When I'd get stuck in the mud, he'd always say, "No matter what happens, just keep on writing!"

Lastly, I am grateful to the Steve Harrison Team:

I'll never forget the day I was in Germany and spotted your email about this extraordinary program. It fired up all my cylinders as I instantly realized my teenage dream of writing a memoir would finally come to fruition.

I would like to thank:

Sarah Brown, my supportive coach, Cristina Smith, project manager, Valerie Costa, my dedicated editor, Kimberlie Cruse, video producer, Christy Day, designer, Steve Scholl, proofreader, Maggie McLaughlin, Geoffrey Berwind, consultant, and Steve Harrison, the visionary who pulled this prolific program together with his extensive literary expertise.

Yes, indeed, it does take a village.

About the Author

After graduating from American University in Washington, D.C., with BAs in Political Science and International Studies, Tania was hired as an international flight attendant by the iconic Pan American World Airways, which set her on a course to explore six of the world's continents. After Pan Am's bankruptcy, Tania's career expanded even more, to flying VIP charters, the White House press corps, convicts, film crews, refugees, military personnel, pilgrims, and medical transplant teams . . . "everything," Tania admits, "except rendition flights!"

The ensuing stories and anecdotes from these diverse adventures begged to be told. Tania's love for writing began when she was attending high school in England. She composed meticulous accounts of interactions with her extraordinary cosmopolitan classmates, many of whom were offspring of royals or celebrities. Tania has documented her most intriguing stories vividly, supplemented with previously unpublished photos.

The USAF awarded Tania the Civilian Desert Shield and Desert Storm Medal for Outstanding Achievement in 1991. During the first Gulf War, Tania flew troops close to the war zone. In 2021, Atlas Air presented Tania with a Certificate of Appreciation for serving in Operation Allies Refuge, airlifting Afghani civilian translators to America.

On Butterflies' Wings is her first memoir and will be part of a series.
Visit Tania at: https://taniaanderson.vip
Facebook: On Butterflies' Wings
Instagram: @onbutterflieswings

Free Offer

As a free gift to readers of my book, I am offering a bonus chapter. Download a compelling story entitled *Superstowaway! Don't ask me about the mile-high club, ask me about stowaways—it's a much better story.* Growing up disadvantaged in northern Nigeria, my affable, intrepid housekeeper Suley was determined to embrace a brighter future for himself at all costs. That he did, with grit, grace, and a burning desire to be part of the American dream.

https://taniaanderson.vip

Made in the USA
Columbia, SC
04 November 2024

45670601R00189